Kee]
of the
Red Clay
Kingdom

a memoir

M A R Y   G R A C E   L Y O N

For permission requests, contact Mary Grace Lyon at
marygracelyon@yahoo.com

or visit marygracelyon.com for more information.

Designed by Anamaria Stefan

ISBN (Hardcover) 979-8-9912227-1-6

ISBN (Paperback) 979-8-9912227-0-9

ISBN (eBook) 979-8-9912227-2-3

1st edition 2024

for Mom and Dad

I W.T.D.B.

CONTENTS.

Prologue   7

Dreamer   16

Son   23

Boy   43

Survivor   73

Georgian   94

Damn Good Dawg   112

North Countryman   133

Physician   145

Bridge Builder   158

Daddy   170

Partner   197

Retiree   222

Hamiltonian   241

Caretaker   271

Husband   282

Papa   292

Nonagenarian   302

Immortal   328

Epilogue   341

Afterword: Family History   353

Acknowledgements   369

References   423

About the Author   425

6

Prologue .

Dirt roads make me remember. I'm not sure if it's the grainy texture in between my toes or the splashing red puddle memories that make me glad. They represent the vanishing fragments of my ancestry, trails beckoning me to secret fishing holes, Indian burial grounds, and a lovers' oak tree bearing pocketknife scars. Five generations of my family have explored these same stone covered paths I walk today.

One still leads to the flat rock in Standing Boy Creek where the neighbors gathered on Saturdays to wash their Model Ts. Another guides my feet to a tall brick chimney now choked with vines and fire ant hills, remnants of a country cabin I imagine Yankee soldiers burned. The trails take me back to happier times. They forge well beyond the dilapidated stand where my cousin Andy shot his first buck and past the field where I drove the Jubilee tractor from the safety of Papa's lap.

If my grandfather's trees could talk, they would tell of moonshiners and arrowhead hunters and bass as big as Labradors. They might reminisce about young skinny dippers and Miss Mary's warm pecan pie served on a quilted picnic blanket. They would keep hidden the dark sins of the past, how the last hooded hangings in Harris County took place just over that knoll. And they would tell why for forty years the aged sheriff sipped his coffee with his back to the wall until his death.

His hills would whisper about a wound so immense in a little boy's heart that it took this whole parcel of land and five decades of cultivating its red earth to fill it up. No written history can capture these moments past, only stories upon stories, retold over decades of sweet tea, cornbread, and berry picking. In our southern foothills, you can easily gain a few pounds in pursuit of back porch truth.

Over generations, my family managed to master the art of mealtime storytelling. It's in the fabric of who we are. In the same way some families pass down wealth or status, furniture or recipes, my family hands down this gift, if you will. Most of our seasoned and best loved storytellers have either exchanged this life for a better one or are now scattered across different states. But I can vividly remember my grandfather masterfully telling us about his life between hurried bites of food and sips of sweet tea. I used to think he ate at a doctor's pace out of habit, expecting the next emergency; now I wonder if it was because he had so much to tell us, and chewing somehow robbed him of the time. Either way, stories like his were meant to be shared and preserved.

These writings about my grandfather and our family are important for my children and their children, our extended family and friends, and those who come after us. But even if you don't know me or my blood kin, this story is for you, too. It's about hardship, overcoming, courage, generosity, family, and something a lot bigger than one man. My desire is if you randomly picked up this book, you might find in these pages hope and inspiration. I pray you laugh and cry and my words bring to mind your own family lore... and then you go and tell your tales to your children. After all, our stories and their tellers are only a generation away from extinction.

You are welcome here, however you found these words. Pull up a porch rocking chair, pour yourself a glass of Southern sweet tea with a lemon slice, and prop your feet up. You get bonus points if you happen to have some hot biscuits, butter, and muscadine jelly. I don't claim to be the best in our line of storytellers, but I'm going to give it my best bulldog try.

This story, my family's story, in many ways begins as an inkblot on a southeastern United States map. Our people have lived as far south as Miami, to the west in Arizona and California, and way up north in New York, but somehow we migrate back to our roots in the tiny town of Hamilton, Georgia. Our history will forever be mingled with this ground, embedded in its sticky red mud and hammered deep in the earth with each fencepost.

Parcels of land heading north along Highway 27 from Columbus, Georgia have appreciated in value over the last several decades, but price and worth are not the same thing. When someone asks, "how much," they want to know what money can buy, but the true value of something can be far more intangible. The worth of our family land hinges less on its location on a map and what we produced *from* it, and more on the sentimentality of what it has collectively produced *in* us. We have not grown mass crops to sell or operated any kind of commercial working farm. There aren't even any structures other than a dilapidated old barn. But so much has been built here, it's impossible to measure.

Our tract of family land gloriously reflects the unassuming greatness of its longtime caretaker: my grandfather "Papa," my hero, Seaborn Anderson "Andy" Roddenbery III, M.D. During half a century of his life, he pieced together over 400 acres of property in this rural area of God's country. His patch of tall trees and red clay is home to more than deer, blue heron, and rainbow trout in the fall. No other place on earth holds this exact recipe of reverie. For me, the land is a dim reflection of what heaven must be like.

Although the vast acreage has belonged to our family for over fifty years, I don't believe anyone can truly own stones and dirt. It's a strange idea to master something thousands of years old, to attempt to lord over creek water that slides right through your fingertips or rule over trees awakened only by the wind. The wild submits to no man, and the strongest and most experienced outdoorsman can't fully subdue it... not even the old Eagle Scout.

Inside the perimeter of the property lines, the many longings Papa had as a child were realized- a place to take off his shoes, to go fishing, to know the curves in each path like friends to grow old with. Best of all, it's a home that can't be taken away or moved. Here, the roots stay firmly planted and the only changes are the cloud shapes overhead and the color of leaves in the fall.

Out on the land, sweltering summer sunbeams burst through clouds in the late afternoons, illuminating familiar dirt paths and the crooked spring fed creeks of our clan. A distinct cacophony of croaks and chirps reverberates in the silence and morphs into a melodic symphony bursting with life. Each babble of the brook sings of a fawn's first steps, a spring hatch of velvety ducklings, or a crawdad's clumsy march. And at dusk, a coyote's eerie shrieks rise to an ethereal moon, just as they have under a thousand starlit skies, long before my ancestors even set foot in the New World.

Even though the land is now a part of our family, this place has a history that precedes us. The stories of those who came before us, some known and some forgotten, intermingle with the ground. Before I ever stood barefoot in this pasture, I am keenly aware that these same blades of grass bent under lost arrowheads, a stranger's carriage wheels, or someone else's shotgun shells. Aged, gnarled branches deep in the woods point to ancient bones and relics mixed with the red dust; their tales lost to the steady passage of time. The breeze alone seems to know and whisper the names of the ones who walked these trails long ago.

Over the decades, my grandfather's faithful influence drew us back to the land. Aunts, uncles, cousins- and now our children, grandchildren, and great-grandchildren- are grafted together here with decided permanence. This ground, though sacred and immovable, could never *ground* us as a family. The grounding had to happen over time- through joy, sorrow, love, and loss only the passing of years could accomplish in each of our lives. Most of the kids and grandkids moved away and learned lessons on our own terms, looking for a better way of living or a version of worldly enlightenment beyond the confines of the rural South. I moved halfway around the world to Asia only to realize so much of the good, the many things I value, and the love that holds my world together was right here in Georgia all along.

That is something my grandfather knew. He never needed to leave to be reminded of it. When he was growing up, the South's vast farmland dripped with peaches and watermelon. Line after line of peanuts, tobacco and cotton scarred most of its earth. Even though he spent several years north of the Mason-Dixon, he hightailed it back as soon as he could and settled contentedly with his young family in the state of his birth. Owning a parcel of it was the realization of a lifelong dream.

As an old man, he loved to walk or ride through his small slice of Georgia. Papa delighted in the jolt of his rusty red pickup truck as it tumbled across the rolling hills of pasture, windows down and the sun lighting the tip tops of hardwoods. He lived to surprise wild turkeys scattering through the brush and longed to happen upon the elusive twelve-pointer, majestic and commanding against a blanket of evergreen.

At his fishing pond, occasional ripples from catfish splashed and churned the murky water into a kaleidoscope of earth tones. He would sometimes lift his gaze in wonderment to the intermittent brushstrokes of azure sky peeking through the peaceful tree canopy overhead. It all seemed wild and untouched, except for the water tower barely visible over the tree line that read "Go Tigers" for the local county high school. Even now, I can clearly envision him casting his line, humming as it glided over glasslike water until it plopped and sank. I saw him do it a hundred times.

Papa's love for us often looked like work boots and a walking stick. He somehow found ways to unite his children and grandchildren in simple tasks- mending fences, feeding cows, or hauling limbs. Forty years after my first memories here, I can hear him narrating the tales of his paradise to us with wonder and humility. I would bet most of his grandchildren can still find our way down each path almost as effortlessly as if he was guiding us himself. Now our inheritance measures largely in the youthful memories we created here, with him and with each other: in shared truck rides, fire pit storytelling, jars of caught fireflies, and paddle boat rides.

His preserve provides a beautiful and familiar place to be together on our leg of the journey, a spot for our family and friends to gather... to tell stories and remember. The constant and loving presence of Papa and his land gifted us the grace to fly far away and simultaneously offered us an unencumbered way home. It birthed in our family both a foundation and a compass, a common magnetic soul to ground us and woo us back to its wild, and ultimately to him and to each other.

The land is the enduring ellipses at the end of Papa's remarkable earthly legacy. It is the last tangible piece of his love and patriarchal provision and the spectacular backdrop of his final chapters. Our history with this magical place and with our beloved patriarch ensured we would stay a family long after he was gone. That's what the best stories can do, bind us together through even one man's true and faithful love. The keys to his kingdom won't fit without one another.

To truly understand my grandfather's life, the land, and why it matters so much to all of us, I need to start at the beginning. Let me go back and tell you my favorite story about my grandfather, the little boy with a darling, mischievous smile named Anderson Roddenbery.

Dreamer

●

Atlanta seemed as far away from Macon, Georgia as a flight to Paris from New York through his twelve-year-old eyes. The distance didn't matter, only the getting there did. Without any parents around to prevent him, his imagination and his feet were free to wander. He started out walking from Macon early in the morning on October 10, 1927, after sending word to his grandmother in Atlanta that he would be staying the night. It was a different time then, when folks would hitchhike fearlessly on back roads, before interstates carried the masses from city to city, and before children had to be warned about predators.

He didn't recall with whom he rode that day- who pulled over and stopped his motorcycle to let the dreamer on board.

When asked what business he had in Atlanta, he smiled and proudly stated that he was going to see "Charles Lindbergh, my hero." In fact, Lindy was everyone's hero. He stood for all that would inspire decades of paper airplanes to be launched from little boys' hands. There was something magical and surreal about his flight over the Atlantic. It was more than an accomplishment for transportation. It was the triumph of a nation, and nearly every flag-waving American revered Lindbergh's name.

The tires kicked up a dusty trail that disappeared into the slight breeze of that morning. Anderson watched the clouds become changing shapes and wondered if they appeared the same from way up in the sky looking down. It was one of those nearly perfect days, one that lives on the tip of your memory however long ago it was. The kind of day that no matter the weather, it seemed sunny outside; no matter the company, it was the best conversation you'd had in a while. Hope hung in the air like honeysuckle vines heavy with spring buds. It was a day that should only exist in little boy dreams.

Young Anderson heard Colonel Charles Lindbergh would be passing through Atlanta after his successful flight across the Atlantic. As part of his patriotic and celebratory tour, he would lay a wreath at Pershing Point to honor those who died in the Great War and receive an honor from the city of Atlanta. Pershing Point is located on a main thoroughfare through the heart of Atlanta at the junction of Peachtree Street and West Peachtree Street, not too far from where Anderson's mother grew up on the corner of Piedmont Avenue and 6th Street.

His grandmother still lived in that home, and he stayed at his grandmother's just long enough to lay his head. When the dew was still good and thick on the ground, young Anderson's eyelids flew open in eager anticipation of the day ahead. He walked alone to Pershing Point before sunrise, staking out his spot like a tailgate parking space the night before the Georgia vs. Tech game. It was quite probably his only chance to see his hero in person, and he did not want to take any chance of missing it.

Through the adult eyes of its author, an article in "The Atlanta Constitution" painted the day as a display of great patriotism and honor for the flying colonel "Lindy."[1] Lindbergh was traveling from Candler (present day Atlanta-Hartsfield International Airport) to Grant Field, and this was one of many stops along the way. The brief visit was colored with members of the Old Guard "in fall regalia" escorting Lindy from his automobile. Traffic was at a dead halt down Peachtree Street as hundreds of people crowded to catch a glimpse of the famed Lindbergh.

The short ceremony was quite formal and proper.

Anderson barely noticed the flags and decorations or the many important people in Atlanta who were poised to witness the presentation. A poem was read, and Lindy placed a wreath on a memorial to Fulton County youths who died in the War. The Atlanta chapter of the United Daughters of the Confederacy donated an emblem that was pinned on Lindbergh by a representative from the United Confederate Veterans. The emblem had a Confederate flag on one side, a Union flag on the other, and they were connected in the center by a United States flag. Southern patriotism was on its best behavior.

What the article does not mention is the bright-eyed boy who grabbed hold of this moment in history, so to speak. Kneeling beneath tall oaks burning with the orange and red of fall, he watched the events taking place. He wasn't really listening to the words of the poem and failed to marvel at the many men in uniform like most young boys would do. Instead, he crouched like a soldier behind a barricade next to the memorial named for World War I hero General John Pershing. Choked with anticipation, he waited for his hero to pass, not really knowing what he would do or if he would speak when the magical moment finally arrived.

On the walk back to his automobile escort, Lindy smiled and waved at the many bystanders. His tall frame seemed to float above the crowd of people like a bobber on a lake until he approached the spot where my grandfather had been waiting for the past several hours. His grand and slender silhouette did not disappoint the imaginary version Anderson had conjured up in his head. Lindy's broad smile and handsome physique complemented his happy blue eyes.

As Lindbergh glided by, little Anderson lurched out into the path. With trembling hands, he made a split-second decision to grab onto Lindy's coattails. The lanky man spun around and looked right at my grandfather, his piercing eyes glimpsing down into his round boyish face and his small, wounded soul. Lindbergh flashed his handsome smile and winked at the eager lad. He may as well have handed him a million dollars.

That day still lived in my grandfather's mind as bigger than life itself, and to hear him recount that day put you crouching and waiting with him, Charles Lindbergh at your fingertips. Of the threads of memories filling his mind and spilling out into beautifully woven stories, it was my favorite one I ever heard him share. He told it more often and with more passion than almost any other, even as his memory failed. That small moment in time passed for hundreds of spectators without a thought about little Anderson, but I believe those same few seconds in time brushed with greatness changed the course of his life.

This story about my grandfather reminds me of another life altering touch of one man's cloak which gave healing to a wounded woman. She had lost everything- her friends, her family, her home. She spent her entire fortune on doctors and healers who tried to make her well. All of them failed. She endured great suffering for twelve years and was an outcast in her own city because of her sickness and the constant bleeding she endured.

One day she heard about a man who could make the blind see and the lame walk. She thought, if I could just touch this man's coat, I will be healed. She journeyed into the city where she heard he was passing through and she fought through a huge crowd of people for just a glimpse of the man. When she saw him, she crept up behind him and grabbed ahold of the hem of his garment, just for a brief moment.

He turned around and said, "Who touched my clothes?" His friends who were with him didn't understand what he meant, because there were hundreds of people pressing in all around him. It could have been anyone. But the man looked around to see a woman trembling with fear. She fell down at his feet and told him what she had done. In this middle eastern culture, someone who was sick was not even welcome in the city gates and could not touch anyone. But instead of showing anger at her cultural disobedience, the man said to her, "Because you believed, you are healed." And she was. She immediately stopped bleeding.

I wonder if his eyes might have twinkled, and the corners of his mouth turned slightly upward to see such a desperate woman who believed so much that one touch of his clothing would heal her wounds. She had great faith. She knew her worthless status in her culture because of her sickness, but she carried great hope of being well. She risked everything for her dream, for one touch of the divine.

I think my grandfather believed deep down that one touch of greatness, one ounce of belief in a hero would somehow lift his soul higher. His heart leaped in his chest when he reached out for the great man's coattails on that fall day nearly 100 years ago. When Lindy passed and Anderson grabbed his coat for that tiny second in time, his hurts did not matter.

He began to believe that the impossible was in fact possible, that a drunken father's casual abandonment would not define him. This could be the beginning of a purposeful life, somehow transforming that invisible boy by his encounter with greatness. Best of all, he began to see that something damaged could be redeemed. The bleeding stopped. His wounds started to heal.

Son

John...his name must have been a forewarning to the path his life would take. His grandfather, the good country doctor and entrepreneur, Seaborn Anderson Roddenbery, and then his father, Seaborn Anderson, Jr., the United States Congressman, shared the same stately name. They distinguished it by the goodness and charm of Georgia gentlemen now nearing extinction.

They were of the generation whose arms tired from tipping their hats to each lady who passed when they walked into town. They were men who were made by the sweat of building their own homes, board by board, and defending what they claimed to be their land against the nearby Creeks. They were educated men who gave back to their communities and neighbors and whose obituaries encompassed entire columns of newspapers. "Seaborn Anderson Roddenbery" was a name of honor and regional fame.

Anderson's father's name, however, was John. It was a common name for a man who would fight and ultimately fail at being anything but ordinary his whole life. The good name of Seaborn Anderson skipped right over John and landed on his son, my grandfather. Maybe much of the strength and staying power skipped him, too. Or it could be that all of the greatness that he might have had poured into his firstborn, my grandfather, at his birth. Anderson's father John (my great-grandfather) was a complicated man. That is the best and most common way he has been described to me. I have no memory of him, even though I met him as a young girl at least once. To try to truly understand him would be nearly impossible, like trying to paint a picture with water. I'm still going to try.

John William Roddenbery (my great grandfather) was born in Cairo, Georgia, the first child of Seaborn Anderson, Jr. (the Congressman) and Johnnie Roddenbery. He attended grade school in Thomasville and high school at Riverside Academy, a private school in Gainesville, Georgia, while his father was serving in The United States Congress in Washington, D.C.

He grew to become a good-looking man of average height and weight. His eyes and hair were both a common brown. According to his children, he was born and raised with a silver spoon in his mouth, and his every desire as a child was gratified. Even in his youth, he was quite charming and personable. He ran around the neighborhood with the likes of D. Abbott Turner, who later became one of Columbus, Georgia's leading businessmen.

His father highly valued education, and strictly enforced John's studies, at times homeschooling him if travel to and from Washington interrupted his schooling. His father's impossible expectations of him as the firstborn son haunted John at a young age, and he began toting the long family tradition of high achievers on his back as a boy. He could probably have coasted along and followed his father into politics or law, but he never really enjoyed learning and resented his father's pressure to perform well in school.

By the time he enrolled at the University of Georgia, the future felt uncertain for John. Everything that is, except for his God given gift. John never felt so alive as when he was making music. He had one of those voices that you might never forget. Had you heard him effortlessly climbing the scales in perfect pitch with a clear and entrancing tone, you may have thought this tenor could be one of the greats.

Once at the University of Georgia, he was free from his father's constant pressure. He joined Alpha Tau Omega fraternity, but his greatest joy was performing as a singer in the University Glee Club. His beautiful voice often charmed audiences as the featured soloist of the group. In the long line of physicians, businessmen and public servants, John branched out from the restrictive family tree, a gifted performer and singer. He dreamed of the lights on Broadway.

At his father's urging, John applied for law school and was accepted upon his graduation from UGA. His plans abruptly changed when his father died unexpectedly, and John was forced to return home to help his family. He was never able, and I believe never wanted, to return to school and become a lawyer.

John met Mary Carle Hurst when she was eighteen and he was twenty in Thomasville, Georgia. Mary Carle was a master pianist, and their love of music and the stage quickly knit them together. They were soon married on July 11, 1914, and they moved into a colonial style home belonging to his family in Thomasville. His love of the stage and musical abilities should have given his future certain promise, but he lacked self-confidence and thought he would try his hand at a more practical endeavor: farming.

After all, John's grandfather had started the Roddenbery Pickle empire out of a bunch of sugar cane fields and rows of peanuts in Cairo, Georgia. It was in his blood. His grandfather, however, did not grow up eating off silver utensils. I don't think John's hands ever grew accustomed to dirt and callouses. His fear of failure kept him from really sticking anything out to the end, and an impatient farmer is about as valuable as a sterile rooster.

According to his daughter, my great aunt Martha, John became increasingly restless, impulsive, and unfocused. He was a complicated person who shifted from charming and pleasant to unhappy and unpredictable in an instant. His pent-up anger erupted almost without warning. His children felt he was unreasonably envious of their very beautiful and popular mother, Mary Carle...

She is still so grand in my mind. The only thing fake about my great-grandmother Mary Carle was the costume jewelry dangling from ear lobes and around her neck and both wrists, and the caterpillar-like eyebrows she blindly drew above her hazel but cloudy eyes. No animal print was too gaudy, no hat was too flashy! Her entrance into and exit from a room were enough to inspire the jealousy of many women throughout the course of her ninety-one years.

My only vivid memory of my grandfather's mother Mary Carle was when I was about seven years old, and I traveled to Savannah to visit her on her birthday with my mom. She was turning ninety, though she confided in my mom that she was "one hundred" that day. Ninety seemed about the same as a hundred to me, and I remember being afraid and awestruck at the same time when she approached me.

I knew she had been an accomplished piano player, and she did not let the blinding glaucoma she developed in her mid-thirties deter her musical career. She pulled my face just inches from hers so that she could see my faint outline. It scared me a little bit, and I fought the urge to pull away from her even though I was afraid of her deep wrinkles, foggy eyes, and long, stringy gray hair.

The silver strands of her waist length hair were pulled back away from her face. She was still beautiful underneath the years. I could see the traces of the "Miss Atlanta" who christened the first plane to take off at Candler Airfield in Atlanta, now Hartsfield International Airport. I remember she was proud as I played my violin for her.

Later in life, she lived in a small trailer in Savannah where she could easily navigate and still do just about anything. It was the first trailer I had ever been inside. I was shocked by how small the living space was. There was no real furniture to speak of and everything inside seemed as old as she did. It smelled musty and ancient.

I barely remember the details of her home because the stuff seemed so small and unimportant next to just being in her presence. She had a way of drawing you in and making you feel like the only person in the world. She was at peace in her circumstances and grateful for her home in the Biltmore Gardens Trailer Park. Even entering her tenth decade in her modest home, she gave the impression of a beautiful and grand lady in a great house.

In the 1980's, my family lived in an upper middle class ranch style home on a dirt road fronting Lake Waunatta in Winter Park, Florida. The home had a huge grassy yard of over an acre, an old inactive water well, and was covered in sun faded cedar shake shingles. There was a pool, and the playhouse above the carport is still in my mind the most awesome place for a child to hide and play.

We had plenty, but there were others with much more and many with much less. I don't remember ever needing things we couldn't have, but I also grew up not thinking things were that important. I must have inherited that from my parents. I certainly understood that the measure of someone's worth is not dependent on where they live or where they come from. But if I'm honest, the inside of that trailer startled me. Seeing her meager means awakened in me a deep gratitude for all that I had and a compassion for those who had little.

Mary Carle loved her trailer because she knew where everything was. I suppose when you can't see, all the shiny and beautiful things lose their hold on you. She and her second husband, Bob Hofer, made homemade wine in that mobile home with their TV advertised Ronco wine-making kit. "Wine o'clock" arrived each day at 5:00 p.m. as they called it, and they would enjoy a glass of homemade pinot together.

Bob was ten years her junior, and he flew a crop duster biplane around the wetlands near Savannah well into his seventies. She would say he took such good care of her, and he told her every morning how beautiful she was. It was a sincere love discovered late in life; a story foreign to Mary Carle's earlier years.

Mary Carle's youth seemed promising enough. She was the oldest daughter of Rosa Lee "Rozzie" O'Kelley and Carl Earnest Hurst. Rozzie, Mary Carle's mother, was one of six children, five girls and one boy. Both of her parents died young, and the only son, Lubba Lochern O'Kelly, was fifteen when he began to raise his five sisters. He worked at a sawmill and purposed not to marry until all of his sisters did. According to my great aunt Martha, Rozzie was by far the most beautiful of all the girls. "She was quiet, soft-spoken, with a gentle manner and lovely smile."

Carl Hurst was walking with a friend by the house where Rozzie lived. At the time, she was nineteen years old and was perched on a swing on the front porch. Carl said to his friend, "See that young girl sitting on that swing? I don't know who she is, but I am going to marry her." And he did that same year on June 15, 1894. Carl was sixteen and Rozzie was nineteen. He kept his age a secret from her for many years, but Carl always loved and cherished Rozzie.

Carl was both a well-educated and a polished gentleman of average build. He had the bluest eyes my great aunt Martha had ever seen, and they always appeared to be smiling. Of English ancestry, he was a direct descendant of Tobias Hurst, the first Hurst to set foot in the New World. In August 1618, Tobias along with forty men under the leadership of Sir Edwin Sandy landed in Jamestown aboard the English ship *Treasurer*. Many generations later, the Hurst family was well established in the South.

Carl attended the Baptist Church in Atlanta and no one on that side of the family recalled him saying a cross word about anyone. He had great charm, was well read and well spoken. He enjoyed writing and was a master of math and figures. He had a warm and pleasing personality.

Rozzie was a true Irish beauty. She wore dark black hair long enough that she could sit on it. Her eyes were wide set and a beautiful shade of grey. She had an enviable complexion that only the Irish can boast about. Gentle and charming, she had few but fine clothes, which she wore with great style.

In the early 1900's, Atlanta was earning a reputation as a bustling and beautiful city in which to live. Carl was an avid golfer at a time when Bobby Jones and golf were becoming very popular. He earned several golf trophies of his own. He and Rozzie were excellent ice skaters, and both loved to dance. They frequently visited Piedmont Driving Club and ice skated in Piedmont Park.

Carl Earnest Hurst and Rozzie Lee O'Kelly Hurst had only one child for fifteen years. She was my grandfather's mother, Mary Carle Hurst, a beautiful little girl with blazing blue eyes and dark hair. She had her mother's Irish complexion. She was born in Cordele, Georgia on April 28, 1897, and soon after, the family moved to Atlanta where Mary Carle lived until she married.

When Mary Carle was quite young, she was diagnosed with a "leaking heart." Mary Carle recounted her mother rocking her, singing to her, and crying because she was afraid her baby girl was going to die. She would pat her mother's face and say, "please don't cry Mommy." Although she did have a heart problem that became more serious in later years, she led a very active, long, and remarkable life.

Mary Carle lived with her parents in their home on the corner of Piedmont Avenue and 6th Street in Atlanta. She was three years old when Santa brought her a toy piano for

Christmas. The next day, her parents were astounded to find her sitting on the floor playing "Suwanee River." When they asked her what she was playing, she replied, "Suwanee Pond," a favorite story of hers to tell.

In grade school, the children marched in and out of school to the music of this small child. She had never had one music lesson but could play anything she heard. Her Uncle Arthur Flowers had no living children of his own and viewed her as the favorite niece. He bought her a brand new upright piano when she was nine years old. From that point on, music was her life.

Her father Carl was the City Auditor for Atlanta and the Secretary for the Atlanta Chamber of Commerce. With his connections, the family was able to attend plays, operas, concerts, and appearances such as the famed Italian tenor Enrico Caruso and other popular artists and musicians. These activities further cultivated Mary Carle's love for music and the theater.

Her parents noticed at an early age their daughter's God given talent for playing the piano, and her father thought it was important to give her an opportunity for exceptional teaching. A very famous musician, Professor Alfred Barili, lived a few blocks away. When she was ten years old, her father decided he would take her to the professor's home.

Alfredo Barili was a pianist, teacher, and composer. He was born in Florence, Italy in 1857 and was a famous concert pianist in Europe and America by the time he was ten years old. His poor health in later years ended his performing career, but he composed and taught selectively from his residence in Atlanta. Many of the South's finest musicians owed their training to him at this time. One of his best-known compositions was "The Cradle Song" for piano, and he was honored by a request from Washington for a manuscript of this composition that resides in the Congressional Library.

One spring morning, a proud father walked his little girl down the street, up the front steps, and knocked on Professor Barili's door. Barili was surprised to see a father and young lady on his doorstep and even more surprised to learn the father's intent to enroll this child in one of his classes. Barili was polite and listened to the request, but he explained that he did not accept children for piano lessons. He only worked with well advanced players who wanted additional instruction or fine tuning.

In his quiet way, Carl asked, "Will you please just listen to her play?" When she had finished playing, Professor Barili said, "I will take her, but she must work long and hard." She was a devoted and diligent student for many years, and the Professor molded her raw talent into a work of art. Sometimes when her father would come to pick her up after her lesson, he would find her seated at the piano playing while Professor Barili laid on his couch listening to the notes dancing off her agile fingers.

Barili had a famous aunt named Madame Adelina Patti who was a soprano from South Wales. She began performing in places like New York City at age seven and later had her own theater called the Patti Theater near her home in Craig-y-Nas Castle in Wales. Famed opera composer Giuseppe "Verdi declared her the greatest singer he had ever heard, and others—from musicians to royalty to an unanimously adulatory opera public—eagerly concurred."[2]

Professor Barili visited his beloved aunt many times in her castle in South Wales, and on one of his visits he told Madame Patti about Mary Carle and her remarkable talent. On Madame's next tour to Atlanta, she presented Mary Carle with a "Medal of Excellence in Music." This was Mary Carle's most prized possession. My great aunt said that "music was her gift from God, and it often sustained her" through trying times.

In her teen years, Mary Carle was very popular with girls and boys. Her mother kept abreast of all the latest styles in clothes. She would go to the fine department stores in Atlanta to get an idea of the latest styles and what her daughter would look the best wearing. She made all of Mary Carle's clothes, including her hats.

Family legend maintains Mary Carle was the first lady in Atlanta to carry a "swagger stick." It was a stylish lady's walking cane, with a handle adorned with inlaid stones. She was photographed walking down Peachtree Street with her swagger stick and was featured in the Atlanta Journal, or so legend has it. I have so far been unable to come up with proof!

Marist College was across from her home growing up, and her father said there were always boys hanging over the fence vying for dates with Mary Carle. She would climb into a small, simple buggy as happily as she would climb into a stylish carriage. Her father attended every dance she ever went to as a chaperone. He would arrive when she did and go home when she left. She was expected to be home by the time her father got there.

In the early 1900's, Atlanta and Houston had a battle to grow their populations to 100,000. As part of a promotional effort, Atlanta ran a contest to select the most beautiful girl in Atlanta. Mary Carle won this contest. There were "booster buttons" everywhere with her picture on them, and most people were wearing them around town. She kept one of these buttons for many years as a personal treasure, although we could not find the button or the "Medal of Excellence in Music" after she died.

Mary Carle, my great grandmother, was not only lovely to look at but quite lovely to be near. Everything about her was melody: her walk, her talk, her laughter and smile. Somehow, she could make dark things bright, sad things happy, and ugly things beautiful. Her eyes found the good things, her ears seemed to hear only pleasant melodies, and her heart could usually find the positive in a person or a situation.

Unless that person was her first husband, John. Her courtship with my great-grandfather, John Roddenbery, must have been a whirlwind romance...the beauty queen and the son of a congressman. With her good looks and his irresistible charm, they made an outstanding duo. At one point, she tickled the ivories, and he sang off Broadway. The two were both very spoiled growing up. Mary Carle as a young woman had never made her own bed, cooked an egg, made a piece of toast, or boiled water. She had not been exposed to "indecent speech" as she called it.

As a newly married woman, she was preparing to have her husband John's sister Mary Upchurch and her husband Worth over for dinner. They had a few chickens on the farm, and Mary Carle had seen the neighbors chase a hen into a corner and catch it around the neck. After they caught it, they would swing the chicken around while holding tightly to its head. Then they would pluck the feathers off and cook the hen.

She decided the process looked easy enough and she set the menu for chicken that night. Once she finally caught up with one of those chickens and had it by the neck, she began to swing fiercely around and around in a circle like a windmill. She then released the dizzy hen, that instead of lying dead on the ground shook itself, clucked, and ran away.

Mary Carle was so upset she called John crying. When he saw her in tears and heard the explanation of the botched slaying, he said, "You don't just swing your arm around. You hold the chicken's head in your hand and make small, quick twists of your wrist." Needless to say, they did not have chicken for dinner that night.

Mary Carle's trauma in the kitchen was not quite over. Not long after that, a leak sprang up in a spigot in the kitchen. Mary Carle called a plumber named George. After examining the problem, he explained he couldn't fix it because his partner forgot to bring the part he needed. When John arrived home, he noticed the leak and asked Mary Carle why it had not yet been fixed. She replied, "That son of a bitch didn't bring the right part." Stunned silence followed. John asked, "Who?" She timidly answered, "I don't know his name. The plumber just said that 'son of a bitch.'" She had never before heard the "b" word.

Over time, a dark shadow eclipsed Mary Carle's personal life and eventually invaded her vision. She was diagnosed with glaucoma in her thirties. The disease formed a blindness over her eyes that lasted as long as she lived and threatened to rob her of her musical gift. She decided to learn to play the piano by memory. If she heard something once, she could easily play it on the piano. Her hands always glided across the keys with resplendent flair. She smiled the whole time she played. "Spread that out amongst yourselves," she would say, as she kissed her fingertips and waved it among a crowd, even one as small as her family in the living room.

Mary Carle loved each of her three children with a devoted, unfailing love. Later when the youngest, Mary, was terminally ill, the three children sat together at Mary's breakfast bar in her kitchen and reflected on the people they had become and how each in their own way was able to emerge from a tumultuous childhood self-confident and loved.

They all attributed their triumph over untold difficulties and trials to the love of their mother. She not only loved each of them so completely and unconditionally, but she led all three to believe they were truly wonderful. She rarely scolded or punished them. In her eyes, they were not only good, but the best! How magnanimous was her gift to them.

Her support was so great, so constant, so accepting and affirming that Mary, Martha, and Anderson basked in the warmth, understanding, and love of their mother long after her death. She made each feel the possibilities of their wonderful capabilities and importance. They were each children of grace. My Great Aunt Martha later wrote "her keen, artistic mind, her remarkable talent, and her joyous spirit were hers until her death on October 11, 1989."

It was after all, the eve of terrific change. I was surprised by my own tears that night as though some voodoo doll with my name on it was being stabbed with pins in some faraway place and making me feel a deep and inexplicable pain. On the way home from pizza dinner, I drove with her almost two-year-old hand in mine. I left my palm open until I felt her tiny fingers wrap around my pointer finger.

We sat that way for the last two miles in the dark and quiet of a Friday night. An hour past her bedtime, she sat with her small green Crocs crossed and resting on the back of the passenger seat. Her free hand was wrapped around her baby as she stared out the window and held my hand. It was one of the last nights where it would be just us, before her little sister would enter the world.

When I was a girl, I used to love to hold my dad's hand. If

I am honest, I still would if I could. Sometimes, my dad would press down on my nail with the tip of his finger so it would dig into his calloused skin. I could not stand the way it would make my fingernail bend under the pressure. I'm not sure if he even realized he was doing it. I married a man who does the same thing.

For some reason, when my daughter did it this night, I could only smile as she rhythmically rotated each of her fingers and pushed down hard on my nail. I know both our worlds were about to change, and we would never have this quiet moment back again. It was surely gone as quickly as it came.

I know she will never remember it, and it probably means nothing to anyone but me. It is one of those memories a mother holds deep in her heart, a stash of sweetness for the long days ahead when things don't turn out just right. It was a memory of innocence and dependence for when the back talking and eye rolling begin.

I found an old picture published in the *Atlanta Journal*, simply captioned "Beautiful Mother and Child." From Mary Carle's lap, my grandfather Anderson looks happy and peaceful. His mother is radiant, with no real lines on her face...a proud mother with her darling son. I wonder if he ever gripped her finger on a quiet night or with what song she lulled him to sleep. Could she have felt all those warm feelings I had that night in the car with my daughter? How could she ever let herself believe she could leave him? I hear a lot more about fathers leaving, and I can justify that better somehow. And maybe John leaving was the catalyst for their whole family to be torn apart.

I wondered all my growing up years what would cause a woman to leave her children to be raised by someone else. Now that I have been a parent for eighteen years, I understand that a mother should never judge another mother. Most of us are just doing the best we can. We are trying to survive and trying to give our children the best lives possible.

Mary Carle struggled as a blind, single mother in 1930's rural Georgia, but she could entertain on a cruise ship and could help provide for her children if she traveled. She believed this might be better than a disabled, single mother at home with no income. Her kids usually lived with friends of the family but more often with other relatives in her absence. Even after glaucoma took the leaves off trees, petals off flowers, and dimples off her children's cheeks, her pen found its way to paper often enough to write the most beautiful letters. They usually arrived from somewhere off the coast, on a cruise ship in the Atlantic Ocean, addressed to her Seaborn son living somewhere in middle Georgia. It was those sincere letters of love and encouragement that lifted him up in her absence.

Boy.

One year before Anderson entered the world, the Great War began raging an ocean away. Uncertainty and fear penetrated the air like machine gun bullets, and it seemed almost everyone wanted to know how they could help. The times called for unprecedented frugality. Next to nothing was thrown away, and little boys and girls were made to finish every bite on their plates. People purchased only absolute necessities and many simply did without.

When my grandfather Anderson was born on August 6, 1915, his parents John and Mary Carle beamed with joy. In the long, dark shadow of a murderous war, pockets of life and light emerged, and a baby boy brought hope into their otherwise

bleak lives. John and Mary Carle lived in Thomasville,
Georgia at the time of Anderson's birth. He was named
Seaborn Anderson Roddenbery III after his grandfather and
his great-grandfather.

When it was time for a second baby, the small family had
moved to Florida and away from the Thomasville farmland.
Martha was born on July 3, 1917, in St. Augustine. John was
an ensign in the Navy, and the War hurled many concerns and
uncertainties at the young family. Baby Martha was taken to
live with her maternal grandparents who lived on the St. Johns
River in Jacksonville, Florida. It was the first of many times
the Roddenbery children would be passed around to relatives.

John, Mary Carle, and little Anderson soon headed to
Charleston where John began training school at the naval base
there. In the city, there were open-air butcher stalls where the
scraps of unused meat were thrown aside. The rancid stench of
raw meat permeated the streets like fresh turd on a hot day. The
constant shadows of buzzards overhead drew dark, swirling
circles on the ground below, and the market workers would
gaze up at the grotesque birds, jokingly calling them "eagles."

John was commissioned as an officer in the United States
Navy and was preparing to go to battle. The family nervously
awaited his departure. The Roddenberys had only been in
Charleston a short while when word spread that the War

to End All Wars was in fact over on November 11, 1918, just before John was called to active duty. Hundreds of people jammed the streets of Charleston celebrating, and amid the chaos, John and little Anderson stood frozen in time.

Three-year-old Anderson could not see past the people on every side of him, and he grew increasingly afraid as firecrackers popped off on the sidewalks and streets. People celebrated wildly with riotous screaming, and Anderson's terror intensified when he lost sight of his father. The raucous curtain of people closed in on him and just as he knew he was lost; he felt a stiff hand on his shoulder. John suddenly reached down for his screaming child, picked up his small frame, and placed him on his strong shoulders.

From way up high, the South Carolina sun melted his fears into joy. Anderson glanced up and down the street. Strangers hugged one another, streamers floated down onto the tops of peoples' heads and rested on low bowing tree branches. Through an alleyway, he glimpsed the shimmering ocean, and as the streets around him erupted in praise, the Central Powers clear on the other side of the vast water were silently retreating, bloody and beaten up.

This glorious moment stood fixed in time- the suddenly warm sunshine, the loud cheering and dancing, the strong shoulders of his dad. The memory would resound in American minds as the end of a great war far away from their homeland, but for Anderson, it was only the beginning of a battle that would rage under his roof. It was one of the last moments when his father alleviated his fears instead of giving rise to them.

Following the Armistice, the family moved back to St. Augustine, Florida. The nation's oldest city was founded in 1565. Its rich Spanish and British roots from previous occupations brought a wealth of cultural heritage and opportunity. The oldest masonry fort in the continental U.S., then called Fort Marion (now returned to its original name Castillo de San Marcos), spread out like a beached starfish on the northern side of the coastal town. The fort took 23 years to build and was completed in 1695. Its coquina limestone construction could resist fire and was virtually impenetrable. It seemed the perfect backdrop to a new beginning for the Roddenbery family.

They moved into a house on San Marco Avenue near the old fort, less than a mile from where the river's mouth spewed tepid water directly into the Atlantic. Their home sat on a strip of land nestled between the Matanzas and San Sebastian Rivers, within spitting distance to the water. The architecture waffled between Spanish and Victorian, and a skyline of Palm trees zigzagged against the bright blue tropical canvas. The Atlantic's roar constantly called to the children, and it seemed to breathe on them, it was so close. They could taste the salt in the air on an aggressive breeze, and as Anderson looked up, his face would nearly always find the light beaming down on him.

They lived there for a few happy years while John ventured out as an entrepreneur with his own business. He owned and operated the Ford Automobile Agency in St. Augustine. The Model T Fords he sold had a crank on the front that had to be turned to start the engine. In its still primitive state, Florida had very few paved roads, and nearby the closest thing was a narrow brick road running from Jacksonville to St. Augustine. The auto industry waited as impatiently as a hungry toddler for the infrastructure to catch up.

Oil millionaire tycoon Henry Flagler brought the railroad to St. Augustine nearly three decades before to boost his booming resort business, most notably his famed Ponce de Leon Hotel. It was the first hotel constructed completely of poured concrete and one of the earliest designs to be wired for electricity. Flagler's friend, Thomas Edison, oversaw the installation of the generators himself, while Louis Tiffany of Tiffany & Co. designed the stained-glass windows in the vast dining room. This Spanish Renaissance style hotel quickly became the choice destination of the rich and famous and was named for the explorer who searched unsuccessfully for the Fountain of Youth there.

From the street, the hotel resembled a hovering mother bird corralling her young into a tropical paradise. The palatial building sat perched on King Street with a wing stretched out on either side toward the street, encircling a lush courtyard. The tiled roof covered the top of the hotel like the small, soft feathers on a grand peacock's head. The towering twin spires flanked either side of the rotunda and emerged from the rooftop in two decadent crowns. Against the white stucco facade, the stained-glass windows were like emeralds and sapphires adorning the tail of the great bird. Even the walls dripped with luxury.

John Roddenbery had only begun his journey to find success and notability but would fare no better than de Leon in finding his own elusive treasure. The Roddenberys arrived unfortunately just as St. Augustine tourism began to decline. The expansion of the railway further south to even warmer Miami made it a less desirable destination for northerners. The hotel as well as the economy struggled. The marvelous hotel is a mainstay in St. Augustine, and now serves higher education as Flagler College.

The oceanfront town certainly had its romance, and the children found pleasure in the beautiful city. They ran in the surf of the beaches, played on their street amid the hustle and bustle, and paid little mind to the sweltering Florida humidity.

It appeared their wandering family would find its balance on this skinny stretch of land that seemed to float on the eastern shore of Florida.

The children had a wonderful black nurse who cared for them. They called her "Aunt Florida." She watched after the children during the day, often nestling Andy and Martha on her starched lap. They snuggled against her bleached and perfectly ironed apron, basking in her tender touch and breathing in her scent of Octagon soap. Her arms were warm and strong, and most importantly available to comfort the two small children. She hummed low and soft to them as she went about her daily work.

Aunt Florida took the children on afternoon walks through the neighborhood. The homes in old St. Augustine sat narrow and deep, with only about five yards between them and between the front of each house and the sidewalk. It seemed like everyone had some type of fragrant, beautiful flower growing in their tiny front yard, irresistible to the touch of a young child.

One day Martha was walking along with Aunt Florida among the palm tree lined streets and picked a few flowers in front of one neighbor's house. A very aggravated woman stepped out on her porch and up onto her "high horse," and she gave little Martha and Florida a good lip lashing. Aunt Florida put her hands on her full hips and said, "Ain't no flowers too good for my baby to pick!"

Florida's bold and protective words always stayed with Martha. While her parents' relationship at home began to crumble, that small incident gave Martha the confidence to stand up for and believe in herself. The unconditional and accepting love of Aunt Florida was forever sewn into the fabric of her heart.

The wide palm branches offered welcome shade from the brutality of the Florida sun. Aunt Florida's strength and affection shielded the children from the outside world, but nothing could protect them from the turmoil at home. As the children perused the sunny neighborhood with bloom embellished sidewalks in St. Augustine, John grew restless for adventures that had passed by him. His deflated dreams constantly eluded him. The voices inside him grew louder and his consumption of alcohol to silence them ever increased. His own father's disappointment and disapproval overshadowed his every endeavor. He was expected to go to law school and follow the family tradition of politics, service, and entrepreneurship. None of those things panned out.

The pressures of his personal and public life mounted. John became increasingly impatient with Mary Carle and the children and blamed and criticized them for any minor misstep. His shifting moods gave way to an unpredictable and insatiable rage that would erupt and land on Mary Carle first, Anderson second, and usually subsided before Martha caught any wrath. What started with verbal assaults became physical punishment.

Despite the domestic unrest, Mary Carle became pregnant with their third child. During this period, the Ford Automobile business began to struggle, and John felt like a songbird trapped in a cage. His voice was his one great gift, the thing that awarded him the applause of the masses. It was the God-given jewel in an otherwise lackluster crown. Broadway melodies beguiled him and involuntarily spilled out the way blood trickles out of a fresh wound.... except that John's wounds were now decades old scars that were incised and healed over so many times he had almost forgotten the original offenses. Unfortunately, his demons kept impeccable memories. The words of the show tunes spoke of true love and unbridled happiness and sang little of the depression and desperation stalking him. Imprisoned in a life he saw as beneath him, his selfish desires called to him louder than the constant dredge of family life.

Many times, when the children were young, John would disappear without explanation for several weeks sending no word to his family. I am not sure if anyone knew where he went on these outings. If they did know, they never talked about it. Wherever he went, alcohol was plentiful and close at hand, to be sure. He did not speak of his times away. He would simply return, remorseless, but with bland acceptance of his life as it was for another short, undetermined stretch of time.

Mary Carle experienced his abandonment too often in her married life. In the fall of 1919, Mary Carle was expecting their third child, and delivery time was near. John did not leave any money for groceries or other needs when he slunk out of town in his hand cranked Ford car. Mary Carle's anxieties about the new baby coming, two small children to care for, and her absent husband sent her into a panic. She called her Aunt Jewel in Macon. Jewel told Mary Carle to pack up herself and her young children and drive to Macon.

Without many options, they dusted off the sand from their shoes and headed north for the golden orange hues of Georgia autumn. Jewel's husband, Arthur Flowers (the same one who bought her a piano as a child) showed extreme generosity toward Mary Carle and her children many times over the course of their lives. Arthur and Jewel had no living children; they had one child who died in infancy. They warmly welcomed the Roddenberys and cared for them in Macon. The baby, Mary, was born in Macon Hospital on November 4, 1919. Shortly thereafter, they returned to St. Augustine a family of four, without a reliable or steady patriarch.

Eventually John returned to their home in St. Augustine and joined his growing family with no explanation or apology. Mary Carle needed him too much to protest- needed his income, his help, and his presence in the home, albeit unreliable. It was a different time, and women- especially a single mother- had little opportunity. At the beginning of the 20th century, divorce was not only unheard of, it was downright shameful.

They resumed some sort of family life. The very gentle and loving personality of Mary Carle overshadowed her overbearing and unbridled husband. Her smile, her musical voice, her demonstrative affection, and artistic qualities served as a cocoon for her three children during these formative years. They were somewhat protected and shielded from much of his negative influence. As they grew older, they developed a cautious fear of him and then a bitter anger.

When baby Mary was a few years old, John decided to move his family from bustling St. Augustine to a very small town called Hastings, Florida, about forty miles away. Farming was the main attraction in this area nicknamed Rattlesnake Alley, and John decided on a whim he wanted to farm potatoes there. Whenever he felt aimless in his career, it seemed he gravitated toward growing crops. He found an old house with a farm and brought his family to live for a short time in Hastings.

Their new country life was foreign to their former city life in St. Augustine. The modest white wooden home had a wide and airy back porch, perfect for barefoot running and banister swinging. Around the sides of the home, the woods thick with brush and wildlife welcomed curious children. When the bright butter sun finally melted down into the treetops, a cacophony of animal calls and chants made a lullaby of sorts. The unfamiliar lowland chorus of treefrogs, crickets, Whip-Poor-Wills and Nighthawks, and the low "hoooooo" of an occasional owl put the young children on edge in the beginning. But after a week or so, they came to expect and look forward to the soothing nighttime symphony.

The earlier owners left behind a pen with four white rabbits in the back yard and only an old sofa in the living room. The cotton tuft rabbits were great entertainment for the young children who loved to chase and cuddle them. The sofa, on the other hand, became an object of duress for Mary Carle. Just before they moved in, John killed a rattlesnake that had made its nest in the old couch. After that, Mary Carle lived in constant fear of baby rattlesnakes lurking in the house. Whenever she expressed her concerns to John, he would howl with laughter. He seemed to revel in her discomfort and fear.

One of my grandfather's favorite childhood memories came during this time in Hastings. Anderson was six and started school that year, and Santa Claus brought him a wonderful Christmas present. Anderson awoke to find a small, untamed Shetland pony. The mean, temperamental thing came with a bridle, saddle, and a small four wheeled carriage adorned with a cushioned seat.

He decided he wanted to ride the wild pony even though it incessantly tried to bite and kick him. Anderson stood outside the wired corral fence to entice the pony with a bucket of sweet feed. When the pony reached its head over the fence, Anderson slipped the bit into its mouth and secured the bridle over its head. Then he put the blanket and saddle on its back. The first few rides were treacherous, but the pony became better mannered as time passed and his owner's determination prevailed. Occasionally the children would hitch the pony up to the wagon, but the little horse still had a mind of its own. A ride in the wagon usually turned into an unexpected adventure on a makeshift path through the woods with the passengers screaming, ducking and dodging tree limbs and bushes.

It wasn't long before Anderson realized the pony was also a "gift" for his mother. Mary Carle would load up a laundry bag with soiled clothes and hitch up the cart to the pony. They would ride on the narrow dirt road to the home of their washer woman, Liza. The ditches on either side of the road were mostly barren except for some underbrush and palmettos. The desolate dirt path had no sign of houses or people until they would finally arrive at Liza's house after what felt like forever. She would unload the laundry and dump it in her big black pot set on bricks. Between the bricks were burning coals. The steam from the boiling water and fumes of lye and Octagon soap burned the hair inside of their noses.

After a year in Hastings, John again moved his family to Fort Pierce where they lived along the Indian River. Though their parents' relationship kept fracturing further apart, the Indian River acted as the perfect escape from trouble and felt like paradise to the three young children. The natural beauty of the landscape and surroundings were colorful and magnificently lush. Fruits and foliage grew abundantly. In their playground of beauty and bounty, they romped and played, ran and stumbled, laughed and cried. They learned how to play together and leave one another out, how to be kind and heartless, how to be selfish and selfless. They did a lot of growing up together on the banks of the river.

Fort Pierce is a little more than halfway down the east coast of Florida in St. Lucie County. It is known as Sunrise City for its magnificent morning sky and is the sister city to San Francisco, the Sunset City. It was named for the nearby fort with the same name which was built in 1838 to protect U.S. interests during the second Seminole War, thought to be the costliest of the U.S. battles with Native Americans. The war ended with the forced removal of 4,000 Seminoles to the west, leaving about 350 Seminoles who would eventually rise up again a third time.

John's oldest sister, Louette, and her family lived in Fort Pierce. Her husband, Gardner Nottingham was the mayor. They had two young boys, Gardner, Jr., who was about eight years old, and John, who was six. Anderson was seven at the time, and the three boys would play together at his rambling house with its spacious grounds and myriad of fruit trees.

The house had thick, reddish-yellow tall grass in the back. It was the perfect hiding place for little boys. They crawled on their bellies like army men, elbow after dirty elbow, propelling their bodies along through the coarse terrain. They played hide and seek for hours in that yard, as well as simultaneously avoiding unwanted play guests who wore dresses and looked like little sisters.

Farther away from the house was an old windmill formerly used to pump water. By the time the Roddenberys moved in, the house had running water, so the windmill was not used for anything practical. It was, however, the perfect apparatus for all kinds of childhood games. Anderson dreamed of flying, and the windmill served as the ideal vehicle to test out his little boy theories.

One afternoon, Anderson called little Martha to come out with him to the windmill. "I'm gonna climb up it. You wanna come with me?" he asked, with a sly but convincing grin on his face. Martha was desperate to play with him, so she swallowed her fears and struggled to match her brother's steady climb to the very top of the windmill. She put her hands where his had been and stepped exactly as he did on the rickety makeshift ladder. Once they reached the top, they could see the roof of their home, the tops of trees, and the scrubby prongs of palmettos that melted together like grass from up high.

Suddenly, he pulled out an umbrella he had earlier stashed near the top and said, "You know if you jump off here and hold the open umbrella over your head, you can fly down to the ground like an airplane. You wanna try it?" He deceived the silent Martha, "I've done it before. You try it." Martha desperately wanted to be brave and so badly wanted to play with her older brother, so she quietly contemplated her options. A few moments later, as little sisters do, Martha burst into tears crying for her mother. When Mary Carle appeared, she called them both to come down off the windmill. Immediately. That was the end of that game. The windmill was off limits from that point on. Its era culminated almost as soon as it began, but Anderson's unquenched interest in flying still flourished.

The relentless presence and regular tattling of two younger sisters left Anderson wanting for other boys to play with. He eventually befriended a little black boy who lived nearby. Born and raised in the South, Anderson learned from his friends and neighbors to disdain "Negroes" and to hate "Yankees." Every child growing up in Georgia in the 1920's heard of General Sherman's "scorched earth" policy, leaving ashes and desolation in its wake from Atlanta to Savannah. The previous generation handed down stories of Yankee troops pillaging and burning the southland and left a bitter aftertaste decades later in the mouths of nearly everyone south of the Mason-Dixon Line.

Because slavery was indisputably tied to the Civil War, or "the War of Northern Aggression" as it was known throughout the South, most whites hated blacks. "Negroes" became objects of wrath absorbing post-war disdain and much of the Southerners' misplaced blame for hardships. Consequently, Anderson grew up despising black people. Even so, the widely accepted lines of race and class did not apply to children young enough and lonely enough to ignore them.

Anderson's new, young friend had skin the color of mahogany stained wood. His round, white eyes had dark brown centers, and they would widen like saucers when anything was exciting or a little bit scary. When he laughed, his eyes narrowed to slits and his large white teeth shined. His new friend was active and jovial, but a bit shy. He did not seem bothered by the milky color of Anderson's skin. And in turn, Anderson was so glad to have another boy to romp and play with in the Florida wilderness, he didn't much mind that his new playmate was dark-skinned. Anderson nicknamed his new playmate "Sambo", and they had a lot of fun in those great outdoors.

The next-door neighbors had luscious peaches growing in their yard, and the two would sneak over the fence and feast on the neighbors' forbidden fruit. When John came home one day, he caught the two boys playing in the neighbor's yard eating peaches. John's rage at his young son exploded out of him. "Anderson, just WHAT IN THE HELL do you think you are doing?"

He immediately removed his belt and jerked Anderson over the fence. He grabbed him by the shirt and threw him to the ground. John whipped his young son uncontrollably, slap after slap with the leather piece of punishment. Whap. Whap. Anderson's little white fingers, still sticky with sweet peach juice, grasped through the grass, dug into the soft dirt and anchored him to the earth. Whap. He gritted his teeth together. Whap. Whap. Whap. "No son of mine will ever steal."

When his father finally relented and wandered away, Anderson eventually let go of the ground. After a few minutes he slowly sat up, his face dirty but dry. The whelps on his backside throbbed. No matter how hard and how often his father beat him, Anderson never shed a tear. He resolved to never let his dad see him cry.

After seeing this brutality of a white man on his white son, Sambo ran for home and didn't come around much after that. This was no place for a young black boy to get caught stealing peaches. Anderson fell back into the rhythm of playing with his sisters and steered clear of his father as best he could. He spent most afternoons outdoors where he was free from John's critical eye and heavy hand.

Despite the bad, there were glimpses of the father John could have been, the kind of dad children longed to have. One such time happened on a routine drive home from school. When Anderson's cousins Gardner and John visited from across town, the three little musketeers would invent projects to fill up the long, hot afternoons. One day, they had the wonderful idea to turn the backyard into a zoo. In the land of snakes, lizards, gophers, turtles, and alligators, any animal that couldn't stand up and walk on two legs was fair game. They spent weeks catching and stocking their backyard zoo and creating habitats with shoe boxes, crates, holes, and tubs of water.

After the cousins went home, Anderson continued to add animals to his growing zoo. One day when John was driving his three children home from school, they spotted a young alligator crawling its way down into the ditch on the side of the dirt road. "Anderson," he exclaimed as he stopped the car, "I believe an alligator is just what you need for your zoo."

A grinning John put it in park and instructed the children to stay put. He took the strap off Anderson's books, this time using the belt to win the admiration of his young son. He stepped out of the car holding the oval end of the strap, and he disappeared into the ditch. Three pairs of eyes and noses pressed against the window of the car. The anxious children held their breath, wondering who would emerge victorious from the roadside battle. A few long minutes later, John came up from the ditch with the leather strap around the alligator's jaws, lifting the scaly beast up so they could get a mouth-gaping look at it. Anderson squealed with delight, and Martha and Mary cowered in fear.

At about the time when John was maneuvering the alligator into the trunk of the car, John's oldest sister Louette drove by in her automobile. She halted the car in horror at the drama unfolding before her. She was on her way to see Mary

Carle, and she jumped out with all the protective instinct of a mother bear screaming, "John Roddenbery, you put these poor children in my car, and I will take them home. You take care of your alligator!" The children piled in Aunt Louette's car followed by John and the alligator, and as my Great Aunt Martha said in her retelling, "the circus traveled on down the road."

Now that they had an alligator, they needed to decide what to do with it. John had a large wooden crate big enough for a piano at the house, and they baited the five-foot-long reptile to wriggle inside. John nailed chicken wire across the top to seal it in. With the arrival of the newest and largest reptile, business at the zoo was booming. The children's friends from class and other neighborhood children came and paid their admission. The gophers grew so large the children could stand on their backs and ride them, the rabbits did what rabbits do and multiplied, and the alligator grew and grew.

One morning Mary Carle went outside to feed the only tame animal at the house, the cat. She was shocked to notice the wooden crate empty with the wire ripped open. There was no sign of the alligator. John drove around surveying the property, but with the swamp water so close by, he determined the alligator was as far away from the zoo as it could manage by now. Without the main attraction, the zoo closed. All they had

left was the cat, which tired of being thrown up and down by
bored children after the demise of the zoo.

Summertime on the Indian River had its drawbacks. The
sun was merciless, and if there was any slight breeze, it would
bring with it swarms of mosquitoes as big as dragonflies. The
air was stifling and oppressive, and the insects punished anyone
who went outside, especially at dusk.

Mary Carle supported a strict nap schedule from two
to four o'clock every afternoon for herself and the children.
She would put thin mats down on the floor in the large front
room for their long, hot, resting time. Sleep was usually not on
the children's agenda, but they had to be quiet and still for the
required time.

Sometimes Mary Carle would gather them up and get
them ready to go out on their dock on the river. There was a
small, fenced in area to the left side of the dock. It was sandy
and shallow there, and the children were allowed to bathe
freely because the fence kept them from going into deep water.
The children wandered out to the dock, and Anderson and
Martha went down to the end and peered into the murky
brown water.

Anderson already knew how to swim. When he was
three years old in Charleston, his father threw him into the

ocean on the premise that he would be forced to swim. He learned on his own survival instinct at a very young age. Martha could not swim, and Anderson decided while standing at the end of the dock that it was her turn to learn in the same manner he had learned. Martha stood peering over the edge of the wooden planks into the murky darkness beneath when Anderson gave her a swift push off the deep end of the dock into the dark, cool water of the river. He watched the top of her head submerge into the swampy water and huge ripples disrupt the still water in every direction. Almost immediately, she bobbed up screaming and splashing for help.

When Mary Carle noticed Martha was missing and heard the ruckus from down below the decking, she ran, jumped in and pulled Martha to safety. Anderson undoubtedly got a stern talking to from Mary Carle, and he promised to never do something so reckless again. Deep down, he was both relieved and satisfied knowing his experiment worked and at least his sister made it to the surface kicking and yelling. Though still a mischievous older brother, Anderson began to emerge as the young patriarch of his family with a desire to protect and teach his two younger sisters.

Religion and church peppered Mary Carle's childhood. Prayers and Sunday school at the Baptist Church in Atlanta had been an integral part of her life. Though John's parents had been devout Baptists in Thomasville as well, he never went to church once he had any say so. Mary Carle was determined to go to church in Fort Pierce, and she would wake, dress, feed, and drive her three small children alone to the Episcopal Church. They landed there because the church needed a pianist, and it was the closest church to their house. Mary Carle played the piano for the small church in the adult services, and the children attended Sunday school. It was a way for their mother to use her wonderful gift.

Anderson knew about the Ten Commandments, and he understood the rules and the consequences of breaking those rules from his father. For the first time, Anderson heard about something greater than those rules. He and his siblings learned about Jesus and the Bible. Anderson heard that God loved him just as he was. There wasn't anything he did or could do to earn God's love. It was a free gift. His mother's love felt a lot like that kind of love. It was this time in his life when he put his faith in Jesus as his Savior. That decision would mark the trajectory of his life. Once the Lord grabs ahold of your heart, He never lets it go.

The roaring twenties hit Florida with a boom, and real estate development began to take off. John jumped on the "land wagon" as it was called. His minimal background in law served him well in his new venture, and for the first time in his young life, he did exceedingly well financially. He dove headfirst into real estate and rode the wave of prosperity it brought for a time. He could barely even hear the tunes on Broadway anymore, and he hardly felt the pull to the stage.

He decided to invest in a new development called Maravilla right outside of Ft. Pierce. Sometimes he would take the children with him to visit this and other areas where he was building new homes. The dust rose in clouds from the turned-up ground as builders struggled to clear the thick underbrush. They were building Spanish-style homes there, now a landmark in Florida architecture. John was one of the first to break ground in a new Maravilla subdivision with the home he built for his family.

While it was under construction, the family moved from their spacious home on the Indian River to a hotel on the outskirts of Fort Pierce. The large hotel was made of white stucco and trimmed in dark green. When they moved, school had already started, and Anderson and Martha were not enrolled in school while the house was being built. However, John had regular study time with Anderson so he would not fall behind in school. John kept him up to date on all of his schoolwork from their little hotel room, much the same way John's father had taught him.

When they moved into their new house, it was like being on vacation. Everything was crisp and new, unlike anywhere they had lived before. It was typical Spanish construction, two-story, and made of stucco. The house was tan, garnished with bright striped awnings held in place by large black spears on either side of each window.

As a result of his newfound success, John seemed more patient and pleasant than usual. He settled more deeply into family life than he ever had, and he found a balance between work and home. The family reserved Sunday afternoons for driving. John often ended a happy afternoon riding around town at the ice cream shop. It sat at an angle at a fork in the road outside the downtown area. The children would start salivating blocks before reaching this most coveted stop. Sometimes John would ride right on past the magical destination as though he didn't know it was there. Then he would laugh and say, "Oh, I was just wondering if anyone would like some ice cream." The chorus would erupt from the back seat, "Yes, daddy, yes!" The marvelous treat was served on a paper plate with not one, not two, but three scoops of ice cream...pink, yellow, and green. During these glorious days for their family, most Sundays had this delicious ending.

While there were many good days for a period, John's simmering discontent and aggravation with the demands of family life eventually chased him down. The carefree outings with their father soon collapsed back into tiptoeing through the house in a quiet dance of avoiding him. John would come home after drinking and the deep well of anger spewed out of his tongue and his hand onto Mary Carle and young Anderson.

His children were all afraid of him, but he never laid a hand on Martha or Mary. He was, however, quick-tempered with Anderson, and punished him severely for small mistakes and offenses. He regularly took off his belt and whipped him until their mother cried and begged him to stop. Lash after lash of the unrelenting belt beat down on his backside. Anderson winced and stayed rigid while his father whipped him, but he stayed true to the promise he made himself. He never, ever cried.

His quiet disobedience toward his father resided deep inside a hardened heart. His body obeyed, but his mind and spirit stood opposed like clenched fists. Perhaps if he had cried out, his father might have shown mercy, but his little heart was already closed off toward his father. He kept his hurts hidden, and the quiet pain collected inside like frying pan grease into a tall Crisco can.

It came time for the children to start school again. Anderson was in the fourth grade, Martha was in second grade, and Mary was supposed to be starting kindergarten.

The whole family got up, dressed, and piled in the car. When they got to school, Mary Carle got out of the car and opened the door for the children to file out.

Mary grabbed her mother around the knees tightly screaming, "I don't want to go, I don't want to go!" Mary Carle calmly said, "It's alright, darling, mother will go in with you." John sat quietly but always listening intently for any sign of pampering. At the sound of Mary Carle's offer, John jumped out of the car and yelled, "No you will not go in with her. Mary Carle, get in the car!"

He reached down and pried Mary's tiny hands from her mother's legs and ordered Mary Carle into the car. She slowly and reluctantly got into the passenger's seat and quietly sobbed from inside the car. She was too afraid not to do what John told her to do, but she was torn over Mary's obvious fear and emotion about leaving her. John quickly got in the car and drove off with Mary Carle crying and looking back at two wide-eyed children and one despondent one standing on the sidewalk together, but all alone.

Martha and Anderson were disturbed and shocked at their father's lack of sympathy for their baby sister Mary. They had seen their father be cruel to their mother many times, but when they saw the hurt and heartbreak in their mother's tearful eyes and Mary's inconsolable wailing, they knew they were the only ones able to help Mary through this difficult day.

Martha was scared too but was too proud to show it. Anderson was a little nervous but had to stifle his own insecurities to take care of his sisters. Martha and Anderson walked Mary to her classroom. After Martha had been in class for about an hour, there was a knock at the door. Mary appeared in the doorway holding her teacher's hand, sniffling with tears still running down her face. Her teacher said, "I had to bring her in here. She wanted her big sister and would not stop crying."

Mary sat at the desk with Martha all that day without ever making a whisper. She occupied herself by rolling her little handkerchief into a "baby in a basket." Each day after that, Mary spent all day in Martha's class at her desk, until the family moved away for good in 1925.

John was a strict father, and he let his children know what he expected and that they should live up to his expectations. The ramifications could be serious for disobedience. One particular morning the family was having grits for breakfast. Grits for breakfast in the South is somewhat of a regular ritual. If you have ever tried grits, you may know that they can be tasty when hot and seasoned, but unpalatable as cardboard when cold. One of the certain rules in the Roddenbery house was to finish what is put before you on your plate.

The other children finished before Anderson, and the longer he piddled with his food, the colder and more awful his grits became. "Anderson, eat your grits," his father barked from across the table. No response, no movement. His mother intervened, "John, the grits are cold, and the children have to get to school." John demanded, "Anderson, you will sit here until you eat your grits." Mary and Martha went on to school, and Anderson sat until he eventually ate his cold, hard grits.

It was similar to another time when, before breakfast, Anderson walked over to the neighborhood golf course to collect lost golf balls. Just as the family was finishing breakfast and getting ready for school, Anderson walked in the front door. With a look of great wrath, John said, "You should not have gone to the golf course. You should not have taken the golf balls. Mary and Martha have had their breakfast, and I am driving them to school. You may not eat breakfast, and you will walk to school."

Their mother cried, "Oh, John!" Anderson's calm, stoic face matched his quiet, "Yes sir!" Mary and Martha rode to school with their father in silent fear of him. On Anderson's long, lonely walk to school, Aunt Louette came to his rescue again, probably tipped off by a deflated and concerned mother. Louette let Anderson in her car and drove him to school.

Survivor.

If you lived through an event like John F. Kennedy's assassination or the Japanese attack on Pearl Harbor, those moments might stay with you forever. You may remember exactly where you were and what you were doing when Princess Diana died, or the first plane hit the first tower. The earliest memory for me when history was burned into my heart and branded into my conscious was when I was eight years old.

I watched in 1986 from my Lakemont Elementary school playground in Winter Park, Florida as the Space Shuttle Challenger sliced through the bright blue sky and suddenly exploded mid-flight. We were immediately ushered back inside our classrooms, and even as a third grader, I knew something terrible had happened. We watched the flights for years in the Central Florida sky, and even felt the walls and windows quake sometimes when the Space Shuttle broke the sound barrier.

It usually looked similar to a jet piercing the clouds leaving a perfect white line of chalk in its wake. On that morning when the vertical line of thick, white smoke dissipated midway through the heavens and spread out like fireworks, I knew I had just seen a tragedy. I put my head down and cried.

I remember the faces of Christa McAuliffe's parents as they replayed the launch on the news. She had been chosen as the first teacher to go into space, and her parents were in Cape Canaveral watching with a crowd of excited spectators. They had never seen a launch in person, and their faces looked unconcerned when the single spark in the sky suddenly turned into a burst of smoke. Theirs were the faces burned in my memory, and although the whole nation mourned, none did so much as the families of those on that failed mission. The next year when I was nine years old visiting Arlington National Cemetery, I paused at the memorial for the Challenger victims and thought only of the McAuliffes.

On April 27, 2011, an EF-5 tornado hit our town. All of us in Tuscaloosa, Alabama would be able to tell you the exact place we were at 5:09 p.m. With a mile-wide fury, the tornado ripped through my city with a vengeance like a kid playing "52 pick Up," scattering houses like cards and sucking up and spitting out everything in its path. In a matter of minutes, five thousand homes were lost, more than 600 injured, and 41 lives gone forever. I was pregnant, huddling in our closet with my husband and two young children listening to our meteorologist James Spann on TV shouting at people to get to a safe place saying, "This is a once in a lifetime storm. This is a tornado EMERGENCY!"

In the aftermath of its destruction, it has been called the second worst tornado in the history of the United States. After those terrifying moments, I witnessed in the faces of my friends and neighbors shock and horror, disbelief and terror, grief and confusion. Those of us without damage struggled through a kind of survivor's guilt. We felt so blessed and thankful to be relatively unharmed but so devastated for the many who were hurting.

I look back on tragedies like Hurricane Katrina and the Tsunami in Thailand, and I think about how easy it was to look through the glass on my flatscreen and feel so bad for "those people." It was even easier to change the channel or simply shift my gaze to avoid the images of pain and destruction from a distant tragedy. And then in a day or so

I went back to my regular routine, unaffected by how their lives were changed forever.

This time was different. For weeks I saw the faces of "those people," a two-year-old little boy who lived a few miles from my house, his forehead nearly scalped, and his skin held together with stitches. I have heard about three babies' bodies lying in a makeshift morgue, waiting to be identified. I know of a woman who found the body of a college student hanging from a tree in her backyard, and I have friends whose homes simply disappeared with absolutely nothing left.

Though my house and family were unharmed, I cannot separate myself from this loss. I can't simply turn away and erase the images of strangers suffering. I daily drove in my car, passing by the piles of debris and numbers spray-painted on doors marking the number who died there. I could not open the paper without flipping past the "People Looking for People" section, at one time overloaded with almost 400 missing names. And instead of two strangers' faces burned into my memory, they are the tear-drenched cheeks of my friends. Until you live through this kind of tragedy, you truly cannot feel its devastating weight. It has in many ways broken my heart.

As a child, my grandfather Anderson lived through one of the most devastating hurricanes in U.S. history, and I now understand why in all his prolific storytelling, he never told me about it. There are just some things you don't want to relive, some experiences that confined to mere words feel like an injustice to those who suffered. I read about his family's experience only through the writings of his sister Martha after they both had passed away.

Amid great prosperity in the real estate expansion of Florida, the population of Miami and Dade County had doubled to over 100,000 people over a six-year period. New buildings seemed to sprout up overnight near Miami Beach dwarfing the swampy landscape. The mangroves across Biscayne Bay were bulldozed to make way for unprecedented growth. However, the giant land boom in Florida collapsed in the middle of 1926, affecting the Miami skyline and leaving it peppered with the skeletons of partially finished buildings.

Many millionaires in the fall of 1925 woke up as paupers under the next summer sun. Good citizens missed mortgage payments and skipped out on tax bills, and they lost everything they had. In an attempt to stay afloat amidst failing businesses and an eroding real estate market, John began traveling from Fort Pierce to Miami to drum up business and make new contacts. This particular time, he brought his family with him to Miami while they awaited his performance as a tenor concert soloist at the Miami Biltmore Hotel. He did a good deal of concert work from 1924 to 1926, and he was at last slated to try out with the Metropolitan Grand Opera Company in the fall of 1926 when disaster struck, once again derailing his musical career.

As children, Anderson, Martha, and Mary spent a great deal of time in Miami. The family always stayed downtown at the Rutherford Hotel, located about two blocks from the harbor where the yachts and ships docked on Northeast Third Street. The manager was Mr. Bill Foley, a close family friend. The Rutherford was a popular destination with a gracious dining room, often appointed with fresh flowers on each table. It was a small hotel only three stories high, which proved to be its saving grace in the Great Hurricane of 1926.

The children always looked forward to visiting Miami. At that time the downtown was a secure environment for the children to play safely and happily. Miami lived in their minds as a joyful place, full of unbridled exploration and lounging in the sun. The beach was a wonderland with powdery white sand, a plethora of seashells for little hands to gather and throw, and sprawling palm trees for shade. They built sandcastles, waded in the warm water, and drank cold fruity drinks in their summer paradise.

The Rutherford was a block away from the tallest building in Miami. From their first-floor room they could look out and see the tall, slender building. The original plan called for a thirty-story building, and in those days, thirty stories qualified as a skyscraper. But because of a lack of finances, the building, known as the Realty Building, towered at only twenty stories high, which was still altitudinous.

There was a Jewish temple down on the corner from their hotel. The children were fascinated by the recessed wall around the basement windows which sat below sidewalk level. The coping around the windows was about four feet high, and sand riding on the ocean breeze would get trapped there. To the children, the windows looked like sunken sandboxes, and they would frequently lower themselves down into them and peer through the glass.

The Roddenberys often visited the elegant home of Mr. and Mrs. Elliot Shepherd, close friends of their parents. Elliott Shepherd was the eldest grandson of the Vanderbilts. He was a tall, slender man with dark hair and a small, neat black beard. He always dressed in Miami best- cream-colored trousers and an open necked, short sleeved shirt. His delightful wife was petite and a little on the stout side. She had beautiful skin and pale blue eyes and dressed very simply, even plainly. They lived in an expansive home on Miami Beach.

Three things fascinated the children about the house. The first was the large entrance to the home with a fountain in the middle of the Spanish tiled floor. The home also had a gun room on a sunken level that boasted a large number of guns, rifles, and pistols of various makes and unique histories. The third attraction was the tower on the roof of the house. Mary and Martha were allowed up into the tower to play, and they would excitedly carry their dolls with them, pretending to be princesses. They spent many hours making believe in the castle tower.

On one occasion, Mrs. Shepherd planned an evening of entertainment in her home. She arranged chairs in a semi-circle around the great fountain in the foyer. A myriad of flowers adorned the floor and sides of the fountain. She asked Mary Carle to play the piano for her guests. Mary Carle happily accepted, always pleased to share her talent.

The leisurely life in Miami and the casual lifestyle suited the children and their young parents just fine. On one of his better afternoons on September 18, 1926, John came in the room and said, "Come on everybody, let's take a ride to the beach." He often made decisions on the spur of the moment, and everyone grinned at this idea, looking forward to playing by the water.

They all threw on their swimsuits, piled into the car and started across the causeway to the beach. Suddenly John slowed down and said, "Look at that sky. I don't like the way it looks." Black clouds loomed at the edge of the horizon, and they swirled and danced like a panther circling its prey. The air was stifling, stale, and eerily still.

Mary Carle remarked that it was probably going to be just a usual summer shower, but John remembered that the Seminole Indians from the reservation in Miami were at that moment traveling in droves on foot as far inland as they could go. They determined a hurricane was brewing in the Atlantic by listening to the sounds emanating from the ground. An ominous feeling got the best of John, and he quickly turned the car around and headed back toward the hotel.

Twelve days prior, the great storm was born near the Cape Verde Islands off Africa, and it moved stealthily across the Atlantic until it reached the Caribbean. It was reported in St. Kitts on September 14th, the Bahamas on the 16th, and by the 17th, it was poised to slam into south Florida. This was 25 years before named storms, so it later became known as "The Great Miami Hurricane" or the "Big Blow" because it was the most destructive hurricane on record to have hit the United States up to that time.

At 10 a.m. that Friday morning, the Weather Bureau in Washington, D.C. issued a weather warning, calling it a "very severe storm" that would pass through Nassau that evening and then onto the Florida coast. The newspaper ran the advisory, but few took it seriously. Two months earlier, a small hurricane brought heavy rain and a breath of wind causing little damage and much complacency among residents.

The last major hurricane to hit south Florida was in 1910 before Miami was very populated. Over the next decade, a 440 per cent population increase landed 30,000 or so people there in 1926. Although some ignored the warning, most just had little understanding of the danger of a hurricane. Just before 6 p.m., Miami weatherman Richard Gray received orders from the Weather Bureau in Washington to issue hurricane warnings. In 1926, there were hardly any avenues to warn people. Only a handful of people owned radios, and south Florida had only one radio station through which to broadcast the news.

The white sand beaches and palm trees of Miami quickly disappeared under a black cauldron of boiling clouds. The waves began to churn restlessly in the nearby ocean and the white caps broke against the shore with increasing intensity. By the time the Roddenberys reached their precious hotel, an ominous blanket of fury covered the sky.

As the young couple raced their three young children inside, they found that the already fierce winds had blown open the locked French doors surrounding the lobby area. Mr. Foley and the other men in the hotel busied themselves trying to get the doors closed again, and John immediately ran over and tried to help. It took several men at each door to hold them closed and the rest would put large strips of lumber across the doors and securely nail them shut.

Mary Carle hurried the children into their room. She shut the door and pulled the mattresses off the beds, lining them against the walls and windows. She pulled her children in close to her, wrapped her arms around them like a mother hen, and they waited in a huddle on the floor. The power was already out all over the city, and although it was daytime, the world around them had grown exceedingly dark.

Around 2 a.m. the storm finally came ashore, and they heard a bellowing wind and the sounds of splintering wood and cracking mortar under the merciless winds. Loud sirens seemed to come from every direction, and fierce lightning popped and cracked. They heard large objects flying through the air and crashing into windows and skylights as thunder shook the walls of their small hotel. Huddled in dim silence, they listened to the wrath of the hurricane beating their beloved city like a blind mule.

By the time John came up to the room, Anderson and Mary had fallen asleep on the floor with Mary Carle beside them kneeling and praying for their lives. Martha recalls her father scooping her up to sit beside the window and watch the hurricane ravaging the city. It is the only time she can remember him holding her lovingly and protectively in his arms. They watched lightning flashes dance across the windows of the tall building across the street. John told her to look at the twenty-story tall Realty Building, which by this time was swaying like a reed in the wind.

The Hurricane struck the shore of Miami with staggering force. Vicious winds ripped open doors and tore the sheets off startled sleepers. Sixty miles wide and 100 m.p.h. strong, the great storm buried cars beneath mountains of sand and pushed the ocean's waves deep into Miami's downtown. The Broward Hotel on Las Olas Boulevard flooded four feet into the lobby. Boats in the harbor splintered and stacked like mulch in a plant bed. South of the Miami River, a twelve-foot swell flooded West Flagler Street and lifted the roofs off houses.

A police reporter for the Miami Herald, 24-year-old Henry Reno, was ordered by an editor around 3 a.m. to run over to the Weather Bureau and "find out what the hell is going on!" Venturing out with his flashlight, dagger-like rain soaked him as he dodged between electric wires and flying objects. The force of the wind knocked him to the ground, and he sought refuge in the Seybold Arcade until a lull in the storm that morning. He survived to make it back to the station (and to later father the first female U.S. Attorney General Janet Reno).

By 6:30 a.m. the next morning, everyone thought the thunderous rain and fierce winds butchering the city of Miami had gone. Little did they know it was the eye of the storm that had come ashore, and a chilling albeit temporary calm permeated the city. The lobby of the Rutherford Hotel became a refuge for the injured and confused people caught out on the street during the storm. Their hotel was one of the only buildings still intact in the area. Many of the people pouring into the open lobby were injured, some seriously, and everyone was frightened, wet, cold, and dumbfounded.

John decided to walk to the nearest store to find food and canteen burners to bring back to the hotel to make coffee for the masses pouring into the lobby off the streets. It was still and quiet outside when he left. When he got to the nearest store, the smashed windows revealed food and cans floating in the deep water inside the store.

Other residents were moving around downtown, kissing the ground and venturing out in their cars. Several blocks across town, weatherman Richard Gray ran out of his office on Flagler Street at the Miami Weather Bureau shouting, "The storm's not over! We're in the lull! Get back to safety! The worst is yet to come!!" Thirty-five minutes later, the winds returned with more fury, measuring 140 m.p.h. in Fort Lauderdale. A 12-foot storm surge flowed up rivers and canals causing mass destruction. Most of the casualties came after this second strike of the storm because so many people were out on the streets thinking the storm had passed.

About the time John arrived at the store, the Hurricane again battered the wounded city. The wind and rain pounded at him suddenly, and he fought his way back to the hotel. A piece of metal of some kind came hurling toward his head, and he threw up his right hand to block the blow. The force of the metal hit his hand and then his head, knocking him unconscious and ripping open his palm.

Two black men from the nearby Nassau Islands saw what happened and dragged John into an alleyway between two buildings. They were talking in their native dialect, and John was regaining consciousness as he could make out them trying to decide whether to stay with him and be killed or run for safety. John regained consciousness and the three of them helped one another to safety. They returned to the hotel and John had his wound bandaged up before trying to help the other injured people funneling into the crowded Rutherford.

People gradually emerged the next morning to inspect the damage. Across the street from the hotel, the Myer-Kyser Building had a large base and a narrow extension of several stories. After the storm, this building was a topic of amazement. The entire building was twisted like a stacked wooden Jenga game, but still standing. The storm leveled other buildings, and the carnage down every street deemed the city unrecognizable.

The children looked around in shock and terror at the view of the hotel lobby that morning. It looked more like a makeshift war zone hospital than a luxury vacation spot. Injured and frightened people were lying on the tile floor while others wandered blank faced and distraught. Many, including their father, sprang into action helping everyone they could. It was one of the few proud memories the children had of their father.

Amidst the chaos, they witnessed with amazement a long black limousine pulling up in front of the hotel. Its shine and grandeur surrounded by mass destruction looked like a new penny in a sewer drain. A fine-looking gentleman sat in the back seat. The uniformed chauffeur got out of the driver's seat and came around to the back door of the vehicle. After opening it, he bent down and lifted the handsome looking man from the car.

The man was a double amputee, and the children had never seen anyone like him before. They stared in gob smacked amazement as the chauffeur placed him in a wheelchair and pushed him into the lobby of the hotel, which was now serving as part hospital and part morgue. The man was a doctor who came to offer medical care to the stream of injured people. As the children watched this man in his disabled state helping wounded and dying strangers, they were profoundly impacted by his generosity and kindness. Anderson saw a physician who despite his own suffering was pouring his life out to aid others. The image burned into his mind.

The Big Blow claimed as many as 372 lives and more than 800 others were missing and never found. Six thousand people were injured. Property damage in south Florida after the storm was the highest in U.S. history, $159 million in 1926, more than $100 billion in today's dollars.

The Hurricane destroyed a levee near Lake Okeechobee, and 15-foot waves ripped buildings from their pilings in the small town of Moore Haven. Whole churches and houses floated by. Nearly a third of the 900 people in the town drowned in the floodwaters, and it remained submerged for eight weeks after the devastation of the storm. The storm hit Pensacola and Mobile before disbanding.

The Roddenberys survived the Hurricane with their lives intact, faring far better than many in Miami. One survivor said that "the devastation- buildings, corpses of people and cattle- will never leave his memory." All electricity and phones were down, and the Roddenberys left the ruins of south Florida anxiously to see how their home in Fort Pierce survived the storm further up the coast. As they approached the outskirts of

Fort Pierce, they could see that the winds and rain had caused considerable damage, though not in comparison to what they saw in south Florida.

When they approached the driveway to their home in Maravilla, they were relieved to see it was still standing, but as the car etched closer, they could see it had suffered severely. The large iron spears supporting the awnings had ripped through the glass paned windows. They could not get into the front door because of the mounds of sand and mud piled on the floor. Mary Carle knelt with her face in her hands and wept. Their home had flooded and most of their belongings were ruined. The loss was devastating to their family.

Damage control in Miami added to the destruction from the storm. With land sales already down, some Miamians combated the news of widespread tragedy. Miami promoters made a makeshift radio station that broadcasted messages that Miami was "down, but not wiped out" as many national headlines portrayed. Thankfully for the estimated 25,000 people left homeless, donations and relief efforts poured into the city despite the dishonest claims of the promoters.

John did not accept tragedy or any type of sadness well. His thoughts immediately jumped ahead to helping the hurricane victims since they had seen firsthand the destruction and grief caused by the Hurricane in Miami. He and Mary

Carle decided they would give concerts in Atlanta and New York to benefit the victims. Mary Carle's piano playing would accompany John's magnificent tenor voice. Together they decided to travel and raise money, and John would regain his coveted place on the stage in the process of helping the storm victims.

The Roddenberys were not alone in their relief efforts. Once railroads tracks were repaired, publishing tycoon William Randolph Hearst sent a train equipped with doctors, nurses, supplies, and water-treating units to bring relief to the shattered communities. As soon as a relief headquarters opened in Miami, John took charge of the food committee desk as chief assistant to Herman Mangles. He stayed committed to his post until all those in need had sufficient food. It was one of John's finest hours.

With the concert tour in the works, the family left Fort Pierce and traveled to Columbus, Georgia, where the three children were left with their grandparents and enrolled in Wynnton Elementary School during Anderson's fourth grade year. From Columbus, the couple pressed on toward New York City to begin their concert tour. John apparently earned and saved enough money from the Land Boom to pursue his singing and theatrical career, if only briefly.

He studied voice in New York and Mary Carle

accompanied him on the piano during his practices. Following the benefit concert, he starred in a production of "The Student Prince" and appeared in several supporting roles in operettas. He also landed the leading role in the musical Schubert's "Blossom Time," which had an extended run at the Roxy Theater on Broadway. The couple rubbed elbows with theatrical celebrities of the twenties and attended many gala parties, all while their children were being raised in Georgia without them.

John's drink of choice was always a Manhattan, and he would swirl it around in the bottom of his glass inhaling the bright lights of Broadway and exhaling smoke from his Lucky Strikes. Though he experienced some brief advancement in his singing career, he was still unsettled and restless. In spite of John's budding success, he drank even more often and to excess, and their marriage began to crumble.

The family was disjointed and spread out for a long period of time. John continued to pursue his musical career but experienced a lot of rejection. He was unable to cope in a healthy way with his increasing depression and began to take it out on those closest to him. John's neglect, alcoholism, and physical abuse caused Mary Carle to eventually leave him.

From that time on, the family was permanently fractured. John was never again in their home or a part of their lives while the children were young. Though John was not very involved in his son's life, his absence left an emptiness in Anderson's young heart and an uncertainty about where he would go and who he would become. Eventually, Mary Carle and John divorced, which was unheard of for the most part and scandalous at best in the 1920's. Their divorce created a vacuum that seemed to suck all the life out of the Roddenbery home.

John chased away everyone and everything truly valuable with an emptied bottle and a balled-up fist. He lived a life of regrets and sank deeper into rage and depression, but his love for Mary Carle never waned. He told his daughter Martha toward the end of his life that he never sang a single note after Mary Carle left him.

After the divorce, Mary Carle, who in her thirties was legally blind, continued to pursue a career as a pianist to earn an income. Many times, Anderson and his two sisters were traded in for what seemed like the applause of strangers, stretching the generosity and compassion of relatives. This began a string of moves that were hard for the children to even piece together.

Each of the three Roddenbery children experienced the same instabilities, tumult, awkwardness, and uncertainties in their formative years. They were affected in various ways by their father's harsh influence and also by their mother's gracious charisma. The effects of these opposing characteristics manifested differently in each child.

Mary became sweet and pleasant to be with. She was lovely to look at and developed all the talents needed to keep an attractive home. She and her husband Cluese were deeply in love with one another, and although they experienced some trying times, she never lost her loving ways and gentle heart.

Martha grew headstrong but also fun to be with. She was a good leader but hard to control. She lacked discipline and effort to achieve, though she was intelligent. While growing up, she was totally unfocused and lacked goals or direction.

Anderson became determined to be the best in every area of his life. He studied and disciplined himself. He took advantage of every opportunity to succeed. By hard work, discipline, and determination, he not only made the best out of every situation, but he also usually made every situation better. Study, work, and responsibility were his trademarks.

While each member of the Roddenbery family struggled to find their footing, another ominous cloud loomed overhead. For the next several years, Miami slowly recovered from the physical blow in 1926, but another storm was on its way. This time it would be an economic crisis that would affect every person in every city across America.

Georgian.

The Great Depression in the 1930's hit the South with even more punches than that Miami Hurricane. Nearly everyone struggled to keep or find work and have enough food to fill the stomachs of the people they loved. In a time of such intense collective suffering, young Anderson lived with the knowledge that he was one more mouth to feed and one more body to clothe. He was one day away from being sent to live with someone else, through no fault of his own.

His childhood geography was so discombobulated that he forgot he ever attended Wynnton Elementary School in Columbus, Georgia. A Columbus native once noticed his black and white picture displayed in the lobby along with his fourth-grade class several years ago. It was the same school that would later educate all four of his children. It's funny how the place he forgot would later become his home and the city he grew to love and build his life work.

Much of the period after the children were left in Columbus was a blur. Eventually, after going to six different elementary schools (mostly around the state of Georgia), the trio ended up back in Macon with their Aunt Jewel and Uncle Arthur Flowers when Anderson was entering eighth grade. Because of the many moves during primary school and sometimes in the middle of a school year, Anderson fell about a year behind in his coursework. He started at Lanier, an all-boys' school in Macon that focused on academics and athletics.

The three children enjoyed the large yards in the front and back of the house, flat areas ideal for playing and exploring. Martha's interest in acrobatics kept her legs up the air more than they were on the ground, and Anderson became an avid fisherman and Boy Scout. Scouting was a way for him to escape and test his abilities against the forces of nature.

Anderson quickly won over peers and parents alike with his personality and talents while living in Macon. Brewing underneath his golden boy exterior was resentment and anger toward his father. At the time, he did not know where his father was or what he was doing. The intense social stigma attached to divorce at the time, and especially in the South, often led Anderson to let people assume his father was dead.

Anderson was embarrassed in small town Georgia for his classmates and neighbors to know the truth about his family. He came from a broken home in a time when shame circled divorce like a buzzard rounding roadkill possum. Anderson always felt loved and valued by his mother and she wrote frequently but it could not replace her physical presence in his life. He never heard from his father. He and his sisters had no parents present and no home of their own.

During his time being passed around between relatives, Anderson grew to love the wild outdoors because trees and lakes were basically the same in south Florida or middle Georgia. While the road underneath him roared past with each move to a new town, the earth under each tree and every lake was solid and familiar. It was a consistency and a sameness he could count on when everything else felt out of control and strange.

I wonder if it was my grandfather's vagrant status as a child that propelled him to become such a steady, dependable man. Constantly uprooted, sometimes not knowing where he would lay his head the next week, made him appreciate each day for what it was. His need for home became deeper with every move and every barrage of new faces and names to learn, so that when he finally placed his roots down in middle Georgia, the red clay, though softened from the rolling waters of the Chattahoochee River, would never let him loose.

There is a mystery about nature, a conflict of the inner man. Anyone who has spent time in the wild has learned to respect what is natural, spontaneous, and beyond human control. It can be peaceful and serene one moment and then fierce and powerful the next. There is no certain safety in the outdoors. Along with commanding respect, the wilderness can evoke a desire to conquer and lord over it. It is what draws people in and what spews many of them out.

As a young man, Anderson admired the trees and animals of the woods. They were like constant friends. He learned hiking and fishing and grew his skill as an outdoorsman. On one particular Sunday, his Boy Scout troop attended Mulberry Methodist Church. At the end of the sermon, the pastor invited all who wanted to give their life to Jesus to come forward. Anderson stood and walked to the front. He fondly remembered this experience and shared it with his daughter many years later.

At twelve years old, Anderson joined the Y.M.C.A. in Macon and became seriously involved in swimming, basketball, volleyball, and religious activities. He went to Benjamin Hawkins Boy Scout Camp in Byron, Georgia where he earned twenty-eight merit badges. He later became a counselor at the camp in Byron where he served four summers as their bugler boy. As his Boy Scout badge collection began to fill up, he finally felt he was good at something. Anderson was at camp when it became time for him to win his final badge in bird identification. This would secure for him the coveted Eagle Scout title.

He gets a wistful, boyish look on his face when he recalls how his scout leader took him out to a cemetery flooded with old gravestones and rotted flowers. Among the tall weeds and trees flocked native birds of all kinds, free to live and roam among the rows of deceased. The moment a call echoed off the gravestones, his scoutmaster demandingly called out, "What kind of bird is that?" Anderson nervously answered back his best guess, palms sweaty, eyes surveying the landscape for a glimpse of the fowl.

Finally, after about a dozen of these exercises, he heard one last call through the pines. His scoutmaster acknowledged with a grin that if Anderson answered correctly, the Eagle

Scout status would be won. Anderson paused for a moment to be sure before stammering out, "The gray slated junko."

"That is correct," the scoutmaster exclaimed! The Eagle Scout badge was finally his, and it remained one of his prized possessions his whole life. The sliver of fabric donning all his hard-earned badges was eventually displayed proudly in a glass and wood shadow box on his wall for many years.

Life in Macon fostered Anderson's love of the outdoors in other ways, too. It was there he started playing football for the first time on the neighborhood sandlot team. One afternoon he was out in the dirt playing with the other boys who lived close by. They would meet up as soon as school was out. Often the boys played well past dusk until they were called home to eat dinner, before they themselves became supper for the overgrown mosquitoes.

One afternoon in an especially physical match, Anderson fell to the ground after a play and his mouth met violently with another boy's knee. Intense pain pulsated through his jaw. When he reached up with his hand and felt the inside of his mouth with his tongue, he realized quickly there was a gaping hole where his permanent front tooth had been. He looked around in the dust and found the bloody ivory nub, root and all.

He thought through his few options. He could bring the tooth home and fess up to his aunt and uncle who had recently taken him in, but he feared retribution for any trouble he may cause his new hosts. Or he could he simply shove that tooth right back in his mouth and hope that no one would be the wiser. He opted for the latter. Anderson showed up at the dinner table a little bit dirty but never letting on about the throbbing pain in his gums. That same tooth, though slightly crooked and discolored, eventually took root. When he smiles even as an old man, it's a visible reminder of his gall and determination.

Another favorite pastime took him deep into the woods: hunting arrowheads. The area around Macon (an old hunting ground for Creek Indians) was primed for exploring and collecting Indian relics. Anderson amassed a huge collection of arrowheads, and he cleaned and polished each one to perfection. He took great care in organizing and displaying his prized possessions in flat boxes he lined with felt, and he labeled every arrowhead with the proper identification. They looked like jewel boxes to his younger sister Martha.

When Martha's class began studying Indians, she decided to take the boxes of arrowheads to school for "Show and Tell" without ever asking her brother. Anderson arrived home from school before his sister, and he immediately noticed his collection missing. When Martha arrived carrying the evidence of her offense, Anderson laid into her with incredible fury. He became so outraged screaming angry words at Martha that Aunt Jewel came rushing into the room. "Anderson, calm down. If you let your anger get out of control, you will be just like your father."

Aunt Jewel's words really shook him up and made a lasting impression on him. It was in those tense moments Andy determined never to be like his father, and he chose to learn the capacity to forgive. From that point on, Anderson began to truly bridle his anger. He deliberately put away the tendencies of his father. The arrowheads stayed a lasting treasure for my grandfather. Through each move and stage of boyhood, he kept his trophies close at hand.

After many tumultuous years, when John and Mary Carle eventually divorced, she returned to Macon to be with the children. The full truth behind the couple's split stayed hidden behind closed doors. Alcohol often released John's demons to hurl emotional and physical abuse at his wife and son, and he could easily be portrayed as an unfaithful man. John had a long list of offenses from which to choose. Once the divorce papers were filed, John had no communication with his children or their mother. He moved to France soon after the split and got remarried there. Anderson did not see his father again until many years later.

After the children were reunited with their mother again, she grabbed the attention of a traveling salesman. She was a shiny object adorned with beauty and talent and was an easy attraction for the peddler. He was a smooth talker and very charming. Dark hair swooped evenly to each side of his bony face, and his even darker eyes shifted constantly. The lanky salesman wore cheap, ill-fitting suits, and he reeked of sweat and the same wretched cologne he carried around with his wares. His features were pleasant enough, but his odd mannerisms and strange accent gave him away. He wasn't from these parts. In short, he was a walking, talking stereotype.

On several visits to their home to visit Mary Carle, this man would admire Anderson's impressive collection of Indian arrowheads. The man would ask to see them, and Anderson would lift them out of his trunk box by precious box. He proudly showed the man the velvet backed display cases with each individual arrowhead- polished, tacked, and labeled to maximize admiration. Many happy fragments of his splintered childhood were contained in those boxes.

When Anderson looked at his collection spread out

before him, he could envision the creek beds he scoured across Florida and South Georgia, the paths he explored, and the mounds of dirt he sifted through. Of all the things he lost and left behind with each move, the arrowheads were his mainstay. With no real father figure in his life, he enjoyed the odd man's interest in his most prized possessions.

During one of his visits with their family, the salesman packed up his many boxes and bags and left very suddenly. Several hours later, Anderson had an ominous feeling deep in his stomach. He ran to his room and discovered his trunk filled with his precious cases of arrowheads had vanished with the salesman. The boy who never cried when his father beat him or when his front tooth was knocked out knelt down on the hardwood floor next to his bed and wept. Hot, bitter droplets ran down his cheeks and he buried his boyish face in his hands. He stayed there for hours lamenting over his incomprehensible loss. His arrowheads could never be replaced. It was one of the most devastating days in his life as a child.

The Depression swept across the country during Anderson's first year of high school. Money for a single, divorced mother in Georgia was hard to come by. Luckily for Mary Carle, she had her wonderful gift of music. She worked more than one job to provide some income for herself and her children. One of her jobs was to accompany silent movies at the Rialto Theater.

Anderson, Martha, and Mary enjoyed free admission to the movies because of their mother's job. The black and white pictures rolled across the screen and Mary Carle's perfect execution would rise and fall with the action of the films. Sometimes Anderson would take a girlfriend to the movie. If he had any extra money, he might also take her to the soda fountain down the street. To one lucky girl he said, "You can have anything you want as long as it does not cost more than a dime."

Mary Carle accepted a job playing the piano on the Ocean Steamship Company fleet of cruise ships out of Savannah. Through the rest of their growing-up years, their mother's presence would come and go with the current of the water and the boats that carried her too often away. As soon as another ship would dock, another group of vacationers would board to Boston or New York, and she would return to the water perched atop her piano bench, leaving her children at the mercy of the next willing guardian.

Although her eyesight failed, Mary Carle's fingers danced across the ivory keys in the ballroom of "The City of

Birmingham," the flagship for the fleet. Anonymous women curtsied, men bowed, and they smiled and danced until late in the evening. The stranger filled room enjoyed her laughter and charm while the children suffered through another loss of their only remaining parent. Though they had several compassionate relatives, they could only truly rely on one another.

After Anderson's first year of high school, Professor Donald Ward, in charge of Industrial Education at Lanier, asked Anderson to live with him and his wife for the remaining three years of high school. They never had children and welcomed the thought of Anderson (now nicknamed "Andy") in their home. The Principal of Lanier High, Major Paul Anderson, fostered this arrangement. Major Anderson paid Professor Ward $50 a month for Andy's board. Andy happily repaid this debt many years later when Major Anderson needed some financial help. Professor Ward saw great potential in Andy, and he and his wife supported his athletic and academic endeavors like loving, present parents.

Andy thrived at Lanier High School for Boys. He was elected president of the senior class and maintained a straight "A" average. He played baseball for one year, basketball, and three years on the varsity football team as halfback and fullback. He was not a standout player, but he led his team to a Georgia

High School AA state championship during his senior year. His team played Savannah Boys High, Tech High in Atlanta, Benedictine in Savannah, and Miami High School. His sister Martha was a cheerleader and traveled to the games.

Despite this lingering unhappiness about their father and their loneliness for their mother, Andy and Martha meandered through high school with ease. Both were popular and enjoyed many parties and dances. They were thrilled when their mother was in town and gave them an opportunity to entertain their many friends at the family home in Macon. It was the summer before Andy graduated from high school, and Martha recalled the day with sweet reminiscence.

They set up the expansive tree canopied backyard with paper lanterns, picnic tables, plenty of food and drinks, and prepared homemade ice cream. Andy and Martha shared many of the same friends because they were close in age, and they happily invited them all to their party. The crowd of teenagers ate and drank and laughed. After supper they went inside to enjoy dancing, which was a common after dinner pastime for that era in middle Georgia.

The large sliding pocket doors separating the living room and dining room were pushed back to allow the maximum amount of space for the dance floor. Mary Carle let them roll up the heavy, ornate rugs, and they pushed the furniture out of the way to make room on the slick oak floors. The lone piece of furniture left inside the room, the piano, sang under the frenzied fingers of the greatest piano player in Macon, their mother Mary Carle.

The beautiful playing and laughing called out the fireflies, and as the sun disappeared, the lighted glow of the windows illumined the happy teens dancing on the eve of adulthood. Their voices and melodies could be heard on the street outside. Andy and Martha beamed with pride to finally have the chance to respond to the many parties they had enjoyed in other friends' homes, and they swayed to the tunes of their mother's magical piano playing.

During high school years, Anderson became more commonly known as "Andy." In the heart of the Depression, with no parents around to finance his education or guide him through the process, Andy's dream of going to college seemed about as possible as a pig spawning wings. Andy's Sunday school teacher during high school at Vineville Methodist Church, Mr. Hugh Quin, knew of Andy's desire to go to college.

Mr. Quin had no children of his own, but his nephew, Sid Murray from Newnan, was a midshipman at the United States

Naval Academy and on the Navy football team. Sid came to visit Mr. Quin over Christmas and encouraged Andy to try for an appointment to the Naval Academy and play football. Mr. Quin wanted to help Andy, and he recruited Ellsworth Hall, a prominent Macon attorney to join his cause. Mr. Hall was U.S. Representative Carl Vinson's primary supporter in Bibb County, and Vinson served as Chairman for the Naval Affairs Committee. An aircraft carrier was later named in his honor.

Andy began taking night classes at the local vocational training school studying literature and math to prepare for the very difficult pre-admission examination to the Naval Academy. It wasn't the University of Georgia, but any college education would be a tremendous blessing. Through Ellsworth Hall's efforts, Andy was selected as the first alternate scholarship to the Naval Academy. He hoped to be admitted that year by default or get the appointment the following year.

At the close of his senior year, Andy sat in suspense with his classmates, awaiting the announcement of the most coveted award at the school. The Lanier High School for Boys graduation was held in the Municipal Auditorium in Macon in 1934. The heat from the June night permeated inside the building and filled the room with stale warmth. Andy was seated on the stage as president of the senior class.

He didn't recall much of what was said that night, but he remembers with unfaltering accuracy the moment the headmaster called out "Anderson Roddenbery" for the Best All-Around Student. He could not hide the joy on his face. Bursting with excitement, he accepted the engraved silver Elgin pocket watch. The watch became a family treasure and one of his most prized possessions. On the back is engraved:

Presented to Anderson Roddenbery
by Jos. N. Neel
Post of the American Legion
Best All Around Student
Lanier High School
1933-1934

Along with winning the "Best All Around" student, Andy received another incredible award that night. He was thrilled when his name was called as the recipient of the Charles H. Williamson Memorial Scholarship Fund. Not only would his education be paid for, but he could go to the

University of Georgia, where he had long dreamed of going. Andy later would say that earning this scholarship was his finest moment up to that point.

After Andy came up short of the Naval Academy nomination, Mr. Quin and Mr. Hall had been undeterred in their quest to find the finances for Andy to attend college. Behind the scenes, they had been quietly pursuing another scholarship, the Charles H. Williamson Memorial Scholarship. The Macon-based award was only given every four years, and this year happened to be a selection year. The single recipient would receive $600 a year to attend the University of Georgia. In 1934, this would adequately pay for all expenses in a school year. The scholarship is still active today, and the qualifications included scholastic merit, personal character, financial need, and potential to succeed. Andy was "flat broke," and he easily qualified with his high grade point average.

The fund was established by Charles H. Williamson, the brother-in-law of General Walter Harris. Several prominent men served on the selection committee for this scholarship. William D. Anderson, President of the Bibb Manufacturing Company and Morris Michael, President of Happ Brothers Manufacturing Company, were both on the committee. During his interview, Andy had to convince the men why he wanted to go to UGA instead of the Naval Academy. This was not a difficult task since he had always wanted to go to the University of Georgia. The two previous recipients made Phi Beta Kappa at the University, and Andy placed a certain amount of pressure on himself to achieve the same academic success. He also held lofty hopes of playing football.

After Andy graduated, Martha transferred from the public school to Mount DeSales Catholic School for Girls. The school was run by nuns and Martha thrived there, growing in admiration and love for her teachers. After a year or so, Martha told Andy she wanted to convert to Catholicism and become a nun. She came to him asking for his blessing, since he was the only father figure in her life.

Andy, deeply upset by her announcement because of their strong protestant upbringing, asked her to defer her decision for another year. If at the end of the year she still wanted to become a nun, then he would give her his blessing. After the year was over, Martha joyfully joined the Catholic Church and became a Sister of Mercy with her brother's blessing. She went on to have a highly successful career in Catholic education, rising to the Superintendent of Catholic Education for the Archdiocese in Atlanta. Andy was very proud of all her accomplishments.

Damn Good Dawg

Nearly all of his teeth survived four years intact, which was some small miracle in the mid-thirties. His nose was not so fortunate. Brains rattled beneath soft leather helmets, bones crushed, and skin tore. The ground did not forgive. Still, his childhood dream repeatedly willed his 160 pound, 5'11" frame on that field to be battered and wounded. His blood and bruises gave fresh meaning to the colors red and black.

The dream began more than a decade earlier. As a young boy, Anderson stopped in Athens overnight on the way to the mountains with his parents. His proud father showed him around the University of Georgia, his alma mater. They meandered through Old Campus under a ceiling of knotted oaks surrounded by sections of black wrought iron fence, the once straight railings now zigzagging over the gnarled roots of century old trees. Parts of the fence were removed and melted down to make bullets during the Civil War, but the Arch, the official entranceway to the University, stood tall and magnificent.

"Don't walk through the Arch, Anderson," his father warned. The Arch has always been the gateway to the University of Georgia, the first state-chartered institution in the United States. "You can only walk through the Arch after you have graduated from the University of Georgia, otherwise you will become sterile." It was the same version of the tale I heard growing up when my parents would bring me to Athens and then later as a student. I gave campus tours of UGA for years while attending there, and I made sure to pass down that bit of campus lore. I was always very careful to walk around the Arch until I graduated, as was little Anderson that day.

The University received its charter in 1785, and the original buildings were steeped with rich heritage. Sherman's troops seemed to peek out of doorways from their occupation on North Campus, and ghosts like former student Alexander

Stephens, Vice President of the Confederacy, peered down at him from the rippled glass window of his dorm room. Old College also marked the living quarters of Crawford W. Long, who first used anesthesia for medical purposes. Meandering through campus that day, the Roddenberys treaded on hallowed ground where the wind whispered legends of glory into Anderson's eager, young ears. It was there, as a young boy, that he first dreamed of attending the University like his father and wearing the football Varsity "G."

Andy's hero from Lanier High School, Vernon "Catfish" Smith, had recently joined the football staff at the University of Georgia as Ends Coach. Catfish gained widespread popularity by scoring all of UGA's points in a 15-0 win over Yale at the dedication of Sanford Stadium in 1929. To have Smith on the coaching staff only fed his love of UGA and his dream of playing for Georgia.

In the fall of 1934, a young Andy Roddenbery climbed the steps to Joe Brown Hall, his freshman dormitory at the University of Georgia. In his left hand, he held a small brown leather bag. It held every one of his possessions. His right arm was free to shake hands with the other eager young men making their start at the University. All his classmates were white, and many came from old Georgia money to be able to afford a college education during the Depression era.

The many other bright, polished young men had promising futures. Andy unknowingly rubbed elbows with many future greats during his four years at the University of Georgia. In fact, several of Andy's friends went on to have marked careers. At that time, they were simply his friends, all pursuing an education and embarking on manhood together. Andy shared their work ethic and determination to be successful.

Andy's high school friend from Lanier in Macon, Charlie Harrold, who was a year his senior, had been attending the University of Georgia and would be a rising sophomore by the time Andy would start. Charlie was handsome, popular, and had a wry sense of humor. He went on to become a successful surgeon living on Park Avenue in New York City and stayed lifelong friends with Andy.

His friend Morris Abram became a successful lawyer and civil rights activist, United Nations representative, and a University President. Lamar Dodd was an artist and university teacher and administrator for whom the UGA Art School is named. Spec Towns, who joined the track team, went on to win a gold medal at the 1936 Olympics in Berlin for the 110-meter hurdles. Spec broke the world record three times for that event. He later became the track and field coach at UGA, and the University's track is named for him.

Andy also befriended Dan Magill, who earned varsity letters in tennis and swimming and volunteered as an assistant football coach. He later became head tennis coach at UGA and built the program over the next 34 years, earning the most wins of any coach in NCAA history at that time, including two national championships. He built UGA's tennis complex and brought the NCAA Tennis Hall of Fame there. Magill made countless other contributions to UGA Athletics. He is one of the most iconic Bulldogs of all time. Ironically in 1987, Dan Magill presented my husband Marcus the Jim Causey "Most Promising Left Hander" Award at the Crackerland Tournament in Athens. Marcus attended many events hosted by Dan Magill at UGA tennis.

Aaron Cohn, who became one of Andy's dearest lifelong friends, was then captain of the tennis team. He became a lawyer in Columbus, Georgia and served a long tenure as the oldest sitting juvenile court judge in the country just before his death in 2012 at age 96. He fought in World War II as a major in the 3rd Cavalry and battled from Normandy across France until the Nazis retreated at Metz. Judge Cohn was later honored by the U.S. Holocaust Memorial Commission as an Official Liberator of the Ebensee Nazi concentration camp in Austria in 1945. As a Jewish soldier, he looked at the stacked bodies of the dead and the emaciated bodies of the living prisoners and was forever changed. I was told that the U.S. soldiers made the surrounding townspeople help dig graves for the masses of dead bodies. After all, they knew what was going on there and did nothing to stop it. Aaron and Andy's lives had become intertwined since their college days, and they settled in Columbus as next-door neighbors raising their families together.

Early on at Georgia, Andy committed himself to academics but also wanted to try out to play football. His personal commitment to achieve an "A" average and desire to play football for the newly established Southeastern Conference consumed his thoughts and motivated him. Excellent high school training aided this quest as he was pulled from the ranks with former teammate Wallace Miller to demonstrate tackling and blocking techniques. Andy was excited to earn the left halfback position on the freshman football team.

His teammates were permitted to scrimmage against the varsity, but they could not play in varsity games. They only played three freshman games. Andy scored a touchdown against Georgia Tech at the annual Bullpups vs. Baby Jackets Thanksgiving Day game on a 45-yard run in 1934. Edwin Camp of the *Atlanta Constitution* wrote of him in his "Ole Timer" column:

"In the picture adorning this piece, appear the likenesses of two young men that will not rate All-America. The odds are rather against their making All Conference. But, from my perhaps whimsical and inexplicable viewpoint on football, they belong in the Hall of Fame.

As players, they transcend their physical abilities by reason of their intelligence, their fidelity, and their courage. As students they are standouts among an enrollment of more than 2,000. As to their personal character, I quote the words of Mr. T.W. Reed, registrar of the University of Georgia- the beloved 'Uncle Tom,' who knows more about what's what than anybody connected with the administration in Athens:

'Anderson Roddenbery and Ward Holland are among the real leaders in the college community. They are clean, sober, reliable Christian gentlemen, examples of the very best in our student life. Georgia and the nation will hear from them in the years to come.'

Roddenbery and Holland have been running neck and neck for three years for leadership and scholarship. Each will be graduated, perhaps a term ahead of their class, with the ranking summa cum laude, which is a Latin phrase meaning 'with highest praise (or merit).' Each will qualify for Phi Beta Kappa and Phi Kappa Phi, the two national fraternities whose prime eligibility requirement is outstanding scholarship.

The name Roddenbery means much in South Georgia. By way of speaking, it is indigenous to the soil and typifies culture and manhood. There was an elder Seaborn Anderson Roddenbery who represented the Second Georgia District in Congress and whose untimely death cut short a brilliant career.

The young Roddenbery of our sketch is attending Georgia on a scholarship. It was won, not by brawn, but by scholarship. It was established years ago by General and Mrs. Walter A Harris, of Macon, and awarded to the Lanier graduate making the best record in studies and in manly deportment. It just happened that he was a football player...

Roddenbery is not big (165), not fast, only a mediocre passer, a fair ball-carrier and not a punter at all. But he is as good a blocker for his size as any player in the Southeastern Conference and he is a battler to the last ditch."[3]

When Andy started his football career, the Southeastern Conference was only one year old. After the organization of the conference, athletes could receive scholarships for the first time for room and board, tuition, books, and spending money. In the spring, Coach Harry Mehre called Andy into his office and offered him a "walk-on" scholarship. Andy was flattered and very badly wanted to accept, but he graciously declined since he was already receiving the Williamson scholarship. He could not in good conscience deprive another worthy student of having the opportunity to receive the funds, although he was "sorely tempted."

Coach Mehre also informed him that he would be playing quarterback the next year, which felt like a huge letdown to Andy. He had visions of glory as a ball carrier, but under the Notre Dame system they used, quarterbacks did not run with the ball. His disappointment was assuaged after starting for the Florida game as a sophomore and going on to receive three Varsity letters in 1935, 1936, and 1937 under Coach Mehre. He was the signal-caller, blocking back, and safety on defense, and he started every game as a junior and senior while uninjured.

In the 1930's, rules prevented very many player substitutions. A player was not allowed to sub out and then return during the same quarter. Every single player was required to play both offense and defense, and each team had a first team, plus second and third units. The first team played both ways for the entire game unless injury forced a player out, and he would be replaced by a second or third string player. In the brutal heat of the South, players could only take water sparingly to rinse out their mouths. Water deprivation was believed to improve the conditioning process.

Injured players received little medical attention, and

they relied only on spectator physicians to help in case of a serious injury. Players with sprained ankles or torn ligaments were told to "Run it off!" Lack of proper equipment and fewer rules and restrictions to protect players made for unnecessary injuries. Penalties for blocking or roughing the passer or the kicker were almost nonexistent. Soft leather helmets and no facial gear caused a great deal more concussions and facial injuries than we have today.

Football felt a little more personal because the fans in those days knew the names of each player. The athletes in general were much smaller and slower than today. Most college team lines averaged 190 pounds or less from tackle to tackle. Backs weighed on average between 150 to 180 pounds. Ends were around 165 to 180 pounds. LSU had a 205-pound half-back named Bill Crass who was something of a celebrity. Another well-known player, Big George Whatley, was Alabama's left tackle. At 6'5" he stood head and shoulders above all the smaller linemen.

Three people in particular who played against Andy made distinguished careers after college. Joel Eaves, an Auburn end, later became UGA's Athletic Director. Vince Lombardi, who played for Fordham, became a well-known and successful coach of the Green Bay Packers. Abe Mickal had a distinguished career as an obstetrician and gynecologist.

He played halfback for LSU. The two most outstanding men on Andy's team at Georgia were Quinton Lumpkin and Bill Hartman. They were wonderful athletes and fine men. They both achieved all-SEC honors during their time at Georgia. Hartman was an All-American fullback and 1937 team captain, and an annual award at UGA is named in his honor. Andy would go on to receive The Bill Hartman Award in his later years.

On October 12, 1935, Andy made one of the longest runs on record at UGA without scoring. He caught the kickoff on the one-yard line and ran the ball against Furman 98 yards before being tackled at the opposite one-yard line. As the stadium erupted and the players were cheering, they gathered in the huddle to decide what to do. All his teammates were saying, "Give it to Andy. Let him run it in!!" But Andy was so out of breath he flat refused the offer. His teammate and close friend Bill Hartman ran it in for the touchdown. It was the most exciting play of Andy's career.

His most nervous moment was the first time he started in the Georgia vs. Florida game on November 2, 1935. His hands were so shaky he muffed the first punt return and Florida recovered the ball. It was Andy's only fumble for the remainder of his years playing for Georgia. In practice that same year, a teammate's knee crushed his nose, and a local doctor aligned it without anesthesia. He went on to play the rest of the season with a special leather face mask designed to protect his nose. The mask covered his entire face except for two tiny slits for his eyes. His headgear looked more like that of a knight than a football player, and the images of his intimidating masked face made their way into promotional printouts touting him "The Masked Marvel."

One of my favorite football stories is from the 1935 UGA-LSU game. Huey Long, then Governor of Louisiana, and not a man who easily accepted "no" for an answer, wanted the undefeated 13-0 LSU football team to have a matchup with UGA. He called Harold Hirsch, who was the attorney for the Coca-Cola Company. According to former player Bill Hartman, "Harold told him (Huey) that they couldn't play that year because schedules were made up too far in advance. Huey told him Louisiana was thinking about putting an added tax on Coke. Harold told him whenever you want to play, we'll do it."

Huey Long promised the LSU students he would provide a train for them to be transported to and from Georgia for the upcoming football game. Almost the entire student body, mostly military cadets, loaded up onto a train bound for Athens for the November 16th game. The LSU players arrived at the stadium wearing Confederate grey uniforms. The Hanna Bat Company, headquartered in Athens, handed out promotional 18" souvenir baseball bats to the Georgia students before the game. My mom still has my grandfather's souvenir bat from that day.

The most exciting play of the game was when LSU's halfback Abe Mickal made a surprise fake kick from the end zone of Sanford Stadium. The ball was on the LSU five-yard line and in a Statue-of-Liberty handoff, Jess Fatheree got the ball from Mickal in the end zone and ran it 105 yards for a touchdown. LSU pretty well dominated the rest of the game, and Georgia lost 13-10 at home.

As the time ticked down, the LSU students swarmed into the famed hedges surrounding the field hoping to head toward the goalposts and topple them down as an act of celebration. According to Hartman who witnessed the event along with Andy that day, the LSU students "didn't know there was a fence in the hedges. They started to go through the hedges and got hung up at the fence. When the cadets got hung up, the Georgia students descended on them and started beating them with bats."

When Andy reached the top height of the stadium level at Memorial Hall where they dressed before and after games, he looked down at the field. He could see the Georgia students swinging away at the LSU students with their tiny bats. The medical personnel at the student center were busy into the night sewing up head wounds, and Andy guessed there were potentially one or two skull fractures. He said it was sad to see so many LSU students injured, and it was rather serious at the time. In retrospect many years later, it was amusing to think back on the scene: a sea of rowdy, victorious students getting pummeled by a bunch of angry Georgia fans with tiny wooden bats.

Andy's most memorable game was against Fordham for several reasons. For one, it was Andy's first trip outside the south. And for another, before the game that was to take place in New York City, Andy received a letter with the return address marked "John W. Roddenbery" from somewhere in New Jersey. He was so excited about the upcoming trip, but opening the letter from his estranged father sent him reeling. It was like spending the day playing in the warm sand at the beach, and then, out of nowhere, getting pummeled by a roaring wave. Andy emerged mixed up, dizzy, and speechless like a staggering surfer with the gritty taste of sand in his mouth.

He stared at the letter for a brief time, wondering how long it had been since he had heard from his father. It had been so long he was surprised to learn his father was no longer in

France but living in New Jersey. Inside the letter, his father John told him how he wanted to come to the game in New York and meet with him. As his eyes raced through the words on the handwritten page, all the old resentment and hurt rose from the deep place where he had buried it during his adolescent life. The letters on the page were like black oil bubbling to the surface of an otherwise beautiful and serene pond. After much thought, Andy agreed to have dinner with his father.

He and the team packed up and loaded onto the train car in late November 1936. Teams usually traveled by bus to destinations under 100 miles away, but longer trips were by train to places like Tulane, Holy Cross in Boston, Fordham in New York City, or Miami, Florida. The elegant sleeping quarters and dining cars on the Pullman coaches felt like first class luxury to Andy and many of his teammates.

For most of the players, these trips were the first time they had ventured out of the state. The beautiful Georgia countryside with rows and rows of crops that had always been constant and serene whizzed by in a messy blur on the train. The view out of the Pullman windows appeared more like one of those abstract paintings in a highfalutin big city museum. Generations of dirty fingernails and sunburned necks sometimes convinced these southern boys they have had enough of tractors and tailgates. After college, some of them left in order to make something of themselves, to be something better than they thought their ancestry could provide in the Deep South. Andy remembers after traveling for games, many of his fellow players decided to leave the farm and the countryside for good.

Once settled in New York for the upcoming Fordham game, Andy made plans to meet his father at a restaurant. It was a beautiful setting: New York in the fall with a cool bite in the air. The restaurant seemed fancy compared to any Andy had visited in Georgia, but the mostly empty and formal room only magnified the space between his estranged father and himself.

Andy recognized his father immediately. His skin seemed more wrinkled and ruddier, but his small brown eyes and the firm, formal handshake were the same. The white linen napkins on the tablecloth were starched and pressed. Perfect creases fell across his lap as Andy placed the napkin on his legs just as his father taught him to do at the start of a meal. The restaurant music provided a soft backdrop for the cruel reality. From across the table, the years separated them by a seemingly insurmountable gulf.

A young boy who had grown up without a father in the rural South faced the harsh and unrelenting man who had abandoned his family. His father John had started a whole new family with another wife in a different state. That elephant in the room was sitting smack in the middle of their table for two. A once young, doting son now stared across the table at his aging father as a college student, a football star, and an already somewhat self-made man.

So many questions lingered. How convenient for the absent father to appear now that Andy was grown and a star quarterback on his alma mater's college football team. Perhaps his father was on edge and full of regret. Maybe he was not remorseful but just wanted to reconnect with his semi-famous son for his own pride's sake. There was still so much hurt.

The conversation was surface level and strained. John still lacked the ability to connect in a meaningful way with his son. When his father offered him a little spending money at the close of their time together, Andy replied as he exited the restaurant, "No thanks- send it to Mother, since you never helped her any after you left." Andy stepped into the brisk night air and headed back toward the hotel.

He walked and thought about the dinner for a long time. He thought about the few good memories from his childhood. He contemplated all the things he felt he missed, all the things other fathers did with their sons that he never got to do. He had watched his mother struggle, watched her leave his sisters and him behind more times than he could count to try to earn a living for them. He remembered all the times he let his school classmates believe his father was dead because the truth that his father left was so much more embarrassing.

And then he realized he didn't want to carry that load with him for the rest of his life. He didn't want bitterness and anger to overwhelm him. If he wanted to have a relationship with his father, he would have to come to terms with forgiving him. He didn't think his father would ever apologize for the beatings and the abandonment, but he decided that day he no longer wanted to live with resentment toward anyone.

The words of his aunt long echoed in his mind that he "did not want to become like his father." To Andy that came to mean he didn't want to be angry and mean like his father had been, but he also didn't want to hold onto the past and allow it to consume him. Over time, Andy chose forgiveness, accepting John for the man he was and not holding him hostage for his past mistakes. After that day, he slowly began building a new foundation with the old sailor. His dad came to the UGA-Fordham game the next day and cheered for his son. It was the first step toward repairing what was broken.

Another reason the Fordham game was so memorable for Andy was because the Bulldogs played against the famed "Seven Blocks of Granite," given this title by sportswriter Grantland

Rice. The best known of these were the All-American center named Alexandrovich Franklinsky Wojciechowicz and Vince Lombardi who played guard. Andy called this his most memorable trip outside of the Deep South to New York on November 21, 1936. The game took place on the Polo Grounds. Andy laughed as he recalled Coach Mehre's pre-game talk. In the locker room, Coach Mehre bent down and told his team, "This group of Southern boys has a great opportunity to settle the score with those damn Yankees!!"

The undefeated Fordham team was headed for the Rose Bowl that year. The coaches of both teams had a special bond. They had played football at Notre Dame and coached together at Georgia. Harry Mehre was still coaching at UGA and Jim Crowley was now at Fordham. At the end of the fourth quarter as the seconds ticked down, the score was tied. The scrappy Georgia team crushed the hopes of an undefeated Fordham team bound for the Rose Bowl who needed a "W" to advance. The final score was 7-7. Andy as quarterback had the ball as the game ended, and he kept it according to the custom that the team in possession of the ball at the end of the game got to keep it.

As Andy jogged toward the dressing room with the football stashed under his arm, he was approached by Fordham's intimidating linemen who took the ball from him.

A dejected Andy recalled the story later that day at the hotel to Athletic Director Herman Stegeman (for whom the UGA basketball coliseum is named). Stegeman looked Andy sternly in the face and slammed the football he had been hiding behind his back into Andy's stomach. "Next time, don't give up the ball so easily!" he said with a deep and bellowing laugh.

Stegeman went on to explain to an astonished Andy that Fordham's Coach Crowley learned of the unsportsmanlike behavior of his linebackers from some other players and confiscated the ball. Crowley, who was indebted to Stegeman for helping him get his job at Fordham, came by to visit him after the game. Crowley returned the game ball to Stegeman and the Bulldogs. The old football, autographed by each of Andy's 1936 teammates, was kicked around and thrown in the yard by the Roddenbery children for many years. Even as the signatures eventually disappeared from the old pigskin, the memory of that historic game never faded.

Andy played in other historic games including the October 16, 1937, game against Holy Cross. The team took an overnight trip in two Pullman train cars to Washington, D.C. From Union Station, they were bused to Catholic University for practice and then continued to Boston overnight on the train. They stayed at the Kenmore Hotel. On Friday night they walked to the movie theater and had a choice between seeing "The Bride Wore Red" or "The League of Frightened Men." On Saturday, the team walked across the street for their game at Fenway Park. It was a long train ride home nursing a 6-7 loss.

Georgia enjoyed the benefits of an extraordinary coaching staff during the 1930's. The line coach for the Bulldogs, Ted Twomey, had come from Notre Dame with Harry Mehre and Rex Enright, and Ted became a close lifelong friend of Andy's. The excellent staff was brought in by George "Kid" Woodruff while on his $1.00 a year salary. Mehre succeeded Woodruff as Head Coach, Rex Enright trained the backs, Ted Twomey the line, and Vernon "Catfish" Smith was the ends coach. Johnny Broadnax coached the freshman squad. These men led Georgia into big time football. The emphasis on winning was not so different than it is now. In 1937, a 6-3-2 season record cost legendary Head Coach Harry Mehre his job.

North Countryman .

In the summers from 1935-1941, Andy was a guide and youth leader at Camp Twomey in Ontario, Canada, forty miles north of the U.S. border town of St. Francis. The only way into the camp was to fly into International Falls, Minnesota and then take a seaplane over the Canadian wilderness to land on one of the many lakes. The camp was owned by the Twomey family and operated during summer months under the leadership of Ted Twomey, one of Andy's football coaches at the University of Georgia.

Ted was the line coach for the Bulldogs, a former All-American tackle at Notre Dame, and a member of Knute Rockne's 1929 National Championship team. He was present during Rockne's famed "Win One for the Gipper" speech in the 1928 Army versus Notre Dame game. Ted and Andy became great friends through the years, and it was in part Ted's generosity that would later change the course of Andy's life forever.

The second of six college summers Andy spent at Camp Twomey was marked by an encounter with "Rattlesnake Bill" Watson. He fondly recalled the meeting with laughter and boyish amazement. Andy, along with a group of eight young men, set out from camp in four old town canoes to navigate through the Manitou Lake Region in hopes of finding the famed character who lived alone. I'm not convinced they knew for sure Rattlesnake was a real person, but they aimed to find out.

They spent hours maneuvering through the twisted water paths, and finally they came upon a rustic but large two-story house built on a small peninsula. Rattlesnake Bill emerged to welcome his young audience of strangers. He showed them the ice-cold spring filled with minerals near his house. "The spring is his fountain of youth, and the cold wintry blasts and cool summer breezes fan his spark for life. The soothing, balsam-laden air fills his soul with vigor," Andy later wrote of his encounter.

After introductions and a few pleasantries, Rattlesnake settled into spinning tales for his eager, young audience. "The North Country is a hard country, and it mothers a bloody brood." His wiry gray beard masked his mouth, but the words escaped sharply from Rattlesnake Bill's lips like daggers tearing at their nerves. There were more than a few oddities about this ancient man who shot his first "Injun" as a boy and at 89 still panned for gold on Canadian shores.

Surviving in the narrows near Upper Manitou, Rattlesnake Bill once made seventy-six thousand dollars in one week from striking gold, losing it almost as quickly as he had made it. You can bet every one of his acquaintances showed up for the party he threw when he struck it rich, and afterward they were just as long gone as his loot. "I had rather be poor," he remarked to the group of young men, "because people don't worry me about my money."

Rattlesnake Bill lived by his own code in the vast Canadian wilderness. A murderer, a survivor, and a savior of sorts, he mesmerized Andy and awakened in him a sense of adventure and awe. Bill was one of those characters Hollywood tries desperately to concoct, while the audience is left doubting such a soul truly exists anywhere off screen.

He was the object of much admiration that night, his stories encircling the eight wide-eyed young men like the intoxicating smoke from his pipe.

Andy returned to camp that night and recorded the meeting as follows:

"It is the experience of a lifetime to see his slightly stooped old frame sitting on a pine stump and smoking an ancient cob pipe. His shaggy, gray hair, somewhat thin now, protrudes from his wide-brimmed black hat. His bright blue eyes, sometimes laughing and sometimes sharp and piercing, have seen many strange sights. Sitting there, unraveling yarn after yarn, puffing on his pipe and watching the smoke slowly wind its way up into the blue sky above to join some hovering cloud, those sparkling eyes portray the picture recalled in his mind.

'When I was five years old, I killed my first Injun,' he started. 'My home was in the Canadian wilds near Lake Champlain, and we were surrounded by Injuns. All the whites in that neck o' the woods were making a stand in our house. The windows and doors were barred. The women were readying old muzzle-loaders, and the men were firing them through the cracks in the walls at the Injuns who were encircling the house.

I was helping my aunt load a rifle when we saw an Injun slowly peek around the edge of the window. Quickly my aunt placed the muzzle on the window ledge and the stock on a chair. After she had aimed it carefully, she told me to put my shoulder against the stock and pull the trigger when he stuck his head around the corner again.

I did as I was told and pretty soon, I saw a feather coming slowly around the corner. His head came in view, so I yanked the trigger. The pellet hit him squarely in the forehead and blew the whole top of his head off. It was the awfullest sight I ever seen, and the blood came out in great spurts. I will never forget it as long as I live.

They call me Rattlesnake Bill not because I am so rough, but because of an unfortunate accident. I was driving cattle in the states- in Wyoming I believe- when I heard the cattle creating a great noise. I jumped from my horse to see what the trouble was and stepped on a 12 -foot rattler. The snake bit me three times on my left leg before I could kill him. I was carrying some soda for snakebites and so I put a little over all the fang holes. I did not have enough to go 'round because the snake had bitten me three times. The poison made the white soda turn black.

I climbed on my horse and drove the cattle on to their destination. I felt no ill effects for a couple of days. Then my knees began to swell. I hurried to a doctor, and he said there was nothing he could do. I lay in bed at my partner's house for three months critically ill. After a year and a half, I had fully recovered."

After sitting awe-stricken for some time, listening to his tales, Andy and the campers bid him farewell. With a burst of laughter, Bill invited them to come back again. Andy said he would be back next year, he hoped. Rattlesnake Bill smiled and said, "Well, I suppose I will be here seventy-seven years from now, so come back anytime."

Andy never did return to visit Rattlesnake Bill, but he later recounted "those yarns will always linger in my mind. I will always see him sitting there scratching his head or lighting his pipe; his eyes will never grow dim in my mind." In fact, Andy documented Rattlesnake Bill's stories in 20 handwritten pages after he returned to camp, and fifty years later he read them to us as children.

The long canoe ride back to camp was filled with reminiscences of Rattlesnake's tales. They laughed at the scrappy old man and his adventures in the Canadian wilderness. They likely startled at noises from the banks, leery of fierce Injuns hidden by darkness. The story of Rattlesnake Bill, or rather my grandfather's joy in telling it, would evoke a boyish grin whenever he recounted these stories from Canada.

It was there in the north country that he chose a life for himself, a profession that would open up opportunities for him. It is a tale of a fishhook, a football coach, and a fishing guide in a region of lakes peppering the Canadian landscape like shrapnel on a battlefield. One man's mishap and another man's prophetic words would change the course of my grandfather's life forever.

In the isolated Canadian wilderness in July of 1936, Andy led a group of men and boys to fish in Lake Kaiskons. The lake was a three-hour canoe trip from their base at Camp Twomey. He regularly led expeditions of this type during the summers there. They set out very early in their canoes to reach the desired fishing spot. Included in the group was his beloved UGA backfield coach, former Notre Dame football player Rex Enright.

As the sun sank low in the sky, the big walleyed pike began biting furiously. Coach Enright was sitting in the front of his canoe when the man behind him accidentally cast his fishing lure right into the back of Enright's head. Upon seeing his error, the man behind him swiftly and instinctively pulled back on the rod to dislodge the hook, but the great fishhook embedded painfully deeper into Enright's scalp instead. There was absolutely no getting the hook out. Enright's blood seeped down his face and neck from his painful head wound. He grew increasingly uncomfortable, and the men began discussing their best options.

Darkness began to swallow the lake like a giant fish engulfing a worm. The men decided Andy would go with Coach Enright back to Camp Twomey to have the fishhook removed. The two men set out on foot through the mile long narrow walking lanes between two lakes. Enright could not carry the canoe, so the experienced guide Andy hoisted it over his head and off they went. They then entered the water, with Andy leading the 15-mile trek paddling all the way back to camp in utter darkness. Two miles of the trip were unnavigable so once again Andy had to carry the canoe alone while Enright trailed behind him.

Coach Ted Twomey nervously greeted them at the front dock when they arrived at midnight. Once inside, Coach Enright sat in a large, rustic chair with stout wooden arms. Ted and Andy discussed what should be done. They were hours from any type of medical care. They both agreed the hook needed to be removed so the wound could be cleaned and bandaged, and Rex could find some relief. They settled on boiling a pair of wire cutting pliers and shaving Rex's scalp around the firmly set hook. Ted was preparing himself to remove the fishhook.

The equipment and supplies were prepped, and Rex Enright's hands gripped the wooden chair tightly. The two coaches Twomey and Enright fortified themselves with some brandy. Andy, a tee-totaler and still a college student, stood by expecting to witness the surgery. Suddenly, Ted turned to Andy and said, "I can't do the job. Rex is too good a friend of mine. Andy, you will have to take over." Andy was shocked by the request but realized he had little choice but to oblige.

Andy knew he could not simply yank the hook out the same way it entered because the barbs would become even more embedded into the scalp and cause more damage. He decided he would push the sharp tip all the way through the scalp, clip the sharp barb off, and then pull the hook back down through the hole. With considerable anxiety, young Andy stepped behind the chair and directed Coach Enright to brace himself. As Rex bore down on the chair arms, Andy gave a mighty push upward on the shaft of the large hook. The barbed tip of the hook popped up through the skin, and Andy quickly severed it with the wire cutter. He then reversed the direction and removed the hook with one swift motion. With the great hook extracted successfully, a large cheer erupted from the onlookers who had gathered.

After the kitchen table surgery in the wilderness of Canada, Enright seemed calm and unphased. Coach Twomey was ecstatic and excitedly exclaimed, "Andy, you will become a surgeon!" A career in medicine had never crossed Andy's mind since he had no way to fund medical school. It was a historic moment in Andy's life. Ted's prophetic proclamation seemed to drive Andy forward and away from his earlier assumption that he might join his family's pickle business upon graduation.

Ted persisted in his challenge over the next several months. When they returned to Athens, Ted regularly asked him, "Are you getting your pre-med requirements satisfied?" Andy told him yes, but that he did not have the money or any financial backing to go to medical school. Ted replied, "Don't worry about finances. Just get qualified and I will see that you get the money."

Squeezing in the pre-med required chemistry classes was a bit of a challenge for Andy since he was entering his junior year, but he trusted his friend Ted implicitly and continued with his rigorous academic schedule. Dr. Alfred W. Scott, the famed Organic Chemistry professor, became Andy's faculty advisor. Scott aided him in taking all of the prerequisite classes for medical school and graciously worked around Andy's spring football practice schedule and fall games. Andy was under the gun and had to work extremely hard.

Many of his classmates were surprised to learn of his desire to become a doctor. They assumed he might choose a career in the ministry because of his involvement and commitment to several religious organizations. He served as The University of Georgia YMCA president among other roles. Other people were not very supportive of his decision to go into medicine. The following summer at Camp Twomey, Andy was guiding a group of surgeons on a fishing trip. They all agreed and told Andy he was crazy to consider a medical career with their belief that socialized medicine was just around the corner. Still, he resolved to finish his pre-med requirements and continue on the path toward medical school.

The months spent in the Canadian wild proved to be a needed respite every summer for Andy. He had opportunities to fish and camp and use his Boy Scout training and love of the outdoors. He also got to lead fishing expeditions with many important men, including several of his coaches at Georgia. He was also a fishing guide for Kenesaw Mountain Landis, the first Commissioner of Baseball.

One summer Andy returned to Macon from Canada after months of working outdoors. He was looking forward to seeing his sweetheart from high school and college, Mary Little. Andy walked up to Mary adorned in his darkened summer skin. She had come with friends to greet him, but took one look at him, shot him a glance of staunch disapproval, and turned and walked the other way. Mary was unimpressed with his dark suntan. She was also unwilling to sacrifice for him to go four years longer to medical school. That was their last interaction.

Andy graduated three months ahead of his class summa cum laude in 1938. He played four years of football at Georgia: halfback on the freshman football squad in 1934 and earned three Varsity letters as quarterback (1935-37). He was part of the Biftad Club, Omicron Delta Kappa, the "X" Club, and was President of the University of Georgia YMCA (1937-38), a large and very active religious organization at the time. He was the Rhodes Scholar nominee for the university and the recipient of the prestigious Sphinx Award. He was invited to join a number of fraternities but could not afford to accept. He was a welcome guest at all of them.

He finished his college career in the upper three per cent of his class, having achieved Phi Beta Kappa and Phi Kappa Phi. However, he did not have the fifteen dollars to get his Phi Beta Kappa key. He went to Coach John Broadnax who oversaw finances for the Athletic Department, but the coach turned him down. He borrowed the money from a classmate, Ward Holland, who also graduated summa cum laude.

Physician .

The postman brought three envelopes addressed to Seaborn Anderson Roddenbery, III on a spring day in 1938. The return addresses read "Harvard University," "Columbia College of Physicians and Surgeons," and "Johns Hopkins University." Each envelope contained a letter of acceptance to the most prestigious and competitive medical schools in the country. Andy's good friend and mentor from Macon who was a year ahead of him at Lanier High and Georgia, Charlie Harrold, was already at Harvard in his first year of medical school. This made Harvard appealing to Andy as he wanted to follow in Charlie's successful footsteps.

Getting into medical school was one thing, paying for it was entirely something else. Andy attended UGA solely on the generosity of strangers and wondered if he would be so lucky to have his medical school funded as well. There was no money to be had anywhere. It was rural Georgia in the wake of the shattering Depression, and many were still living hand to mouth. Andy turned to his good friend Ted, the one who nudged him into this dream of medical school, to make good on the promise he made on the lake in Canada. "If you can get in, I'll see to it that it is paid for."

Ted made arrangements for Andy to meet Harold Hirsch at his home in Atlanta one Saturday afternoon. Mr. Hirsch was Chairman of the University of Georgia Athletic Board and the head attorney for the Coca-Cola Company. He reached regional fame for successfully leading Coke's legal battle to protect the secret formula of Coca-Cola. The powerful attorney and the hopeful college student chatted over two cold glasses of the brown bubbly elixir.

Andy began, "Mr. Hirsch, I have worked hard in my studies and have maintained an 'A' average and attained the honors of Phi Beta Kappa and the Rhodes Scholar nominee for the University of Georgia. I have acquired all the necessary courses for entrance into medical school."

"Well done, Andy, those are quite impressive accomplishments. What is it that I can do for you?"

"Mr. Hirsch, I do not have the funds to go to Medical School, and my football coach and good friend Ted Twomey thought you may be able to assist me."

Mr. Hirsch paused, took a sip of his ice-cold coke, and grinned through rippled glass at a nervous Andy. After a pause, he set the glass down on the table and began, "I would be honored to help fund your medical school endeavor. We will need to find a few others to help with the costs, but you can count on me. The only thing I ask is for you to visit after each year and update me on your progress."

"Yes Sir, Mr. Hirsch! This is wonderful news! Thank you so much!" Andy tried to contain himself.

"Where is it that you want to go to school, Andy?"

"I have been admitted to Columbia, Harvard, and Johns Hopkins, sir."

"Have you made your decision?"

"Yes sir," Andy smiled. "Harvard."

Harold Hirsch and Harrison Jones, CEO of the Coca Cola Company, together decided to loan Andy half the money for medical school. Midway to his goal, Andy decided to approach some of the men who had supported him thus far from Macon by awarding him the scholarship to Georgia. These men, W.D. Anderson, Morris Michael, and General Walter Harris loaned him the other half. His loans totaled $4,400.

During Andy's trip to Boston in 1938, a great hurricane hit Boston and postponed his trip. His friend and classmate from UGA, John McPherson, also on his way to Boston, encountered a washed-out bridge in Connecticut that delayed his trip. The two persistent Southerners pressed northward on their mission, eventually joining scores of New Englanders in Cambridge to begin their studies at Harvard University.

One hundred thirty students entered the first year together, with only one dropping out before graduation. All were white males and very few were married. Most of them lived in Vanderbilt Hall, the Medical School dormitory situated across from their lecture halls, labs, and the library. Andy had opportunities to earn some of the additional funds he needed for living expenses when he became the Athletic Director of Vanderbilt Hall. He oversaw the tennis courts, pool tables, and other athletic facilities.

Vanderbilt "Vandy" Hall was built in 1927 to house medical students. The grand building provided a sense of community and a place to have social activities. Prior to Vandy Hall, students lived in local boarding houses in less-than-ideal conditions. Many medical students were far from campus in unhealthy environments, and there was little camaraderie or social interaction between them. At the time, Vandy towered over the surrounding small brick buildings and undeveloped lots. Adjacent to the Faculty of Medicine, the more modern style dormitory clashed against its gleaming marble columned counterparts, a lasting landmark of its multimillionaire benefactor.

The medical school students at Harvard learned under some of the best in the field, including Nobel Laureates, Endocrinologist Fuller Albright, Physiologist Dr. Walter B. Cannon, Pathologists Shields Warren and Sidney Farber, Chester Jones in Internal Medicine and Gastroenterology, and Cardiologist Samuel Levine. Another faculty member, William Castle, first described the metabolism of vitamin B_{12} and the importance of intrinsic factor. His discoveries led to treatment for pernicious anemia, a formerly fatal disease.

Another faculty member, Dr. Hans Zinsser, a leader in microbiology, wrote the textbook that bears his name used by generations of medical students. Another doctor, Soma Weiss, suffered from an aneurism at an early age. He diagnosed the aneurism himself at the exact location of the Circle of Willis in his brain and asked that an autopsy be performed after his death to confirm his diagnosis. Dr. Weiss' self-diagnosis proved to be correct.

After graduation, about 40 per cent of Andy's medical school class of 1942 went into academic careers in medicine. Among these men were Dr. John Kirklin, who was central in the development of the University of Alabama at Birmingham Hospital as a referral center and for whom the prestigious Kirklin Clinic is named. Dr. John Merrill was a nephrologist involved in the first kidney transplant, and Dr. William McConaghey was the leading endocrinologist at the Mayo Clinic. Dr. Oglesby Paul had a distinguished career in Cardiology at the University of Chicago, Northwestern, and Harvard University.

During Andy's four years at Georgia and an added four in medical school, he never saw a black student. He later wrote in his biography "I Swear by Apollo" that during those years it never occurred to him that "a negro had the inherent mental ability to be educated and trained to a professional status."7 During his first year of medical school, he was surprised to be greeted in his opening class in bacteriology by a distinguished black professor, Dr. William A. Hinton.

Dr. Hinton pioneered a serological test for the diagnosis of syphilis. He was a highly respected scientist, and his Hinton test became widely used and was regarded as more sensitive than the previously acclaimed Wasserman. Andy and his roommate at the time Dr. John T. McPherson from

Athens, Georgia were the two southerners in their class, and their classmates joked with them about sitting under a black professor. They took lots of ribbing and they laughed along, but they began having conversations that challenged the racial bias they grew up believing.

Andy and John regarded Dr. Hinton as a giant in the field. Andy felt no shame in his genuine admiration for his teacher, and really for the first time began contemplating his thoughts about black people. His feelings were further tested when a horrible accident took place outside of Peter Bent Brigham Hospital in Boston. Snow and ice covered Shattuck Street at the rear of the hospital, and flakes continued to pummel down from the sky causing very poor visibility. Dr. Hinton had just parked his car and as he stepped out onto the pavement, a passing truck sideswiped his car, nearly severing his left leg. He immediately went into surgery under the supervision of his colleagues and the chiefs, Dr. Elliott Cutler and Dr. Robert Zollinger.

Andy later wrote: "Two days later we gathered for our Saturday morning clinical anatomy class in the Brigham amphitheater. Dr. Cutler, in his inimitable, dramatic style, presented the first patient. Rolled upon the stage in his hospital bed was our wounded but smiling Dr. Hinton, who greeted us with a triumphant wave. A standing ovation with loud cheering and applause followed. The efforts of the finest surgeons had been unsuccessful in restoring an adequate blood supply to the leg. An above-the-knee amputation had already been done.

This chain of events filled me with sadness. At that time, I began to question the basis of my deep-seated prejudice. I realized that this accomplished scientific genius, by education and hard work and despite his color, had made it to the top."

Abe Conger, another Harvard medical student, was from Bainbridge, Georgia and graduated from Mercer in Macon. He had already heard about Andy and what he accomplished at Lanier High School and at the University of Georgia. He was eager to meet Andy after his arrival at Harvard. Abe secured a job at Robert Breck Brigham Hospital in Boston, and he invited Andy to move in with him since there was room for one more. After his first year, Andy left his job as Athletic Director to share a room with Dr. Abe Conger above the morgue at the hospital.

They were just barely surviving between their studies and their work, with little sleep and no real free time. At their most worn-out moments, when they felt the lifeblood drain from their exhausted bodies, they would fall limp as wet noodles onto their beds. Certain days it seemed like only the floorboards separated them from joining the corpses beneath them. During the late nights, long hours, and study sessions, the two doctors forged a lifelong friendship that would turn into an enduring professional partnership.

Allen Callow (who became the Chief of Surgery at Tufts University) later joined them. The "Three A's," Andy, Abe, and Allen, worked in the hospital together obtaining medical histories and performing physical exams and laboratory studies requested by attending physicians. They earned room, board, and a small stipend for their work. During clinical years, the medical school students did lab tests on their patients. They also did urine analyses, blood counts, stool examinations, and quelling tests. These were early tests for pneumonia before the use of antibiotics.

It was in Boston that my grandfather met my grandmother, Grace Graver George. She was a beautiful Registered Nurse from Manchester, New Hampshire and the Assistant Director of the Operating Room at Robert Breck Brigham Hospital. She earned this title at a relatively young age for a nurse. Grace had dark hair, big brown eyes, and a tiny waistline. She was extremely intelligent and hardworking. She was very frugal and had been careful with her finances, saving much of her money. She bought a small car, called an Americar. She met my grandfather over a tray of urine samples she was bringing him while he was doing urine analysis, and it was, naturally, love at first sight.

Andy continued to show promise as a medical student and won several awards, including membership in the Boylston Medical Society, the Aesculapian Club of Boston, the Stork Club, and the Lancet Club. Most of the students were called into the military reserve. Andy received his M.D. from Harvard in 1942 and became the second medical doctor to bear his name behind his great-grandfather, S.A. Roddenbery who started the Roddenbery Pickle Company. Andy went on to Roosevelt Hospital in New York to do his internship in July 1942, where Charlie Harrold had gone the year before. Roosevelt only accepted doctors from Columbia and Harvard at this time. He did not receive a salary but did get room and board.

Andy was spending any spare change on phone calls to Grace back in Boston. Together they decided they should get married, and Grace sold her little Americar to have some money for a place to live. They were married at Marble Collegiate, Norman Vincent Peale's chapel on 5th Avenue in Manhattan on September 4, 1942. They moved into a one room apartment near the hospital. Their Murphy bed folded out from the wall and the train roared by about every hour, shaking the light bulb hanging from the ceiling, and rattling the windows and doors of their tiny place. Grace worked as a private nurse, earning $8 for an 8-12 shift. They ate most of their meals at the hospital.

Andy's active military duty began right after his internship at Roosevelt. In 1942 as World War II was just beginning, he joined the U.S. Army-Air Force and reached a rank of Major with Flight Surgeon status. He was stationed for a time at Drew Field in Tampa from July 1943 to July 1946, and he moved south to Florida with his bride. Grace was pregnant at the time, but they lost their first little boy at about seven months gestation. It was a devastating loss for them, and they buried their stillborn son.

Their second pregnancy culminated with the birth of another son, Seaborn Anderson Roddenbery, Jr. (IV) who earned the nickname "Boots" for clomping around in a grown man's boots as a little child. He was born at Drew Field on May 27, 1944, as was his sister Grace "Ann" who followed less than a year later on May 12, 1945. The birth of Ann kept her father from leaving the country because if you had two children by May 13, 1945, you were exempt from overseas active duty. Andy made the cut off by one day thanks to Ann.

Andy learned his father was living in Tampa at the same time and was stationed at the Naval base there during World War II. He decided to reconnect with his father and his father's second wife and three children. The long days in the service were sprinkled with happy moments getting reacquainted with his father, his half-sister and two half-brothers. Andy had finally put the past behind him and was moving toward reconciliation.

After about three years in Tampa, the young Roddenbery family moved to Emory Hospital in Atlanta where Andy was Assistant Resident in surgery from July 1946 through July 1948. It was the first time Andy had lived on the red clay of his youth in nearly a decade. During their time in Atlanta, my mother Roberta Arden "Berta" was born May 13, 1947, at Emory Hospital. She was named after my grandmother's beloved sister Roberta who went by Bobby.

When Berta was two years old, the family moved to Jacksonville near the St. Johns River. Andy was Chief Surgical Resident at Riverside Hospital there from July 1948 for two years under Dr. Edward Jelks and Dr. Ashbel Williams. They lived about a block from the river and next door to Dr. Jelks who became a dear friend and mentor to Andy. At long last, they bought their first car, a dark green 1949 Chevrolet. With three children under the age of six, this was a huge milestone.

By 1950, Andy and his friend and former roommate and colleague Abe Conger decided to set up a surgical practice together after the war ended. They both wanted to return to Georgia, and the two set off in a car driving around the state looking for the right place to start their careers together. Grace forbade Andy to move home to Macon because his former high school and college girlfriend still lived there, so that was not an option.

The two men traveled from city to city for several days. Andy said when they got to Columbus, there was a sign that said, "Welcome to Columbus, Georgia's Most Progressive City." That sounded pretty good to them! Abe and Andy moved their families there and set up their joint practice in July of 1950.

Bridge Builder

The young doctors set up practice in 1950, in the progressive west middle Georgia city named for the explorer Christopher Columbus. The bustling town is separated from Phenix City, Alabama only by the meandering murky waters of the Chattahoochee River. This section of the river begins the first navigable part of the waterway, which in the city's early days was its lifeline to the world.

Across the river in Alabama's Godwin Cemetery, stands a tall stone monument, stained with mildew but still light against the dreary backdrop of faded silk flowers. The massive memorial points skyward amidst knotted tree trunks and aged gravestones protruding like crooked teeth out of death's throated ground. Black, sharp etchings contrast starkly against smooth white rock:

> John Godwin
> Born Oct. 17, 1798
> Died Feb. 26, 1850
> This Stone was placed here by
> Horace King
> in Lasting Remembrance
> of the Love and Gratitude
> he felt for his friend
> and former Master.

The pre-Civil War memorial costing a hefty $600 was paid for and placed by former slave Horace King, in memory of John Godwin, the master and friend who freed him.

Horace King was born into slavery in 1807 on a plantation in South Carolina to parents with mixed ancestry of black, Native American, and white. Godwin purchased King, and they moved along with Godwin's family and his other property from South Carolina to Columbus, Georgia in 1832. Godwin secured the bid to build the first bridge over the Chattahoochee River in that area in 1832.[4]

Godwin quickly noticed King's intelligence and taught him how to read and write, which was against the law at that time in the South. While working as a slave, King learned the "Town Lattice Truss" design patented by bridge builder Ithiel Town. This new design revolutionized bridge building in the United States and was the genius behind the many wooden covered bridges dotting the South. Many of these covered bridges were later built by King and Godwin.

Under Godwin's charge, Horace King supervised the building of the 900-foot covered City Bridge connecting Columbus to Alabama over the Chattahoochee in 1832. The land across the river had belonged to the Creeks until the Treaty of Cusseta when the Indians ceded the land to Alabama and white people began moving westward. The bridge was built by a joint effort of slaves and free men using mules, hand tools, planks, and granite.

Functioning as an apprentice of sorts to Godwin, King's reputation grew in prominence and respect across the southern states. Well known as a masterful designer and skilled engineer, King oversaw the building of many bridges across the South. He and his master also built homes and developed real estate together in Alabama. King even played a critical role in building the dome and the floating staircase in the Alabama capitol building in Montgomery.

Although King was his slave, by all accounts Godwin treated him with respect and even admiration, giving him much influence and control over his business. When Godwin had a series of financial setbacks, he feared creditors would take possession of Horace King to settle his debts, and he decided to set him free before anything like that could happen. Freeing a slave in Alabama was a legal matter and not always easy to do since whites were largely afraid of free black people. With help from state senator Robert Jemison, Jr., John Godwin petitioned the Alabama legislature to grant Horace King his freedom. It was an act of friendship toward this man who was his property, since King would be very valuable and desirable to other slaveowners because of his ingenious architectural skill.

On February 3, 1846, Horace King finally became a free man. After a mandatory hiatus from the South required for all emancipated slaves, he eventually returned. He worked on many projects with Robert Jemison, Jr. of Tuscaloosa in the western part of Alabama. King was involved in one of the most massive projects in Alabama's antebellum years, the building of the Alabama Insane Hospital (Bryce) in Tuscaloosa in 1860 (this building is now a part of the University of Alabama campus and has been fully restored). He was even later elected to the Alabama House of Representatives, serving from 1869 until 1872.

Horace King and John Godwin were literal and figurative bridge builders. In Columbus, their ingenuity and partnership pioneered the way for people to cross dangerous waters, and their friendship forged a pathway toward some small degree of racial reconciliation, if only in their personal lives. King cared for Godwin's children and his struggling mill business after his friend's death. Despite the many beautiful bridges they built that unified the Chattahoochee Valley, the bitter seed of racial separation between black and white folks in Columbus continued to grow. The long history of racial tension was entrenched in the hearts of most people.

The railroad arrived in Columbus around 1845, and the city became a major hub for the textile industry, dotting the skyline with huge brick structures and tall chimney stacks exhaling long black puffs of smoke. During the "War of Northern Aggression" as some call it in these parts, Columbus was second only to Richmond in manufacturing supplies for the Confederate Army. Many companies in Columbus supplied the South with wool uniforms, cannons, and other machines.

Some factories manufactured bayonets, swords, and firearms, and Columbus even housed a shipyard for the Confederate Navy.[5] Horace King built a rolling mill for the navy and provided logs, beams, and lumber for the construction of the Confederate ironclad gunboat Jackson.

The last land combat in the Civil War happened on April 16, 1865, in the Battle of Columbus. Although Lee had already surrendered and Abraham Lincoln had been assassinated, word had not yet reached the men in Columbus. Fighting ensued, and the Northern troops set fire to many of the city's industrial buildings. The battle cost the city dearly. The Yanks left a blazing reminder that consumed much of the city's soul along with its industry. Columbus would be the last city to take up arms for the South and one of the last to begin to let go of the racial prejudices haunting it after the war ended.

John Pemberton, the pharmacist who created the recipe for Coca-Cola, was wounded in the Battle of Columbus. Pemberton became addicted to the morphine he used to quell his pain from the injury to his chest. He used his pharmaceutical knowledge to develop Coca-Cola as a morphine-free medicinal alternative to the addictive pain killer. Though he created an incredible beverage, Pemberton could never shake his need for morphine. To support his expensive drug habit, he eventually sold his Coca-Cola rights to some businessmen in Atlanta. His son later sold his only remaining shares in the now multibillion dollar product for $1,750.

During the Reconstruction years, Columbus once again boomed. Factories peppered the horizon and The Springer Opera House, the State Opera House of Georgia, was built in 1871. An army training camp emerged to the east and grew into what is now Fort Morgan (formerly Fort Benning). Today, Columbus is home to corporate giants like AFLAC, Synovus, TSYS, Carmike Cinemas, the W.C. Bradley Company, and the Woodruff Company.

By the time the two young doctors Roddenbery and Conger set up practice in Columbus in 1950, any legacy of Horace King and John Godwin's interracial friendship had washed away with the magnificent bridges the two built together. Only one remains, the Red Oak Creek Bridge in Meriwether County, Georgia. The newly minted duo of doctors slid easily back into the familiarities of the Deep South, where blacks and whites were segregated in nearly every way possible. Racial tensions churned beneath the surface of "Georgia's Most Progressive City."

After a few months of practicing medicine in Columbus and seeking other ways to generate income, Abe and Andy set out for Tuskegee, Alabama. They were bound for the Veterans'

Administration Hospital, which was about a 45-minute drive. The rambling building had 500 patient beds and a pharmacy across the street. In September 1950, there were no white patients, no white doctors, and no white staff at the hospital. Andy had never been in an all-black environment before. He was unsettled and nervous at first but took his cues and gained courage from his bold and tenacious partner Abe Conger.

On that first visit as surgical consultants, Abe and Andy visited the bedsides of many patients and heard case presentations by the residents. Abe was direct and challenging to the doctors, calling each by name and demanding answers to his questions. Andy's nerves and the tension in the air made him quieter and more uninvolved than he usually would have been. He was relieved when they left the hospital and started the drive back to Columbus.

Andy questioned Abe about his bold attitude toward the residents because it had made him uncomfortable. Abe told Andy that he had resolved before their visit to be completely color blind and that he would require the same from the black doctors as he would any group of their white counterparts. Andy decided to follow Abe's lead in the future. Thus began the doctors' weekly twenty-five-year service as surgery consultants in Tuskegee.

Andy and Abe made new and unlikely friends at Tuskegee. They befriended Dr. Asa G. Yancey, Chief of

Surgery at Tuskegee, who later became professor of surgery and medical director at Emory University. Dr. Yancey was also later Dean of the Emory School of Medicine. Andy and Asa intentionally made time to talk about their personal lives. While Andy agonized over the difficulties of parenting young children, Asa would share with him how hard it had been for his children to adjust to the South, where they could not even drink out of a water fountain that wasn't marked "colored." These conversations stuck with Andy, and he realized the issues his children were dealing with were very different than what black children faced in Georgia.

In Columbus in 1950, a hundred years after Horace King became a free man, there were only seven black physicians. These doctors had very few opportunities. They were denied membership in the local Muscogee County Medical Society and couldn't attend meetings. Black doctors could only see black patients in the Annex to the hospital, which had only about 40 beds. Both black and white doctors could go to the Annex to see patients, while only white patients and doctors were permitted in the City Hospital, which had about 125 beds.

In 1957, City Hospital expanded with a 100-bed addition and was renamed the Medical Center. Black patients were confined to the south wing and had to stay segregated. Saint Francis Hospital would admit only the black patients of white physicians (there were no black physicians on staff), but they had to remain on the ground floor in the south wing of the building.

In the 1950's racial tension in Columbus seemed relatively good compared to many other cities in the south at the time. Civic and professional organizations like the National Conference for Christians and Jews claimed goodwill toward all people as brothers and sisters under God. With very few public incidents, many whites believed racial discord was nonexistent. This city-wide facade of peace did little to assuage individual tensions between blacks and whites.

In February 1956, one major event in Columbus put a bee in the bonnet of race relations. Dr. Thomas A. Brewer, Sr., a black physician and a prominent civil rights activist, was shot and killed by a white department store owner at his F&B store. Brewer was outspoken against many Jim Crow laws and founded a Columbus chapter of the NAACP in 1939. He organized events to push for voting rights for black citizens and was pressuring the school board toward racial integration. Many people in the white community feared and despised him. Brewer often carried a pistol in his pocket because of numerous death threats he received from the Ku Klux Klan and others.

Brewer's office was located at 1025 1/2 First Avenue, directly over Flowers' F&B Department Store. Brewer and Flowers had been arguing earlier in the day after they saw a black man's forceful arrest. Brewer, believing they had both seen police brutality, wanted Flowers to testify in agreement. Flowers disagreed with Brewer, maintaining that the manner of the arrest was nothing out of the ordinary. Brewer was angry, and Flowers called for police protection in his store because he felt threatened.

When Brewer returned later, Flowers shot him seven times killing him, in the presence of two white police officers who were there on guard. A pistol was found in Brewer's left pants pocket, unfired. A Muscogee County Grand Jury ruled it was a justifiable homicide done in self-defense. Brewer's shooting propelled the black community into turmoil. A local business owner equated Dr. Brewer's killing to the death of Martin Luther King, Jr. for the black community in Columbus.

At Brewer's funeral, an estimated 2,500 people overflowed from First African Baptist Church out into the street.8 Over the next year, most of the black doctors and at least one prominent black lawyer fled the city. Almost exactly a year later in 1957, Flowers was found dead with a massive gunshot wound to his head, also on First Avenue. His death was ruled a suicide. Many believed Flowers was killed to atone for Dr. Brewer's murder. Over fifty years after his death, the Justice Department reopened the case to try to determine exactly what happened. Brewer is now recognized as a martyr of the national civil rights movement.[6]

In 1950's Columbus, the memory of bridge builders Horace King and John Godwin was buried deep with them, washed away like their many bridges with the rising, punishing waters of racial injustice. The legacy of their construction was nearly all gone, replaced by newer roadways with no remembrance of the white and brown hands that together first forged the way. At the same time, the weekly pilgrimage of two white doctors from Columbus, Georgia across a modern bridge spanning the Chattahoochee River to Tuskegee, Alabama somehow became more than a charitable venture. It opened the door for something greater and more challenging than they could foresee.

Daddy.

My great-grandfather John was a complicated man, who lived with many unmet expectations and much unrealized potential. He let his own vices and circumstances dictate the path of his life rather than rising above them. There were several years when Andy had no contact with his father. John had started a new life with a new family and seemed to shroud himself in mystery to hide the bland truth of his self-loathing and disappointment.

Several years after Andy's parents divorced, his father moved to France where he met an American woman named Bonnie. She was from Ohio, had attended Ohio State University, and was an artist and designer. Bonnie was timid and shy, but she welcomed romance with the talented and charming John. Soon into their relationship, Bonnie became pregnant, and after the birth of their daughter in 1928, also named Bonnie, the two were married. Two more children soon followed: John, Jr. in 1929 and Pierre in 1931. They moved back to the states to raise their children.

John tried a lot of jobs but never felt satisfied with any of them. He sold home insurance for a time and then began selling health insurance when the industry was in its infancy. He seemed to always have real estate deals going on, and he had experience with sales back in St. Augustine when he had the Ford dealership. Instead of staying on any one career path, he had many odd jobs like growing water lilies, selling and delivering them.

He used to say, "whatever I do is nobody's business," and truly even his second set of children were never sure what kind of work he was really doing. Daughter Bonnie said she was always embarrassed when people asked her at school what her father did for a living because she didn't know how to answer. She usually told the truth- that she didn't know, and then she would feel so stupid.

John's second family lived in Bellville, New Jersey for several years while the children were in elementary school. During these years, Andy was in college and then medical school. He continued to pursue reconciliation with his father and occasionally visited him and his family. Bonnie has sweet memories of Andy's visits and grew to love and respect him.

In 1949, the three children lived in Ohio for one summer with their maternal grandmother. Bonnie's 5th grade year started in Lancaster before they rejoined their parents who had moved to Miami. This disjointed period for John's second family seemed like Deja vu. After the Pearl Harbor tragedy pushed the U.S. into the second World War, John decided to rejoin the Navy and was stationed in Alaska, Miami, and then Tampa. He ultimately reached the rank of a full Commander at the end of World War II.

According to his daughter Bonnie, John was aloof, difficult, and argumentative. If you tried to stand up to him in any way, it would make the disagreement worse. You could never win. Bonnie said, "He would grab onto a point and rant and rave about it off and on for hours. He was a heavy drinker, and I am sure this had something to do with it. He used to browbeat my mother, was verbally abusive to her, and I do remember him hitting my mother."

Bonnie also said he never seemed to like or enjoy any of his children. She was terrified of him. She remembers her father as a man who loved power and money, who liked to purchase real estate, make money, and accumulate power. He had no use for women, often commenting how women were stupid and not worth much. He was verbally abusive to Bonnie and physically abusive to sons John, Jr. and Pierre. They all felt that nothing they did was good enough or right.

Bonnie recalls only one pleasant period in her childhood, and this was when they lived in Tampa. John was a Commander in the Navy, in charge of supplies at the Receiving Station. The family lived on S. Boulevard and John enjoyed his position there and was pleasant to be around as he was not drinking as much. He spent a lot of time outdoors pruning trees and caring for their yard and plants. Aside from this short time, Bonnie really has no happy memories of her father.

John wanted to stay in the military, but he was getting older and for some reason unknown to his family, he was discharged from the service. His appearance revealed the tumultuous life he had lived, and his aged complexion had the smoothness of a pool hall dart board, ruddy and gnarled from years of self-neglect. By the time old age came for him, regret and disappointment overtook his once bitter disposition. He made peace with his first three children: Andy, Martha, and Mary, but his first wife Mary Carle chose never to be in his presence after their divorce. He was his own worst enemy. According to Martha, when that enemy had finally been put to rest, he became thoughtful, regretful, generous, and eager to make amends.

When Andy became a husband and started to father his own brood, he reflected more often on his own father growing up. He assessed his father's strengths and weaknesses honestly, but he did not speak of his difficult childhood. He kept the promise he made to himself when he was a boy that he would not become angry or mean spirited the way his father had often been. I feel sure the childhood pain and abandonment Andy felt from his father propelled him to be a different kind of dad. He purposed to love his children, to build them up and to invest in them, much like his mother tried to do. Though family life could sometimes be overwhelming, Andy occupied a constant peaceful presence and availability in their home.

Grace was dependable and very intelligent, but emotionally she struggled to withstand the pressures of motherhood. Between the child she miscarried and having Boots and Ann so close together, she had been pregnant and carried three babies in a span of three years. When Berta came along, Grace was completely overwhelmed with three very young children at home. She was resourceful in her parenting solutions to common problems, even though most of her ideas would probably land you in a file on a social worker's desk today. When Berta was about one or two years old, Grace put a metal stake in the ground in the backyard with one end attached to a rope and the other end to little Berta. She staked her toddler out in the yard like a dog. This gave Berta some fresh air and gave Grace a break for an hour or so.

Grace also fashioned a screen door, complete with hinges and a latch for closure, to the top of my Uncle Boots' crib to prevent him from climbing out. To keep my Aunt Ann from thumb-sucking at night, she made a strait jacket from an oversized pajama shirt and pinned the sleeves behind her so she could not access her hands. She sometimes had to go to extreme measures to survive those early years of babies and toddlers with no help and limited finances.

A year into the new practice, the young Roddenbery family of five was finally finding its footing in Columbus. Grace was a good mother and devoted wife. One fall afternoon Andy returned from work to find Grace lying on the bed crying and distraught. It took her a few minutes to collect herself enough to reveal to a surprised and delighted Andy that she was pregnant. The next year, on June 22, 1952, the final Roddenbery child, Edward "Ed" Jelks was born, named for Andy's friend and mentor in Jacksonville.

While working crazy hours at the office and hospital, Andy still maintained the importance of balancing his family life. He was tired most days when he arrived home, but he always made time to listen to his children and coach them in little and large things. He loved teaching them how to do all kinds of tasks while also casting bigger vision for the future, often assuring them it would be a bright one. Family life suited him.

At home, Andy was steady and dependable. Neighbors and friends could always count on him to keep promises or help when it was needed. He didn't like to leave anything undone, and he wouldn't let the sun go down if there was even a light bulb that needed changing. His younger daughter Berta often occupied his lap when he would finally fold down into a soft chair after a long day. His only guilty pleasures were smoking briefly during and after World War II and occasionally mixing a little Crown Royal with his club soda. In the evenings, he changed into his bathrobe and slippers and enjoyed time with his family.

Andy was tough as nails, and he expected the same from his children. When they were sick or had a cold, Grace usually called Dr. Haywood Turner to get them medicine because Andy expected them to tough it out. Boots had severe allergies as a child, and Andy administered regular allergy shots to his young son. After several doses, Boots grew tired of needles and frustrated with his dad for pricking him. He looked up at his dad and said, "I'm going to give you a shot, Daddy!" To assuage his angry child, Andy got a needle and let Boots dig around in his arm while clumsily trying to give him a shot. Boots said his dad never winced or changed his expression.

Andy taught his boys how to play golf. Some of their best memories of growing up were with their dad on the golf course. Andy was not that great at golf, but he was determined to play with his boys because they enjoyed it. He would come inside after a frustrating golf outing and eventually after much thought and self-evaluation he would say, "I think I know what I am doing wrong now." Then he would go out and play the next time, only to diagnose a new set of problems with his game.

While Andy struggled some with golf, Boots and Ed both excelled at the sport. Andy would take Boots out to a driving range on Victory Drive and to play at different local courses. Once they began playing a lot of golf, Andy realized it was cheaper to join Columbus Country Club and play for "free" than to keep paying greens fees at the public courses, so they joined the Club.

Boots worked hard and was captain for the Columbus High golf team. He also went to Dothan, Alabama to play a Future Masters tournament. His dad was his caddy, a very thoughtful and wise help on the course. In the first round Boots shot a 76, landing him in the consolation round. His score in the final round was two under par, winning him the consolation. Boots says it was one of the greatest experiences of his life.

Ed came right along behind Boots, excelling at the sport. Boots often caddied for Ed, who was eight years his junior. Ed traveled to Aurora, New York to a Gary Player national tournament and even won the "10 and under" title. He also went down to Miami for a tournament. The boys spent many hours at Columbus Country Club, sometimes playing as many as 45 holes a day. Once Andy even inspected Ed's hands to see if he had callouses to be sure he was really practicing all those hours he was gone.

He also taught his boys how to fish and hunt dove, quail, and ducks. Andy's skill as an outdoorsman shone on hunting expeditions. He had a keen sense of direction and knowledge of nature, and he loved being out in the woods teaching his boys new things. Boots remembers getting a Daisy BB gun when he was eight. He aimed at things in the neighborhood- one time shooting at a bird in a bush and accidentally shooting out a car window instead. In the beginning, he had to be able to run pretty fast to make up for his lack of marksmanship.

When he was twelve, his dad took him to Bainbridge down to their relative Stuart McKenzie's house to hunt doves with a shotgun. Stuart married to Rosalind, Andy's Aunt, his mother's much younger sister. In Bainbridge, the McKenzies and their neighbors each had large tracts of land. They would figure out where the birds were that day and all hunt that parcel together. When Ed was a little older, his parents would put him on a greyhound bus to Bainbridge by himself to hunt.

Andy was a strict disciplinarian as well as a loving supporter of his children. When a child needed punishment, Andy would take him or her into a room and sit face to face. He would lecture for about five to ten minutes about character and doing the right thing and often a spanking would follow. One of his best points that we grandchildren also heard was how you only have one reputation, and you never want to do anything to spoil it. It is much easier to keep a good name than to try to improve a bad one. I have passed that one along to my own children.

One time, Boots smarted off, "Dad, quit giving me that flowery speech!" The prolonged lectures were made more agonizing because of what they anticipated was coming next. One leather belt he used for spankings had gold metal circles on it. Before he started spanking, he would say the classic phrase, "this is going to hurt me more than it hurts you." After as many 5 or 10 licks, they would never want to do anything bad ever again.

Every summer the family of six made the long trip to Manchester, New Hampshire. Andy promised Grace when she moved to Georgia that he would take her to see her parents once a year. This annual pilgrimage was before Interstate Highways or air-conditioned cars. The Roddenberys piled into the station wagon, starting out with the four children in the back. After a while, they would end up three in the back and three in the front (Berta in the front middle because she got car sick and would throw up).

After yelling "Cut it out!" a few times, Andy would have enough of the inevitable teasing and bickering from the backseat. Before they were even out of Georgia, Andy would usually pull over and tell all four children to line up against the car. He didn't care who was causing the problems or who was bothering whom, every single one got a spanking. Peace would reign for hours after the attitude adjustments.

On one of their trips to the Northeast, an excited Andy woke the sleeping children as they approached New York City. The buildings were so tall and shiny against the crisp fall sky, and it was like nothing they had ever seen in Georgia. "Kids, wake up! Look at New York City!" he exclaimed with a childlike exuberance. A sleepy Ed rubbed his eyes and peered out the window with excitement, "Look...There's a crow!" he squealed.

Grace pinched pennies to make ends meet when they were establishing the new practice. One way they tried to save money was by Andy giving the boys haircuts at home. The style at that time was a shorter crew cut for boys. Andy set up the step stool in the kitchen and took the clippers to older son Boots' hair without incident. Then he got set for the next haircut and removed the guard and brushed off the clippers.

Little Ed climbed up in the chair and Andy draped the sheet around him. Unexpectedly Andy got a phone call and stepped away. When he returned, he was noticeably frustrated after his conversation. He turned on the clippers and in one smooth motion swiped them straight down the middle of Ed's head. To his horror, he had forgotten to put the guard back on. He mowed a perfect skunk stripe all the way down to Ed's scalp, a reverse mohawk!

At the sound of his father's gasp, little Ed reached his hand up and felt his smooth skin down the middle of his head where his hair had been. With one hand glued to his head, he ran to the mirror. He looked up at his dad with teary eyes and yelled, "I'm gonna kill you!" Andy did his best to blend the remaining hair on the top into the middle, but it just made Ed look like a balding old man. To remedy the problem, Andy drove Ed to Dave McGee at the Blue Jay Barber Shop to get it fixed. The barber looked up and said to Andy, "In the future, you take care of the doctoring and leave the haircuts to me!"

In their despondency, Andy and Grace sat the other three children down to talk about the incident. They ordered them not to poke fun at their little brother, which to a child was more like an invitation to do exactly that. Andy bought Ed a baseball cap to wear (which was not at all in fashion at the time). Of course, the three children at once began their relentless teasing of their baby brother. Friends began to question Ed, "Why are you wearing that baseball cap around?" The siblings devised an entrepreneurial plan surrounding their brother's misfortune. The neighborhood kids could come over and pay a dime each for Ed to lift his cap and give them a peek at the worst haircut they had ever seen.

The Roddenberys lived on Stark Avenue in Columbus next door to Andy's longtime college friend Judge Aaron Cohn and his family. The kids were all around the same age and played together frequently. Their families were so close, when the Cohn children came down with the chicken pox, Grace sent the Roddenbery children over to play so they would get the sickness, too. One evening when it was time to leave for Jewish temple, the Cohns could not find their son Leslie. They looked in all the usual places, and up and down the streets until they finally found him. Leslie was going door to door selling Christmas cards with Boots Roddenbery!

Berta, the younger Roddenbery daughter, and the Cohns' son Leslie were the same age. As little kids often do, they longed to play with their older siblings. Their brothers and sisters, knowing how badly they wanted to be included, liked to dare them to do crazy stunts to be allowed to play. One time, they were told they could play if they lay down together on an old mattress in the garage and kissed each other, which they did.

There was a dilapidated brick pile in the backyard covered with leaves and dirt. Any time someone moved a brick, several roaches would come running out. One time, the older Roddenbery and Cohn kids told Berta if she put her hand by the bricks and let roaches crawl on her arm, they would let her play. To their delight, she wanted to play really badly so she winced and looked away. Then with one quick motion she buried her hand in the bricks. The roach legs tickled up and down her little arm and she earned the right to play.

A lot of the games the children played were harmless and typical things kids would do at their age. They used to hide in the bushes at dark and throw cans behind passing cars. Because cars had no AC and people rode with their windows down, the driver would often hear the can bounce and clank down the street and think they had lost a hub cap. They would pull the car over and inspect each wheel before continuing. The children found this incredibly entertaining.

After a soaking rain one Saturday morning, the Roddenbery kids found a soft, wet puddle of dirt, perfect to make mud pies. They proceeded to pat the soft mud back and forth from hand to hand, making the perfect consistency to launch at passing cars. The children hid in the bushes near the street, and as unsuspecting cars passed by, Boots threw the mud pies at the cars. This was a somewhat harmless prank until Boots landed a mudball directly into the driver's open window. The children quickly disappeared into the shrubbery, but it was obvious who the culprits were.

The car pulled into the Roddenbery driveway. A nurse stepped out, whose once perfectly white starched and pressed uniform was now covered in thick brown mud. When the angry nurse explained to an embarrassed Dr. Roddenbery what his children had done, his usual calm demeanor disappeared, and the children knew they had incurred the wrath of their dad. He gave them all the usual, a firm belt spanking and a very long "lecture."

Addie Spencer worked at the Roddenbery home for many years as a maid, cook, and stand in mother at times. She had beautiful chocolate skin, a welcoming smile, and the most spellbinding singing voice. She earned a voice scholarship to go to college at one time but opted instead to get married, a decision she later regretted. She was a caretaker nearly her entire life as she looked after the Roddenbery family, her own children and husband, and then her mother after she retired.

My mom and her siblings loved Addie. She was warm, pleasant, and nurturing as well as readily available to listen. I remember mom taking me to visit Addie at her home in Columbus when I was an adolescent. Addie's mother was aging then, and Addie was her full-time caregiver. I loved meeting her and I could tell mom's deep affection for her was returned in Addie's easy smile and warm embrace. It was also the first and only time I ever saw anyone eat a pig ear sandwich. It had two slices of white bread, mayonnaise, slathered on the bread, and pickled pig ears between the slices.

When Berta was a young girl, she and her sister Ann were out roaming the neighborhood. Older sister Ann decided to climb up and hop over a chain link fence to shortcut home, the kind with barbs across the top. "Come on Berta! What are you afraid of?" she teased. A determined Berta grabbed onto the fence and started her ascent. When she reached the top, she carefully hoisted her body over with one arm still holding on. When she jumped, she didn't let go in time, and the underside of her upper left arm got caught on the barb and it ripped her arm wide open nearly to the bone. The pain was intense, and blood spurted out everywhere onto her clothes and the ground. Crying, Berta looked up at her sister Ann and asked, "Do you think I'm gonna die?"

Ann, the ever-reassuring sister said, "I don't know...I think so."

They made their way home as fast as they could, and upon their entrance into the house, Addie took one look at Berta's wide open tricep and the trailing blood and she fainted. When Berta eventually got to the hospital, her dad quickly realized he could not scrub out the wound and sew up his own daughter. He asked Dr. Conger to do it for him.

Grace and Andy invested in a country place to the north of Columbus in Harris County. Pine Mountain Valley was very rural but equally beautiful, and this slice of land was near Drs. Bill and Miriam Chambless, some colleagues and friends of Andy. It was the first time Andy and Grace bought land, and it was a significant event in their lives.

Another common lecture from my grandfather used to include "land is a good investment because they aren't making any more of it." The farm had a small home built by Roosevelt's CCC Boys after World War II. It also had a red barn, a small pasture, and a beautiful creek all on ten acres. The Roddenbery family retreated on the weekends to the rolling countryside. The boys enjoyed hunting and fishing and learned to love the wild Georgia land alongside their expert outdoorsman father. In addition to being a weekend getaway for the family, Grace and Andy hoped it would get their daughters away from any growing interest in boys.

Andy bought two horses, one for each of his daughters. King was given to Ann and Tammy was given to Berta to ride. King was a beautiful white horse with some dark spots on his rump. He had a spirited but smooth gait and a pleasant demeanor. Tammy, however, was a spitfire chestnut quarter horse with a white blaze on her nose and a special affinity for biting.

Tammy tried to buck off every rider, no matter how experienced, within the first few minutes after being mounted. If the riders could hold on through her attempts to throw them, I guess she figured they earned a ride. However, on the way back as soon as they could see the barn, both King and Tammy took off in a full gallop and no amount of pulling back on the reins deterred them. The riders had to hold on for dear life.

The kids also came up with games to play when they all got bored in the country. One such game has become an infamous part of our family lore. A few weeks before one particular weekend in the country, the whole family had gone to Great Aunt Flowers' funeral. She was Andy's aunt who helped raise him and his siblings along with her husband Arthur. The couple made an indelible impact on Andy, and he wanted to honor her by bringing the whole family to lay her to rest in Tifton, Georgia. This was likely the first funeral any of the children had attended.

There was an old graveyard on the Roddenbery country property. It was small, about 15 feet square, and surrounded by a knee-high wrought iron broken down fence. Several of the grave sites had about a 12-inch raised cement casing with a huge cement slab cover on top. One of the slabs was broken and a little cattywampus, with just enough room for Boots to slip down inside of it with a flashlight. He was lying on his back on top of the ground enclosed by the cement box, with just enough room for his head to peek out of the broken top.

According to the premeditated plan, as the sun began to set, the two sisters rounded up younger brother Ed and led him over to the graveyard. They marched with their flashlights and chanted in a unified cadence, "Great Aunt Flowers walks tonight. Great Aunt Flowers walks tonight" over and over again. When they finally reached the grave where Boots was lying, he flipped on the flashlight at his chin, illuminating his entire contorted face. The grand effect caused even the girls to scream, and poor Ed ran off howling into the otherwise serene night. The funniest part was the prank scared everybody!

The family moved to Peacock Avenue in Columbus, where they had a dog named Target and a cat named Snoozy. Target was their beloved family pet for many years, and though he was a dog, he may have had nine lives. He loved to chase cars and had several resulting injuries from his adventures. The worst injury happened when there was a grease fire in the kitchen and in her haste to take the pan outside, Grace tripped over Target who was lying on the porch. The flaming grease spilled all over his back. He had terrible scarring from it, and Grace always felt terrible about the incident.

All the neighborhood kids played outside after school until dark. They would eventually all gather at Betsy Parks' house in the late afternoons. Her front yard was flat and grassy, perfect for playing games. They played "IT," "Sling the Statue" and "Red Rover" until mother voices rang up and down the street right at 6:00 P.M., calling their children home for dinner.

There was a convenience store at the end of the street called the "Tote-a-Poke." Outside the store stood a tall branchy tree with a huge beehive, low enough to see and reach with a long stick while standing on the ground. The neighborhood kids often marveled at it, swirling and buzzing as if the whole nest were one huge, angry insect.

Boots and one of his friends wanted to knock the nest down, so they came up with a foolproof plan. They found a large box and cut an arm hole on the right side and two slits for eyes. They fashioned a potato sack to the arm hole so someone could be holding a stick and moving their arm around without it being exposed to flying, vengeful punishers. Boots and his friend decided little Ed would be best suited for the task.

Somehow, they were able to recruit and convince Ed to go along with their ill-fated plan. Feigning bravery, naive and eager to please, Ed suited up in the box with his arm in the potato sack. The older boys gave him a stick to hold, then they backed away to a healthy distance from the tree. Boots motioned to Ed to go on ahead.

Ed was short enough, and the box was tall enough that he could walk a few steps and then crouch down so that the bottom of the box was touching the ground. He took a few steps and then stopped. He peeked out the eye holes and then took a few more steps. This continued for what seemed like several minutes until he finally reached the trunk of the tree. He heard the loud buzzing as hundreds of bees swarmed the nest. He paused.

"Go on now Ed! Hit it!" the boys yelled.

Ed took a deep breath and then with one swipe, he brought the stick down hard on the center of the nest. The boys cheered and for a quick moment, and Ed was elated. It was a direct hit! Before Ed could think or react, the bees furiously descended on the box, covering it like summer flies on a fresh cow patty.

The plan was perfect except for one major oversight. The eye slits were wide open with no protection. As the bees covered the cardboard looking for any crack or weakness, a handful of them found their way inside the eye holes. Ed flew out from under the box, running and screaming, giving the bees easy access to his entire body. Even though he was flailing around, a huge mass of the flying enemies caught up with him and stung him head to toe. The older boys fell over from laughter.

Their amusement didn't last long. Panic ensued when they realized Ed was in serious pain and was having a full-blown anaphylactic reaction to the multitude of stings. After a brief stay in the E.R. at the hospital, Ed returned home with a swollen, painful recovery ahead. They discovered after this stunt that Ed is allergic to insect stings. He still carries an EpiPen with him whenever he is outdoors. If he gets stung badly again, he could have a life-threatening allergic reaction.

All parents have moments that put them to the test, moments when they want to protect their children from hard things. Good parents realize that shielding them from the natural consequences of their actions does not do them the most good in the long run. Andy and Grace had several of these moments with their four children. It was of the highest importance to Andy that his children developed strong character and integrity. He wanted to be a good example to his family of doing the right thing, and he wanted his children to set a good example to others in turn.

The Roddenbery kids knew they had to behave when their dad was around. He worked very hard, extremely long days, always leaving the house by 6:00 a.m.. They did not want to make him angry, so the children did their best to obey and comply when he was around. The four children did, however, enjoy pushing their mother to the limits from time to time. Their maid Addie was somewhere in the middle, a cushion who also knew how to diffuse a situation.

When Boots was in the upper grades, he was taking Ed, his much younger brother, fishing at the Chamblesses' lake in Harris County about twenty miles north of Columbus. They started speeding halfway there in the 1953 two-tone green Chevrolet on Highway 27 heading north. It wasn't long before the flashing red lights of a police car appeared behind them. Boots decided to turn east on Highway 208 toward Waverly Hall, and he pushed the pedal to the floor, racing up the road going about 90 miles per hour. With the law in hot pursuit, they whizzed around curves and turned on a back road, finally slowing down when they believed they had outrun the police.

They arrived at the lake and were enjoying the serenity of the country. The calm and quiet of their fishing spot was interrupted about thirty minutes into their venture. Dr. Chambless approached them on the bank and said sternly, "Your dad is on the phone." The boys dropped their poles and went inside to answer the call.

"You didn't have an encounter with the police, did you?"

"No, dad," remarked Boots, "I outran them!"

The boys didn't account for the officer getting their tag number and calling it in. Because the car was registered in their dad's name, he got the call at work. "Go turn yourself in." Andy ordered, "Meet me at the Harris County courthouse." The two boys solemnly drove to meet an angry father and longtime Harris County Sheriff Sam Jones. Their dad, always devoted to his patients, had to leave an office full of people waiting for their appointments to drive the 30 minutes or so to deal with this situation. He was not happy. "Dr. Roddenbery," the sheriff said, "We didn't realize this was your son."

"Throw the book at them," Andy said through gritted teeth.

The sheriff ordered them to pay a fine and suspended Boots' driver's license.

Boots came by his lead foot honestly. Once when Andy was returning to the hospital for the second time on the same day, he was speeding and got pulled over. He explained to the officer that he was headed to the hospital for an emergency, and the deputy let him go. Several hours later on his way home, he got pulled over for speeding again by the same officer. He asked, "What is your excuse this time, doctor?"

Andy responded resolutely, "Write it up."

Andy immensely enjoyed taking the family to Athens for Georgia football games. On one trip, Ed and his friend Stokely Pound accompanied Andy to the game. Stokely played golf with Ed, but I met him later as the owner of the Ace Hardware Store in Pine Mountain. They always stayed in the Georgia Center, the on-campus hotel where the University's famed mascot UGA has his own suite. On this particular trip the three of them - my grandfather, Ed, and Stokely- piled into the same room. They returned to their room after the game, but the partying continued outside. Late into the evening, they could hear some commotion out in the hallway.

Andy reached his breaking point and went out into the hallway to see what was going on. He found a man verbally assaulting the female who was with him. Andy told him to "knock it off" and to leave the girl alone.

"Are you going to make me?" the intoxicated man mocked.

The young man didn't realize he was barking up the wrong tree. Andy, in his fifties then, grabbed him in a headlock and pounded him in the nose. An astonished Ed appeared in the hallway to find a young man on the ground looking up at Andy.

"Gollee," he mumbled, "for an old white-haired man, you sure do have a lot of grit."

He was a Southern gentleman but was tough when he needed to be.

Andy was relatively trusting of most everyone. He always tried to see the good in people and give them a fair shake. Grace, on the other hand, didn't trust people naturally. Once, a traveling salesman came to call on doctors in the area. An Asian custom suit tailor came to the office and gave a good rundown of his skills. He measured and picked fabrics, and Andy decided to let the man make him a suit if he would do the same presentation for his wife and could win her approval. Grace gave her ok as the man was very convincing. The next day, Andy even referred him to his partner Abe.

When the suits finally arrived, they were ridiculously ill-fitting with lopsided hems. One arm of Andy's suit hung down way below the other. Being frugal, he resolved to wear them anyway, and he and his similarly clad colleague would chuckle about their wardrobe malfunctions together. Grace forbade him to wear the awful suits when she was with him.

Another man came into town and hit up a bunch of the doctors to invest in his project. He was building a state-of-the-art hotel in Warm Springs, Georgia called the White House Inn. This was near Franklin D. Roosevelt's vacation home in Warm Springs where he created a polio treatment facility.

The Inn was on a beautiful tract of land with a gorgeous view of the nearby valley. The developer broke ground and began construction. He built just enough of the foundation and the concrete blocks of the first level to get investors to commit before he ran off with everyone's money. They never heard from him again. Even in my childhood, I remember the cement skeleton of a half-built building choked with Kudzu vines.

Andy was the same man at home as he was in his practice and in public life. He was kind, fair, encouraging, held high expectations, was tough, and worked very hard. Though he wasn't especially funny himself, he had a wonderful sense of humor and loved a good laugh. He was dedicated and loyal, and he pursued excellence in everything he did, even if it was something as simple as tying a fishing line or repairing a fence.

People remember the way he made them feel, as though they were the only one in the room. He always had time for anything you wanted to share with him. Andy deeply cared about other people, was a brilliant doctor, and was tenaciously committed to doing the right thing, especially when it was the hard thing to do. These are some of his greatest legacies to me.

Partner.

May in middle Georgia is the gateway between cool, blossoming spring days and the unrelenting, sweltering heat of summer. The skies seem clearer and bluer than April, and the flowering bounty of springtime azaleas and dogwoods makes you believe anything is possible. In the 1960's, most anything *was* possible for anyone; that is, unless you were brown or black. Then, the possibilities were limited by the shade of your skin.

Early one afternoon in May of 1964, Dr. S.A. "Andy" Roddenbery sat with his medical partner, Dr. A.B. "Abe" Conger, discussing their surgery schedule for the next day. The sun beamed through the windows in their second-floor office suite of the Doctor's Building in Columbus, Georgia. A light rap on the door disrupted the conversation, and Betty Harrison, Andy's secretary, appeared in the doorway.

"Excuse me, doctors, but Dr. Delmar Edwards is waiting in the colored reception room, and he has requested to see both of you."

Both men recognized his name as one of the surgical residents at Tuskegee Veteran's Administration Hospital they had been mentoring. Since the start of their surgical partnership in August of 1950, both Dr. Roddenbery and Dr. Conger had been driving to Tuskegee once every few weeks to serve as surgical consultants at the all-black hospital, seeing patients and training the staff and doctors there.

Dr. Delmar Edwards was then a surgical resident, and both men felt embarrassed to realize that this educated, respected doctor would have been forced to enter the tiny, crowded waiting room for coloreds rather than through the more spacious white waiting room in their building. Every office in the entire building had segregated waiting rooms with two entry doors- one larger main entrance with the Doctor's name and room number and a smaller entrance for "COLORED."

"Send Dr. Edwards back," Dr. Conger said briskly. A tall and slender black man in a dark suit entered the room.

His hair was cut in his usual short style, and he wore large, rounded glasses. He strode over to them with poise and grace, and his mild manner and familiar smile put everyone immediately at ease.

"I know you are both busy with afternoon appointments, so I will get right to the point," he said. "I am aware that you both served as preceptors for Dr. Freddie Smith and Dr. John Winston at Tuskegee for a two-year period. These two years ended their six-year training and allowed them to become board eligible in general surgery for certification as specialists in the field." Both men remembered with pride and satisfaction helping the two young surgeons begin their careers at Tuskegee.

"Have you kept up with them?" Andy asked.

"Yes sir, I have. They both have successful surgical practices to date," Dr. Edwards responded.

After a pause and a deep breath, Dr. Edwards continued, "I don't want to set myself up as a bona fide specialist unless I am adequately trained, and I hope you two gentlemen will be willing to help me...I am wondering whether it would be a possibility for this same combination, Drs. Conger and Roddenbery, to help me qualify for certification in general surgery."

Possibility. The word hung over all three of them in the suddenly heavy air like August peaches on a bending branch. They all silently acknowledged the magnitude of what he was asking. The previous black doctors they helped had received their residency training prior to Drs. Conger and Roddenbery helping them finish out their specialist training. All of this took place at Tuskegee, the all-black hospital.

Dr. Edwards was asking to work alongside them for training in general surgery so that he could earn Board Certification. This would involve seeing their white patients and operating in their white operating rooms with their nearly all-white staff. After each man inhaled and exhaled a couple of breaths, Dr. Conger broke the silence. "What does the American Board of Surgery say about this?"

"I have a letter from Dr. Robert Moore, Chairman of the American Board of Surgery." He pulled out the letter and began to read, "You may complete your surgical residency training under a two-year preceptorship arrangement under the direct supervision of Dr. A.B. Conger and Dr. S.A. Roddenbery. This can be approved provided that Drs. Conger and Roddenbery notify me in writing that they will assume this responsibility, and each make the necessary detailed reports to my office at six-month intervals." Dr. Edwards stopped. He hesitantly raised his eyes from the trembling letter to the two white men, his dark eyes flooded with apprehension but steadied on their response.

And he waited.

After a long pause, Dr. Conger said with a troubled look, "Delmar, this could cause a few problems. What do you think Andy?" He agreed. "We might stir up real trouble in our medical community."

"There are a number of problems that come to mind," continued Abe. "You would be assisting one or both of us in the operating room daily. There will be some patients who will not wish to be cared for by a black physician. Black nurses are somewhat acceptable in the operating room, but black doctors are something else."

His words floated through the air and seemed to land hard somewhere between the two white men and their black counterpart. Long, dark afternoon shadows from the window blinds cut through the light on the floor. Suddenly it seemed as though they were sitting on opposite sides of the railroad tracks.

Both Abe and Andy knew that forming such close personal and professional ties with a black doctor would inevitably create difficulties. They would be sticking their necks out, and there were plenty of people eager to combat their good will. All they really had to gain was the satisfaction of helping a young, black surgeon improve himself and become a better doctor. It was a noble effort for certain, but working with a black man, no matter how qualified, under the current racial climate in the Jim Crow South could be detrimental to both men's careers and their families. They were not sure it would be worth the cost.

The mood was solemn. For a long time, no one spoke. All men were professionally prepared for this endeavor, but personally it could require more than any of them were willing to endure. Abe broke the ice with a stunning statement, "Delmar, you will not really be ready for this until another person looks you in the eye, calls you 'nigger,' and gets in return a smile instead of overwhelming anger."

After a minute, Delmar responded to Dr. Conger, "I have no problem handling that situation. I have lived with it all my life. Let me tell you some true stories. In histology class, my lab buddy was a young, blonde, freckled kid from a small Arkansas town. We were exchanging unknown slides and quizzing one another. My partner gave me a slide and asked me to identify the structure or tissue. My first guess was that it was an appendix. He gave me credit for a correct answer."

Delmar continued, "I proceeded to give him a slide that seemed to stump him and he could not come up with the answer. Suddenly he cried out, 'Oh, oh oh! I have it Delmar! This looks like skin! Yes, that's it! Just plain old nigger skin!' Then my friend, realizing his mistake, began to turn red starting at his neck and spilling all the way up over his whole neck and face.

He apologized profusely, 'Delmar, please forgive me. I love you like a brother and would never intentionally do or say anything to hurt you.' I smiled and said, 'Don't worry brother. Think nothing of it! You are right. That's just plain old nigger skin.'"

Delmar explained that another time, he had a visiting teaching professor in medical school. The man was doing a slide presentation in a darkened room. A student asked a hypothetical question about a rare variable in the situation they were talking about. The teacher responded that if that hypothetical "should ever occur, I should have to conclude there was a 'nigger in the woodpile' somewhere." He did not let the comment bother him.

Delmar was invited to play for his medical school basketball team and earned a spot in the starting five, only to be uninvited because the YMCA was not integrated. He was uninvited to attend the dinner-dance for the graduating seniors of his medical school because the hotel hosting the event did not permit blacks as guests. Delmar had been left in the pouring rain by taxis carrying white patrons, and he was told to eat in the back kitchen of a restaurant in Texas as the leader of an all-white group of servicemen because of his skin color. Unfair treatment as a black man was something he was very accustomed to.

Andy and Abe talked into the evening about their meeting with Delmar. They met at 8 a.m. the next morning to decide whether or not they should take on this new partnership. There were undoubtedly risks involved. Abe and Andy were working hard to build their own practices in Columbus, and they knew that starting a close relationship with a black man professionally, even though he was a doctor, would do more than raise eyebrows. They could not afford to offend their patients, and they wondered if they were foolish to bring Delmar into an all-white medical community, for his sake and for theirs.

They agreed that they would never have sought out this arrangement. However, here they were, in what seemed like an impossible predicament. They wanted to help Delmar, but the roadblocks they were facing seemed insurmountable. They agonized over what seemed like a lose-lose decision. They did not see the advantage of upsetting their patients, their practice and colleagues, and even their families over what felt like an act of goodwill. However, they could not find the grounds to hinder a qualified man from proper training simply based on the color of his skin.

When Andy and Abe recited The Hippocratic Oath at the end of their medical training, the words they said resided deep in their souls and guided them for their practice and their lives. The oath, originating about 400 B.C., has been used to swear in new medical apprentices at the beginning of their training. The classic version of the oath (a newer, modern language version was written in the 1960's) begins "I swear by Apollo..." and spells out in the covenant to "apply dietetic measures for the benefit of the sick" and to keep patients "from harm and injustice."

The oath goes on to promise "I will neither give a deadly drug to anybody who asked for it, nor will I make a suggestion to this effect. Similarly, I will not give to a woman an abortive remedy. In purity and holiness I will guard my life and my art... Whatever houses I may visit, I will come for the benefit of the sick, remaining free of all intentional injustice...".

Segregated schools, buses, public buildings, swimming pools, and water fountains were the norm in Columbus. Hospitals, operating rooms, and doctors' offices were no exception. They were considering a journey that would be lonely, confrontational, isolating, and dangerous, albeit rewarding. They were toying with the most deep-seated societal norm of the south and challenging the hierarchy in the social strata of physicians.

The two white surgeons reasoned that The American Board of Surgery had approved it and so should they. In the end, their consciences won out, and they agreed to try the preceptorship surgical training of Dr. Delmar Edwards. This one decision would lead them to confront their own personal prejudices and those of their colleagues. Delmar, Abe and Andy were three Southerners who shared a geographic heritage but very little else. They were forged together by a common love of medicine and a strange opportunity to partner together and push the bold lines drawn between black and white.

This newfound professional arrangement would transcend cultural and societal norms. It would surpass even their own ideas about what they were embarking upon. In one sense, they were only doing what they thought was right to help a fellow doctor. In another sense, they were marching to war against an institution that did not wish to be challenged. They were running through the taut rope of racial segregation with scalpels in their hands.

Dr. Delmar Edwards moved to Columbus to set up practice in July 1964. Many black people in town still held vivid memories of the vast racial discord. Delmar struggled to find anyone willing to rent him office space. A black man of influence named George W. Ford offered him the space over Coffee's Drugstore in the black section of town. The modest office was downtown and on the corner of 7th Avenue and 8th Street. Ford displaced his wife's beauty parlor which was using the space to make this arrangement possible. It was a small two-room office, on one side was the reception area and waiting room and on the other side was the examination room.

Quietly, Andy and Abe had their doubts about Delmar's ability to withstand the outside pressures of this surgical training partnership. They were pleased to have someone else to assist them in the operating room every morning, but their other white doctor counterparts dug their heels in and protested. They were not willing or ready to accept Delmar as any sort of equal. Delmar calmly but directly began to challenge the existing norms in the hospital.

On his first day in the surgical suite, he made a lasting impression. He asked one of the longtime orderlies, Crocker, about the location of the doctors' lounge. When a dumbfounded Crocker did not respond, Delmar pressed, "Where is the doctors' lounge?"

Speechless, Crocker stared at him and began to break out into a sweat as several others quietly gathered, curious to hear his response. Delmar fully understood the magnitude of his question and continued slowly with emphasis, "In every hospital I know of, there is a room where doctors go while they are waiting for their cases to be called. It normally has a coffee urn and some kind of pastry or danish. Where is that place in this hospital?"

Black doctors had never been allowed into the doctor's lounge or the white dressing room. They had a colored dressing room upstairs in the obstetrics department. Crocker glanced over Delmar's left shoulder at Margaret Webb, the operating room supervisor, who had joined the few onlookers.

As soon as Webb reluctantly gave the nod, Crocker finally responded, "Right this way, sir."

When Delmar walked into the doctor's lounge, every physician except one got up and left the room. Only James Rhea, a tall and friendly young pediatrician, stayed. He walked over to Delmar with an extended hand and introduced himself. One of the doctors who had stormed out of the lounge went straight to the hospital administrator's office to complain. In his rage, he demanded Delmar be removed bodily from the premises. Unbelievably, and admirably, the administrator refused.

Later that afternoon, Delmar got a call from Dr. William G. Reid, a black general practitioner. "I heard you carried your black ass into the doctor's dressing room. Are you crazy?" he chided. He could not believe Delmar's audacity and the subsequent lack of impunity.

When Andy heard about the incident from another person at the hospital, he was disappointed and angered by the response of his friends and colleagues. The past decade spent driving to and from Tuskegee with Abe and the hours teaching and associating with the patients and staff there had radically changed his views on the black race. The conditioned prejudicial scales began to fall from his eyes, and he could clearly see the value and humanity of the many doctors and patients there. As soon as he finished for the day, he had one thing on his mind. Andy drove immediately to Delmar's office.

In the confines of his car, Andy boiled with anger at the injustice of his friend's treatment. He thought about how humiliating it must have been for Delmar. Unsure of exactly what to say, he parked his car and ran up the back stairs. Upon greeting his friend he started, "Delmar, you know you have many friends at the hospital. The treatment you received today is not representative of how many others feel about you. I am so sorry for the inappropriate response by the other doctors. It was uncalled for."

Delmar flashed his easy smile that seemed to wrinkle up half his face. Calmly, he put a soft hand on Andy's shoulder and said, "Please don't worry about me. Actually, I expected this to happen." Somewhat relieved by his friend's response, Andy implored Delmar to keep up the good work while quietly reassuring himself the climate among the doctors would surely improve. The incident did not leave Andy's mind for quite some time, and he wondered how Delmar would make his way forward in such a hostile environment. He resolved to be by his friend's side each step of the way.

The next morning in the corridor of the hospital, Abe and Delmar were chatting about the events of the previous day. Abe listened, particularly interested to hear about the colleague who marched straight to the administrator to register his rage...the one who complained that Delmar had entered the lounge and had asked for Delmar to be thrown out of the hospital on his ear. As Abe's fury was mounting, suddenly that very doctor rounded the corner of the hallway. When the doctor spotted Delmar and Abe talking and noted the rage on Abe's face flashing toward him, he made a speedy detour toward the elevator.

Dr. Abe Conger was not your typical middle-aged professional. In addition to his sometimes-fiery personality, he had the fists to back it up. To keep in shape, he worked out with weights and regularly pounded a punching bag hanging from the ceiling of his garage. His professional loyalty and tenacity made him a force to be reckoned with, and his muscular physique could intimidate men half his age.

As the doctor raced into the elevator frantically pushing buttons to make the doors securely close him in, Abe growled as he sprinted down the hall toward him, "Wait a minute! I want to talk to you!" The doors closed just before Abe reached the elevator, and the metal chariot began its ascent to the third floor. Abe stood there for a minute beating his fists on the closed metal doors demanding, "Come back! Come back here you sonofabitch! I heard what you did! I want to talk to you!"

Andy and Abe each made their support of Delmar known in their own way, but they knew Delmar had an uphill climb to win over the others. One evening, Andy received a call from the hospital administrator asking him to come to his office at 11 the following morning to discuss an important matter he would not disclose. Andy arrived promptly, surprised to find Delmar walking up for his own meeting with the same man. "I hope you aren't in some sort of trouble," Andy whispered to Delmar as the secretary announced their arrival.

"I sure hope not," was his friend's startled reply.

The administrator asked them to sit down in two chairs facing his desk while he uncharacteristically paced nervously back and forth. Andy and Delmar had no idea the purpose of this strange meeting and were eager to find out. He finally sat down, thanked them for coming, and then began a diatribe about his feelings on integration. He believed the hospital was moving too quickly to integrate black and white patients, and he wanted Delmar's help as a black leader in the hospital to slow it down.

He asked Delmar if he would go to different black groups and ask them to pump the brakes on pushing for these radical ideas at the hospital.

Andy sat quietly, taking in the situation unfolding before him. As the conversation went on, it was obvious to Andy the administrator brought him into the meeting as a means to intimidate Delmar into going along with the request rather than embarrass Andy if he refused. Andy resented this deceptive manipulation of his good friend Delmar, but he decided not to speak and to let Delmar handle the situation. He had confidence in Delmar's good discernment and ability to maneuver difficult situations, and Andy decided he would support whatever decision his wise friend made.

Delmar calmly explained to the administrator that he was wholly in favor of integration and if he was asking for a short time for the hospital to get organized, he would be glad to help. But he also made it clear that if this was some sort of stall tactic, he would not be able to cooperate. The administrator, disappointed he was not able to get Delmar's commitment, thanked them and they left his office.

After the meeting, Andy and Delmar seethed about the way they had been exploited by the administrator. He had attempted to use them and their unlikely friendship for his own devious purposes. He had falsely assumed Delmar would be easy to manipulate and that the presence of his white mentor would pressure him to acquiesce, but he didn't know Delmar the way Andy did. If he hadn't already proved himself before, now Delmar left no room for any doubt of his character and his grit.

Delmar felt similarly about Andy and Abe, and he would tell people, "I have the best of two worlds. I work with not one, but two Georgia born and bred, Harvard Medical School educated, well trained, and experienced surgeons." He even called on their recommendation at the bank to be able to get a loan when he was ill for a period of time. They happily vouched for his character and ability to repay the loan, and the bank gave Delmar the money.

Andy saw new depths of Delmar's character and became fascinated with the way Delmar absorbed insults and slights with a peaceful disposition. "How could he resist fighting back? How could he contain his temper and maintain his poise? How could he hold up his head, smile, continue his pleasant manner, and retain a good self-image?" Andy later wrote. 10

Delmar's surgical skill set was equally as impressive. He had good hand-eye coordination, smooth and precise movements, and very good technique. My grandfather felt the only "defect in (Delmar's) surgical armor" to be a lack of concentration in the O.R. when other people in the room were having conversations about other things. It seemed his mind wandered, and his concentration waned. Andy pulled him aside on two different occasions and discussed his concerns with him. After the second conversation, he never noticed again.

Years later when they were visiting in the doctor's lounge one day, they talked about those conversations. Delmar admitted he was frustrated by the criticism at the time, but after an honest assessment, he agreed that he needed to work on those areas. He reflected that in his youth he felt the need to always be aware of everything going on around him as sort of a first line of defense. He could easily become preoccupied with conversations and the moods and actions of people around him because he wanted to be one step ahead of any kind of conflict arising.

Slowly, Delmar continued to win over the doctors at the hospital. Regularly, nurses and doctors would pass along compliments to Abe and Andy about their protege. There were still several who made negative remarks about Drs. Roddenbery and Conger, but never to their faces. In the doctor's lounge one physician would joke that Andy and Abe were using Delmar to do their rounds so they didn't have to do them. This was simply not true. Abe and Andy had heard enough through the hospital grapevine to identify four main critical colleagues and resolved to each talk with two of them face to face.

Andy made an appointment with one of the men and

went to his office to sit down with him. He got straight to the point and told the man that he had been overheard saying that Abe and Andy had no business being mixed up with this black doctor and that some friend should tell them to kick that rascal out of town. He then went on to explain the preceptorship arrangement with Delmar in detail.

"Well, you know what you are doing, don't you?" asked the colleague. "You are taking it upon yourselves to upgrade a Negro doctor."

"Yes, that is exactly what we are trying to do," Andy smugly exclaimed.

"All right, count on me to keep my mouth shut on the subject. If I have anything more to say, it will be to you," the doctor said.

After Abe and Andy made the rounds with the four resistant doctors, they had relatively few incidents. Delmar had to fight many of his own battles, but he always did so with peaceful grace and resolute steadfastness. Gradually, he helped integrate the hospital cafeteria by sitting on the white side, and he in turn gained ground for other blacks at the hospital to do the same. For nearly everyone around Delmar professionally, it was impossible to deny his reasonable activism and his strong character, though he was not afraid to defend himself when necessary.

Dr. David Stein, who was chief of anesthesiology at Saint Francis Hospital enjoyed ribbing Abe and Andy and finding the humor in their arrangement. At the time, Abe was nearly bald, and Andy was prematurely grey. One day in the Operating Room, Stein asked, "Well now, how are the Silver Fox, the Bald Eagle, and the Brown Bear getting along these days? I understand that Delmar Edwards is the only black surgeon in the state of Georgia, maybe in the entire South, or even perhaps in the whole U.S.A. who has not just one, but two white physician's assistants to help him do his surgery." A tense silence blanketed the room. After a few moments, Andy broke into unbridled laughter. Everyone in the room, including the entire surgical team and all supporting personnel, joined in. Those nicknames followed them for years to come.

Dr. Edwards was performing surgery with Andy and Abe as courtesy staff, and eventually he was granted full surgical privileges at Saint Francis Hospital. This good news came after he had loudly joked that if he wasn't given full privileges, he would contact the NAACP and surround the hospital with so many blacks, it would get dark at high noon! In a few days, his privileges were granted. Later, he was appointed to the credentials committee and became chairman for many years.

In 1972 Delmar also became a Fellow of the American

College of Surgeons (F.A.C.S.), the goal of every qualified surgeon in the country. He also served on the Muscogee County School Board, the AFLAC Board of Directors, and received many other honors and awards in the community. Early on, Andy remarked to a friend that the wisdom or folly of his and Abe's decision to mentor Delmar would become evident in time. Dr. Edwards proved in every way his merit and ability, and their gamble paid off.

They became so close that Andy insisted Delmar and his wife Betty attend his children's weddings and sit just behind the family. Andy made special arrangements to be sure the ushers knew where to seat his cherished friends. Delmar said he was called to an emergency that kept him from attending my parents' wedding in 1969, but Andy had his suspicions. They did come to my Uncle Ed and Aunt Becky Sue's wedding on December 14, 1974. To Andy's dismay, Delmar and Betty were seated in the balcony of Saint Luke Church in Columbus.

Later, Delmar explained to Andy they had been running late and had requested to sit in the balcony so as not to disrupt the ceremony. Andy took the opportunity to ask him about Berta's wedding five years earlier to assuage his suspicions as to why he didn't come. Delmar said, "Well, Andy, that was five years ago, and the climate then was a bit different. I didn't want to do anything in any way to mar her wedding day."

Andy responded, "You are kind and considerate, Delmar, to think and feel that way, but you should have come anyway."

Delmar laughed, "You know, Andy, sometimes, I have to protect you from yourself!"[7]

I found a typed copy of my grandfather's resume outlining all the amazing things he accomplished, but what you can't read on plain white paper in common written words is the stuff that makes up a man, the things down deep in his soul. I believe one of his greatest accomplishments was his friendship, formed against all odds, with Dr. Delmar Edwards amid a largely racist southern culture. One of Andy's strongest gifts both personally and professionally was his ability to see right past the surface and down into the guts of a man. What he learned about Dr. Delmar Edwards changed him and a lot of other people for the better.

Andy performed several thousand surgeries during his medical career. Many of our family friends in Columbus and the surrounding area have stories about him caring for someone in their family at some time or another. My uncle shared a story with me about how Andy's care for him saved his eye and kept him from "looking like a freak."

On November 3, 1973, my dad's younger brother

Leighton Alston was in a terrible car accident. He was en route to Columbus from Carrollton, Georgia for naval reserve duty. In the early morning hours still shrouded in darkness, a car suddenly pulled out in front of him. With no time to avoid the collision, he hit the front right wheel of the Ford Torino and careened into a ditch on the right side of the highway.

Leighton was driving a brand-new Toyota, the first car he ever owned with seatbelts. Thankfully, he had fastened the separate shoulder and lap belts, each with manual tension. Toyotas in the early 70's were not built like they are today, and they were not as safe. His shiny new car folded up on impact like a Japanese paper fan. He ate the steering wheel that slammed into his lap. The rear-view mirror dislodged in the crash. He picked it up to see what was wrong with his aching face, but he couldn't see anything except blood.

Leighton was a medic in the reserves, and somehow his training kicked in even through his own bodily trauma. He doesn't know how he was able to get out of the car, but he got his first aid kit from the trunk and tried to tend to his wounds. A stranger approached him on the roadside to help, and Leighton asked him what his wounds looked like. The man could not hide his aghast look of horror. When another approaching car slammed on brakes, Leighton fled back down into the ditch clutching his face with gauze.

The only available vehicle, a hearse, came to pick up Leighton from La Grange, the closest city with a hospital. The driver had no medical training and said he had to turn off his siren when they reached the city limits. My uncle wondered if the hearse driver would be incentivized if his patient died before they got to the hospital. Upon arrival at the Emergency Room, a young doctor told Leighton he would need to go into surgery immediately. Thankfully, Leighton was still conscious and told the doctor to call Dr. S.A. Roddenbery in Columbus, Georgia and do whatever he told him to do.

Leighton's parents were already en route from Wetumpka, Alabama, and once they arrived, they loaded Leighton into the back seat of his dad's car. When they arrived in Columbus, Dr. Roddenbery was waiting with an ophthalmologist and eye surgeon (Dr. Lionel Yoe), an orthopedic surgeon (Dr. Sidney Yarbrough), and a head and neck surgeon (Dr. Ronald Watson). Leighton didn't know these specialties existed since he had only ever been to the Swift Spinning Mills doctor! They took him right away into surgery.

When Leighton woke up in Intensive Care, he had over 400 sutures in his face and head. The tissue connecting his face to his skull had been ripped off. He had deep lacerations in his eyes, forehead, and lips, and his nose was crushed. When he looked at his reflection a few days post-surgery, he thought he was going to look like a monster! Andy later remarked it was nothing short of a miracle Dr. Yoe was able to save Leighton's eye. Although Leighton's nose is slightly shorter than before, most people who knew him couldn't tell. His face itched constantly for over a year while the nerve endings grew back. Leighton was certain he would have been unrecognizable if they had operated on him in LaGrange and it hadn't been for Dr. Roddenbery's help.

His right patella was also crushed, but the surgery to remove part of it would need to happen a few weeks later. After such a long recovery, his muscles atrophied a good deal. Even though he was young, he practically had to learn how to walk again. He is deeply grateful for Andy and his team's great care.

In all his years practicing medicine (1950-1986), Dr. Andy Roddenbery III had no scandals, no lawsuits, and never lost a patient in surgery. He only had two patients who died at the hospital. One lady was recovering from surgery in the hospital and after a few days suffered a fatal blood clot right before she was to be dismissed. The only other death was a man who died after being put under with anesthesia before surgery was to begin. Dr. Roddenbery had many patients who revered and loved him for the excellent care he provided.

Retiree.

When the wind blows hardest off the crest of the ocean, the most difficult thing to do is to look straight into it. Your sights dim, your ears fill with all sorts of static, making it hard to hear even ordinary sounds. As you turn toward the full force of air pounding against your face and chest, forcing you to go nearly deaf and blind, only your heart can lead you. You must depend on it. This is the curse of a man with the ocean in his veins. A sea born man is anchored by his heart no matter how violently his craft is tossed, no matter how hard the wind batters his sails. In the fury of a storm, he must call upon his wits and internal compass to make it through. But when the morning calms, the sea calls to him mercilessly to return to her, beckons him to the wild and fury where the man is both at home and at war. The sea is master and servant, lover and commanding foe.

A surgeon, however, depends on his logic and senses. There is no place for reckless emotion. The heart must relent to the head. The surgeon relies on the minuscule, calculated movements of his hands. He rests on the reliability of his vision. He processes everything about a situation and weighs it against his rigorous training before he can make an educated decision about a course of treatment. He must rely wholeheartedly on his training, his intellect, and staying current with research and procedures. His heart can rarely interfere; it certainly cannot guide the scalpel in his hand.

This was the way Dr. Andy Roddenbery approached his surgical cases, with utmost professionalism and wisdom, and with calculated accuracy. But the true measure of a man, even a surgeon, is not only in how he cuts out what ails a man, but in how he binds up his wounds. Andy's head and hands guided the surgeries, but his heart led his treatment of the people who came to him for help.

His best attribute may have been the way he was trained to see deeper, straight through the skin, past the marrow and the flesh, to find what is really broken. Once the skin is peeled back, the surgeon's eyes see only the insides of a man, not the color on the exterior of his skin. He learned to look completely past the superficial to find the sickness. By seeing firsthand how we all truly look the same on the inside, his head and heart would not allow him to stand by when injustice ran rampant.

People rarely find their passion in life, the thing they love to do more than anything else. And when the passion agrees with the special talents of the person, that is truly a gift from God. My grandfather found his passion in being a physician and lived it out every day, his skilled hands cutting and stitching the physical wounds, his heart listening and caring for the emotional and spiritual ones.

Dr. Roddenbery's horn-rimmed glasses were a stark contrast against his salt and pepper swept back hair. His naturally thin upper lip melted completely away into his contagious, childlike grin. When he laughed, his soft brown eyes sparkled, and they froze intently while listening from the heart. He wore shiny brown or black wingtip shoes (never tennis shoes), a corresponding belt, and khaki pants with his shirt tucked in. He dressed in a suit every day for work and would take his jacket off to put on his white doctor's coat upon arrival at his office.

His average but somewhat muscular build paid homage to his former athletic accomplishments. His many patients were quickly at ease under his soft gaze and kind demeanor. His genuinely warm and welcoming smile and pat on the shoulder or hand while he earnestly listened endeared him to each person. The black community in Columbus felt especially loved and cared for by the good doctor since they were ostracized and cast aside by many white professionals in town. He did not charge those who could not afford to pay him for his services.

Once his practice was well established, Andy was finally able to repay his medical school loans to the generous and powerful men in Atlanta and Macon. He borrowed a total of $4,400 to complete his four years of study and receive his M.D. from Harvard. When he contacted the widow of his Jewish benefactor, Harold Hirsch, she would not accept the payment but asked that it be passed along to a needy young person.

General Harris also rejected receiving any interest on his loan but asked that Andy pay it forward. Through their examples, these men and women instilled in him the virtues of generosity and compassion for others. Thus began one of the secret kindnesses of my grandfather's life: paying college tuition and offering free medical care to many who were deserving and could not pay. Andy committed many years ago to repay not only his financial debts but also his own good fortune for the way sports helped to shape his life.

He later wrote regarding his involvement in sports, "I feel an eternal debt to athletics and to what this has meant to my life. For the joy of competition experienced and for the self-discipline it taught me, I shall be forever grateful." To satisfy some of his desire to give back, Andy served in many capacities locally and across the state of Georgia. For ten years he was on the Muscogee County School Board and Chairman of the Athletic Committee from 1961-1970. This was a complex and at times dangerous period to be on the school board during the tumultuous years of school integration.

For ten years, Andy served on the Athletic Board of the University of Georgia. In 1968 he was chairman of a committee that instituted the cardiopulmonary resuscitation program for Sanford Stadium (the UGA football stadium). This program supplied medical equipment necessary to care for a person in the event of a cardiac arrest. Georgia was one of the first schools to have this program and equipment, and it became a model for football stadiums around the country.

While Andy was on the Athletic Board at Georgia, he invited Vince Dooley, then a talented assistant football coach at Auburn, over to his home. After meeting and spending time with Vince, he reported to the rest of the Athletic Board that Vince Dooley should be the next hire as head football coach. Dooley did come to UGA as Head Football Coach and won the National Championship for the University of Georgia in 1980, with the talented Herschel Walker as running back. Dooley then served as Athletic Director for many years, and the football stadium field is named for him.

Andy later wrote regarding how deeply athletics had affected his character:

"The most dramatic change in athletics I have witnessed has been the integration of black athletes into the system. At graduation from college, I had never seen a black athlete compete in any sport. The success of these men has been phenomenal. It has done more to modify or eliminate racial prejudice than any one factor I have known. It has had a terrific impact on a social evil. Thank God, I am not now swayed by prejudice or bigotry. It reaffirms all that we should have been taught since birth- that man must be judged by his character, behavior and performance of deeds in his lifetime, and not by his race, religion, or ethnic origin."

Andy earned the Lifetime Achievement Award from the Georgia Surgical Association as the pioneer of endoscopy in Georgia in the 1960's. He helped establish the Endoscopy Departments at Saint Francis Hospital and The Medical Center in Columbus. He taught as Assistant Professor of

Surgery at the Medical College of Georgia in Columbus from
1978-1985 and chairman of the Emory University faculty of
Columbus. He also wrote multiple academic papers published
in medical journals regarding the treatment of ulcerative colitis,
pancreatitis, burn patients, hypothermia, and many other
subjects. He was an excellent diagnostician and diligently
studied medical journals throughout his career.

He led as Chief of Surgery at the Medical Center
and then Saint Francis Hospital in Columbus. He served as
President of the Georgia Chapter of the American College of
Surgeons and president of the Georgia Surgical Society. He
was the regional consultant in surgery for the Department of
Education in the state of Georgia. For 36 years, Andy worked
every other weekend as a trauma surgeon in the emergency
room in Columbus. He saw all kinds of injuries from car
wrecks, gunshot wounds, and other accidents. As a result of
the carnage, he regularly told us growing up never to hang
our arm out of a car window and cautioned us against riding
motorcycles.

In the 1960's the Roddenbery children moved away
to college, graduate school, and some had started their own
families. In 1970 Grace and Andy looked for a place to move
out to in the country north of Columbus. They loved having

their place in Pine Mountain Valley to the north when the kids were young, and by now a lot of people were starting to move out of the city. The best and most obvious direction to go from Columbus was north.

Andy never forgot the surreal day when he saw the land for the first time. He was practicing medicine in Columbus, Georgia, and the property was a good twenty miles north up GA Highway 27. When my parents got married on July 5, 1969, at Saint Luke Methodist Church in Columbus, Andy's family came in town for the wedding. His father, John Roddenbery and his half-brother John, Jr., went with him to see the home and the land in Harris County.

Past the two-story columned antebellum home stood a rustic red barn with a small, corralled area. Eventually, a painted wood Georgia Bulldog head would be fastened to the tin roof (I have this faded, aged piece of wood hanging at my house today). A single line of mature pecan trees separated the immediate pasture from the rest of the property, and then a wide-open field and splendid woods extended beyond. The three set out on foot following the sun to the west, wading through the tall waving grasses in the absence of any cut roads to navigate through the property.

A breeze chased them across acres of green rolling pastureland where a Black Angus herd would one day graze.

On the highest point of the land used to stand a white clapboard hospital from Civil War days. Small, colorful glass medicine bottles would be discovered by my grandmother throughout the area. They were hidden underneath decades of debris, soil, and stones.

Down the hill, twin hundred-year-old oaks guarded what would become a dirt road entrance to the immense pine and hardwood forest. To the north a low valley of tangled blackberry bushes and impervious shrubbery marked the property line, and a cemetery was visible up the hill. Under Andy's vision, this area would later become a two-acre fishing pond with paddle boats and stocked bass, bream, and catfish. To the south, he would later build another larger lake. And all throughout the property, for years to come, he would hike with his children, grandchildren, and great-grandchildren. They would search for and occasionally find arrowheads, creating happy memories and amassing a new collection to replace the ones that were stolen so long ago.

Once in the backwoods, they could hear the soft chatter of several creeks skipping over stones and carving out the ground. Regal eighty-foot oaks stretched their branches so thick with leaves, the eclipsed sky could hardly peek through. The canopy of trees dominated the archaic forest in every direction. The ferns and rocks kowtowed in due respect. The men in turn felt dwarfed by the ancient giants and spellbound by the raw beauty all around them.

At some point on the hike, their father John had to stop. A lifetime of bad habits and emphysema chased him down. Andy and his half-brother John Jr. continued, and upon their return they discussed with their father whether Andy should buy the land. John, Sr., who had experience in real estate, told him he thought it would be a good investment. The price tag on paradise was $80,000 in 1970 for the original 80 acres and the antebellum home. The sale of the house came with the understanding that the cook Stella and the handyman Sleepy would stay on as employees of the new owners.

Andy's father John, the very man who tore the notion of home away from his young son, was there when a new home began, one that would host at least five generations of Roddenberys. John, the man who had dealt harshly with Andy as a child, gifted him wisdom and generosity toward the end of his life. He even loaned his son $10,000 to buy the land. As he put it, "Land is a good investment. They aren't making any more."

In that moment, as the sweltering sun illuminated the tops of bristly Georgia pines, Andy looked out over what he had been searching for his entire life. Stately oaks waved in the wind, rope-like grass danced beckoning him closer, streams chimed a muted welcome, and ancient arrowheads hid in the dirt waiting to be discovered. He bought a plot of land to drive his stake down and claim as his own.

Andy and Grace moved to the antebellum home at 105 Hill Street (later 341 Hill Street). For sixteen years until 1986, Andy lived in Hamilton and drove the twenty-minute commute to Columbus for work. Sometimes, he would go back and forth twice in one day if he was called in for an emergency. Andy and Grace hosted their family and many guests over the years for fishing, hunting, and just driving or walking out on the land.

Sleepy, who had worked on the property for many years, became a regular fixture. He was aptly named, as he worked slowly and deliberately, and may have taken more time on break than he did actually working. Nevertheless, he was of some help doing regular chores around the farm. One afternoon Grace and Andy gave him a ride home and discovered he was living in a dilapidated five room home less than a mile away. Andy walked inside and could see daylight through the large holes in the roof! Shocked by the condition of his home, Andy said, "Sleepy, doesn't water come into your home?" In his usual shy and slow pattern of speech, Sleepy answered, "Onlyyy whennn it rainssss."

Not long after that, Andy and Grace decided to buy

Sleepy a new trailer home and locate it on the far edge of their property near GA Highway 116. They outfitted it with electricity and a well. Almost daily, Andy and Grace would take the red truck through their land- winding through the woods, pastures, and through streams in the late afternoons. They would even pick up Sleepy's garbage once a week as he aged and haul it in the back of the pickup to their home.

One time, Judge Aaron Cohn was visiting from Columbus and rode with Andy as he pulled up to Sleepy's place. Sleepy was outside when they drove up. Andy slung two bags of his trash into the back of the truck. Aaron, with his usual good sense of humor, said, "Sleepy...you are probably the only black man in the United States who has a Jewish judge and a white doctor picking up his trash." That evoked a rare laugh from the kind and humble man.

The Roddenberys paid Sleepy once a week. One time he confessed to Grace that he spent all his money after every paycheck. A concerned and frugal Grace decided to set up a savings account for Sleepy, and she deducted a small amount of income from his paycheck weekly to deposit into his savings. Over the years, he was able to accumulate enough money for his retirement and for a few other special purchases.

In the early 1980's, Andy's vision began to fail. After further examination by an eye doctor, he learned that cataracts were clouding his once clear brown eyes, the necessary tools in a surgeon's arsenal. In 1986, cataract surgery was in its infancy, and the most plausible option for him was to retire from surgery altogether. His eyes had become cloudy, but his vision was still razor sharp.

On August 1, 1986, shortly after his retirement, Papa set out to write a biography about his friend and colleague of 25 years, Dr. Delmar Edwards. He mentioned to Delmar several times over the years that he should write his own autobiography, but Delmar had little interest. Delmar thought the only person who would want to read it might be his mother.

Andy felt convinced that the story should be told. The dramatic social and political times produced their unlikely friendship, transcending the traditional segregation of the South. Living and working so closely to Delmar over a quarter century gave Andy deep insights into the man. They had a mutual understanding of one another in a way that only mass quantities of time spent together could create.

Andy and Grace tirelessly gathered facts, and he wrote by hand the entire book. Once written, he dictated while she furiously typed on her old-fashioned typewriter. They titled the book "I Swear by Apollo," the beginning of the Hippocratic Oath that all physicians pledge. The oath, along with Andy's faith, steered the course of his conscience and career. The pledge to "do no harm" was a personal and professional motto. As Andy delved into Delmar's past, of his Arkansas youth in a segregated society, Andy began to relive much of his own past, colored with complex feelings toward black people.

He later wrote, "In my own lifetime, I have seen many changes in laws, attitudes, and customs that have moved our land toward the dream of justice for all. Knowing Delmar Edwards has reinforced what I began to learn long ago- that a person's true worth should be judged not by the color of skin but by character and deeds."

Andy looked straight into the wind of culture, blowing every which way, and he let his conscience lead him down a road few men in his position would ever have taken. He stepped toward a path of reconciliation and love for his fellow man, starting with his own father and continuing toward his darker skinned counterpart. This path culminated when he picked up a pen and started to write.

Andy closed his practice upon retirement, but being thrifty, he held onto most of his office furniture and moved it to the house next door on Hill Street. He purchased this house for his mother-in-law Florence "Flossie" George when she moved down from New Hampshire years ago, but after her death, it sat virtually empty. For a brief time, his good friend Charlie Harrold moved to Hamilton and lived in "the cottage" as it was affectionately called. Later, Charlie married Andy's Aunt Rosalind, who was around their age. Even after Charlie moved away, he and Andy remained lifelong friends. Charlie would call Andy from time to time. He always called him "Seab," which usually garnered a chuckle.

The front living room walls of the cottage were each lined with a row of orange and dark brown waiting room upholstered chairs, the kind that were connected to one another with little hooks on the sides. They still smelled like a doctor's office to me, dank and dirty from years of patients' backsides pressed into them, but strangely sanitary, like the smell of an old hospital corridor. The back bedroom housed gigantic metal filing cabinets with extra wide drawers, and of course his precious slide projector with carousel upon carousel of patient slides.

My dad used to tell a funny story about when he and my mom were dating in high school and having dinner with my grandparents one evening. Andy rushed to finish eating and as the rest of them were finishing their meatloaf, the lights went off and the room went suddenly dark. My dad was bewildered and confused about what was happening until suddenly on the far wall, like a blazing comet in a black night sky, appeared an image of someone's colon. And then another. And then my grandfather proceeded into unfortunate detail about the diagnosis of each patient using a telescopic pointer to highlight the issues. My dad lost his appetite in a hurry. That was not his idea of dinner and a movie.

We had similar experiences as grandchildren. All eight of us were lined up on the carpet, dreading the click of each new slide and counting the minutes until a predictable and prompt 6:00 p.m. dinner would set us free. "This right here is a polyp," he would say, with the delight of a child on Christmas morning. He showed us the literal blood and guts of complete strangers as he mounted carousel after carousel on his slide projector and turned the living room wall into a parade of blistered and bloody colons. His hopes of turning us all into doctors were realized only in my cousin Andy and in my brother Travis who is also in the medical field.

When we visited from Florida, we sometimes stayed in this house next door. There was a pull-out sofa and another bedroom furnished with a beautiful antique mahogany bedroom suit that belonged to my grandmother's mother Flossie. The kitchen was stuck somewhere in the late 1950's, but as a child, I hardly noticed the dated decor. It simply felt warm and familiar every time we stepped over the threshold. When I walked down the back steps, I always thought of how my great-grandmother Flossie fell down them to her death suffering a massive head injury in 1980. She was living in the house and that morning she was leaving to visit us in Florida with my grandparents.

In the years following his retirement, Andy wanted to keep his license active, but malpractice insurance had become outrageously high. He made the difficult decision to retire for good. Even after retirement, he was happy to help anyone in Harris County who needed it if he was able for no charge. He had built a reputation for being especially kind to black folks, starting in the years prior to integration until the present, which made him both a hero and an enemy, depending on your side of the tracks.

If a medical problem needed special attention, he would refer his unofficial "patients" to doctors in Columbus who were more specialized. On one such occasion, he sent a black woman to a physician about her ailment. The woman came back and told my grandfather that when the receptionist had asked her who her referring physician was, she had answered matter-of-factly, "Dr. Roddenbery." The black receptionist looked up at her from her starched white uniform with an expressionless face. She said in an exceptionally drawn-out fashion, "E'rrrrry niggerrrr from Harrrris County, when I ask them who their referring physician is, they say 'Doc-c-t-or-r Rod-d-d-denbery!'."

Andy chuckled at hearing this and his response was,

"Well, that is high praise." When my mom told me this story, I thought back on all of his interactions with people of different races, the way he greeted people, helped them, loved them. It was clear to me in that moment that his best asset was not that he *didn't see* the color of skin, but that he peered straight through it to the inside. He was unchanging in how he viewed and treated *all* people, especially those who were under resourced or underserved.

Andy and Grace built two duplexes in the late 1980's on their property fronting Highway 27. They named the small subdivision "Stonehurst," a combination of their mothers' maiden names, Hurst and Stoneback. Several widows and many others from Hamilton lived there for many years. They paid only a modest rent and enjoyed a lovely country setting.

Andy was retired but he rarely sat idly. The surgeon's hands did not rest. Once we came to visit after he had learned the craft of weaving cane chair bottoms. In almost every corner of the living room sat a ladder-back chair with a brand-new seat. In the afternoons, he would sometimes stand in the pasture nearest the barn. He had an old bull horn carved into a kind of trumpet. He mastered the art of blowing it, much like his boy scout bugle, and he would stand at attention belting out the most clear and beautiful mooing sound from the horn. I still can't figure out how to make a proper noise come out of it, but it was fun for all us grandkids, and now his great grandchildren, to try. My mom keeps it on her mantle, and it is a regular challenge to see who can blow the horn the best.

As the herd of Black Angus cows and bulls meandered through the gate and into the safety of the pasture every afternoon, he sometimes stood among them, still as a statue. He might even coax the cows with a special treat in his hand; Mostly he just stood there, talking low and soft and brushing their backs with his palm if they came close enough. He delighted in seeing new calves born. I remember my childlike amazement finding its mirror image in my grandfather's face one morning when we together watched a newborn calf, not yet able to walk. "Such a miracle!" he said.

Hamiltonian

I was born longing. My family tree was firmly rooted in Georgia, but my brother and I entered the scorching earth in sunny central Florida. Never entirely belonging to either culture, I constantly toppled between the two, sipping sweet tea while playing in orange groves. The magnificence of my sunshiny childhood somehow eclipsed under the faded light of a peach shaped moon. I dreamed of the day when I could attend the University of Georgia just like my parents, my grandfather, and his father. Georgia was somehow carved into my DNA such that I never felt like a native Floridian, even though I am one.

My grandfather used to delight in telling the story of when I was born. He and my uncles, Boots and Ed, had been in South America hunting dove in Columbia. My grandmother Grace came down to Orlando early because my brother came very quickly two years earlier. They were all eagerly anticipating my arrival. The guys were in a private plane on the way back to Georgia and when they flew over Orlando, my grandfather radioed down to the hospital to ask if I had been born yet. The message came back over the radio "No... stork...yet," which made my grandfather chuckle each time he regularly told me the story.

My brother Travis was born in July 1976. I arrived in June 1978, next to last in a string of eight grandchildren on my mom's side. Boots and Donna lived near Pensacola with their daughters Laura and Paige Roddenbery. Ann and her husband Frank Brookins had Tripp and Tate in Columbus and later moved to Athens. Ed and Becky Sue Roddenbery lived in Columbus with Andy (S.A. Roddenbery V), who was my age, and a few years after me came the family caboose, baby Ruth.

Our family of four jumped in the car and headed to Georgia as often as our schedules allowed, which was usually about once or twice a year. My dad's parents, Otis and Mary Owen Alston, were in Wetumpka, Alabama at the time, not too far from Columbus. We made the rounds seeing cousins and aunts and uncles on both sides before heading back to the flat, sandy land we called home. Even though our suntanned skin screamed Florida, we were bona fide Georgians at heart.

The wilting green grass between my toes tickled as I glided deer-like through the two-acre wilderness around our Florida house. Sometimes with my arms spread wide singing "The Hills Are Alive," other times running just for speed, pretending a ferocious animal was chasing me, I raced, arms pumping, in joyful laps around my vast yard. By the time I slowed my feet, fire stoked in my chest.

I stopped, red-faced and found a seat in the bends of the tangerine tree just outside my parents' window to catch my breath. I reached up, carefully, avoiding the inch-long thorns, choosing the perfect fruit- not too soft, not hard or green at all. Leaving the peelings trailing behind, I wandered to our metal swing set, the tart sweetness lingering on my tongue.

My tanned, lean arms glided effortlessly across the slightly rusty monkey bars. I hoisted my lanky frame up on the top of them, walking across while carefully holding my balance, like I was on one of those rope and wooden bridges from "Indiana Jones" movie set. Because my mother had a clear line of sight right out the kitchen window, I did this infrequently and only after careful surveillance for parental interference.

Then I jumped on the blue plastic swing, gripped the metal chains, and pumped my legs hard to reach that soaring point where all I could see were my bare feet overhead and the clouds behind them. The pitchfork legs of the whole metal play set would rock back and forth, leaning off the ground a bit when the weight of my swing reached its highest flight path. My rear end would hop out of the seat when I started the descent from high to low, and strawberry blonde hair folded over my freckled face as the swing cut backwards through the humid air. I decided I'd had enough and waited until I was at a reasonable height before I leaped off mid-air, landing feet, then knees, then hands on the ground.

I made my way over to the tree, the giant Sycamore in the front of our circular cedar mulch drive. At eight years old, I was a head taller than everyone else in my class but too short to reach the lowest branch, so I would drag a metal folding chair out of my dad's work shed and position it perfectly below the branch. Once standing on the chair, I could easily reach the first one and then navigate with my long monkey limbs all the way to the top third of the tree.

I flew up the trunk with ease, palming its strong branches as if they were grabbing for my hands in return. The trunk was light grey and gritty under my calloused kid hands. The bark was ruddy and dimpled with black holes that marched up the tree in crooked lines like an army of ants. I assumed the holes were the proud work of a red headed woodpecker I heard banging away at the trunk fifteen feet up.

From my perch in the tree, I could see the brown shingled roof of our cedar shake house and the expansive sodded yard behind it. Our small nonfunctional well with its own tiny roof looked like a dwarf's house or a hotel for traveling fairies passing through on their way to Disney World several miles away. Behind the house was our giant blue swimming pool surrounded by a wooden deck and then the brownish-green lake.

The border of the yard was a freshly cut square, and I could see my dad on his riding mower, giant radio headset on, rounding the corners, shaving off the outer edges of the square half acre lawn with a haze of grass dust behind him. An hour from now, the work would be reduced to one tiny strip of shin high weeds. He would take one last pass and then head for the carport and settle in front of the T.V. with a giant cup of chewing ice and glorious air conditioner raining down on him.

Beyond the yard, I could see the sun glistening on Lake Waunatta, the main reason my parents settled on this charming house. A few glittery speed boats raced around nearly pulling little kid arms out of socket and violently throwing teenagers off inner tubes. They would emerge with a nose full of lake water, coughing and spitting and begging to do it all over again. I loved exploring the clear water along the lake shore- finding open mussel shells the raccoons had picked out of the grainy sand at the water's edge, pried open, and eaten the night before.

Our dock was a bit rickety and known for inflicting splinters on bare feet, but it was covered, and you could fish off the edge and catch decent sized bass or bream. One time we were playing in the lake and my dad spotted a water moccasin not far away swimming toward us. He usually had a gun handy, and he shot that thing right through the head, its body flailed like a limp lasso spiraling through the air. He could do anything.

Looking down from my tree at the world from the woodpecker's view, everything seemed smaller. My house, my neighborhood, the lake, and even the orange grove across the dirt road became rows of Bonsais from way up high. My brother Travis, who was a good five inches taller and two years my senior, seemed like a munchkin on the front porch. I could see him on the cool cement shaded by our porch roof. His beloved cat, BJ (named for our previous neighbors Bucky and Jessica- because that is who three-year-old boys name their cats after), was lounging lazily on the top of the front porch rail. BJ had splintered his favorite sunny spot with scratch marks from sharpening his claws over the last six years.

Travis was wearing a yellow E.T. shirt and his brownish

black hair was matted like a helmet on his head except for one piece on top that preferred standing up like an angry rooster. He has always had the kind of hair reserved only for princes in fairytales, thick as my great aunt Ossie's Southern accent when she called me "Honey."

Travis was kneeling, with Dad's heavy metal hammer and a line of caps. He was pounding the caps with the hammer, making loud popping sounds one after the other, a hobby that would eventually land him in the ER with a flattened thumb and me with a spoiled slumber party.

My mom's voice broke my afternoon reverie. "Mary Grace? Are you up there?" I could see her neck crooning around trying to get a visual of my exact position. "Please come down...CAREFULLY." I reluctantly started my descent. "Watch what you are doing...*Be careful...*" her voice quaked. I could hear an unfamiliar nervousness in her voice, since my mom rarely worried about much of anything. I knew she was concerned but I didn't understand why. I felt just as breezy up there in the bending branches of the big tree as I did cuddled up on my dad's lap. When I made it to the bottom, she gave me a big hug and a soft lecture on the dangers of falling from that high up.

My mom taught at my elementary school, and she was the kind of teacher every kid loved, especially the bad kids or the ones who struggled. With her beautiful, kind face and her sweet southern voice, she spent time loving every kid and gave special attention to the ones who had the cards stacked against them. Even if Mrs. Alston was your friend's mom, you would still want to go over to her house and play, although your cheeks might blush if she tasked you to call her "Mrs. Berta."

She was still and always the same girl who had been voted "Best All Around" and crowned Prom Queen twenty years prior. She possesses effortlessly that special quality, the nameless indefinable one, that puts everyone at ease and makes them want to be her friend. She carries much of her father's greatness in her 5'6" frame: the same loving embrace, the same gentle and compassionate gaze, the same deep-down integrity.

She has cheeks that make round balls and dimples every time her easy smile flashes across her face. She freely shares her caring brown eyes and quick laugh, doling out generous portions of love in the way she treats each person. My brother and I joke that we know Mom must have sinned sometime because that's what the Bible says, but she must have done it when she was really little because we have never seen her do anything wrong. She hates it when we say that.

After tree-climbing, I wandered into my bathing suit that was slightly too small and rode up in the back a little, and out the back door, slicing headfirst through the water of the deep end with my outstretched arms. I watched the bubbles slide down my arms and up toward the surface. I let all the air out of my lungs and sat Indian style at the bottom of the pool for as long as I could stand it before pushing off toward the surface and floating on my back for a few minutes. Then I flipped my head forward in the water, so my hair was in front of my face and stood up. I pushed my hair back with my hand making a single curl around my face we called Martha Washington hair.

I learned to swim proficiently at two years old, or "drown proofing" as it was called in Florida then. I was two and Travis four when we moved to this house and my mom wanted to be sure we were safe with so much water around. The drown proofing home videos are our favorite home videos. There is no sound, but you can see little Travis waddling into view, suited up in full winter attire for his final exam outfitted in a red knit hat with a white pom-pon on top, boots, jeans, and a winter vinyl-sleeved Georgia coat.

To the musical overtones of "It's Gonna Be a Bright Sunshiny Day," he looks at the camera with one of those open-mouthed Snoopy kinds of shrieks, the kind where you can see clear to the back of his throat. And then suddenly his teacher picks him up and tosses him sideways into the deep end of the pool. Even without the winter gear, he swam lopsided, like a wounded duck, with his right arm functioning at 100% and his left arm at about 60%, and he bent slightly at the waist every time he kicked. The winter clothes amplified the errors in his form, and he looked like a bird trapped underneath a pile of wet laundry trying to fly away.

At eight, I felt as safe and happy underwater as I did high in the lofty branches of that tree. I surfaced to find Dad relaxing by the pool, and he looked startled from the cool water my splash rained down on him unexpectedly. "Hey Gracie," he called out with his watermelon slice grin. His skin was oily and tan and smelled like Hawaiian Tropic, and his trusty oversized plastic Georgia cup was filled to the brim with melting square cubes of ice, the kind from the plastic refillable trays you had to twist and pop out.

His hair, as black as my brother's, was still wet from the shower after mowing the yard. "Let me see you dive down and get this ring!" he called as he shot it high over my head with his rifle of a throwing arm. It sank fast down into the middle of the pool by the drain. I dived in, retrieving it and happily throwing it back.

After a dozen tosses like this, Dad jumped in the pool and rode around with me on his back underwater playing like he was "Shamu." Then he threw me high into the air with his strong athletic arms all the way from the shallow end into the deep end half a dozen times to my squeals of delight before he returned to his spot in the sun. My dad was larger than life.

Even nearing forty, Dad was extremely handsome, and when he occasionally grew out his mustache, we teased him that he looked like Burt Reynolds. He met my mom in high school in Columbus, Georgia, when he was the star pitcher for the Columbus High Varsity team. He was tall and lanky and a bit shy then, but he could throw a baseball like it was a bullet shot right out of the barrel of a pistol. It made that cracking sound when it hit the catcher's glove, the pop that means it came in close to 90 mph and that the catcher might be icing his hand after the game.

Baseball has always been a huge part of Dad's life, so much so that when he was in elementary school playing in the Pony League in Columbus, on the days it rained, he would sometimes cry because he couldn't go out and practice baseball. I saw him once in the church softball league hit the ball so hard and so high that it busted the lights out and caused a widespread power outage that made the nighttime news.

My parents were sweethearts all the way through the University of Georgia and his brief stint in the Army Reserves as a medic before they married in July of 1969. My grandfather tried to convince my dad to go into medicine, but he didn't have the stomach for it. I came by that honestly. When my grandfather took him on rounds with him and questioned him about becoming a doctor, my ever-affable dad laughed, "Doctor, you obviously have not seen my transcripts."

My beautiful mom Roberta, or "Berta" as most people call her, and my tall, dark, and eventually outgoing dad Robert decided to move to Orlando to start their family a few years later when he was offered a job. He was a stockbroker and she taught elementary school. From the time I can remember, we lived almost at the end of a paved road turned dirt called Waunatta Court in Winter Park, Florida. Winter Park is a suburb of Orlando, but they blended directly into one another, and you couldn't tell where one started and the other stopped had it not been for Winter Park's charming brick streets lined with gigantic oak trees. Beautiful fountains and dripping Spanish moss characterized the small Southern gem in the rapidly changing conglomeration of O-town.

We were the second house on the right after the street turned to gravel and dirt. There were no houses on the left, as one of the few lasting orange groves in Winter Park fronted the left side of the road. The man who owned it used to ride around, pushing dirt and drinking beer on his John Deere. He would leave his crunched-up cans and glass bottles haphazardly around the grove, and finding a bottle cap was like discovering a secret treasure. All the kids in the neighborhood were afraid of him. I thought of him like Mr. McGregor, and we were

Peter Rabbit and friends, running and hiding, climbing his trees, playing King of The Mountain, throwing rotten oranges at each other, building forts, and growing up children of the 80's.

The first house on the dirt part of Waunatta was occupied by an elderly couple I knew as Opal and Johnny. Between their house and ours where the road bent, the tire traffic had worn a deep groove in the dirt. When it rained, it transformed into the best mud puddle around, and I remember belting out "Singing in the Rain" while jumping around in my nubby bottomed bathing suit, not minding the lightning that peppered the sky like the freckles on my summer nose. The neighbors on the other side of our house were practicing nudists, whom I only saw from a distance, thankfully, adorned with loosely wrapped towels in their backyard getting water from their well.

If you cut straight through the orange grove to Glenmoor, there were several other kids we liked to play with, notably for me Lisa Porter. The Porters moved from a different state like almost everyone else and brought a few oddities with them. The "Welcome to our OOL. Notice There's no 'P' in it. Please keep it that way" sign hung inconspicuously on the wall by their screened-in pool. We used to trade Garbage Pail Kid cards. In an eight-year-old's life in the mid 80's, going to the 7-11 and blowing what little cash you had on Big League chew, a Coke Slurpee, and a pack of GPK cards was like going to Vegas for your bachelorette party.

I almost learned to roller skate on the pavement of the first part of Waunatta with my neighbor friends Giomara and Sandra. They laughed as I, laced up in Gio's skates with the colored laces and protruding stoppers on the front, fumbled and tumbled my way across the cracks in the sidewalk with each of them at an elbow. Despite their efforts and some punishing scrapes on my knees and thighs, I never really got the hang of it, except to be proficient enough to attend the school skate parties at Semoran Skateway.

I was unnecessarily terrified of anyone asking me to couple skate, where you hold hands and skate around in the dimly lit rink and a song like "Say You, Say Me" blared through the speakers on either side of the rotating disco ball and twirling neon spotlights. I was afraid of falling and pulling a poor guy down with me, thus sealing my social fate for all time. But no one ever asked as I wasn't that popular with boys in elementary school, and my social life and my kneecaps survived intact.

I dried off from the pool and slipped into shorts and a T-shirt and helped set the table for dinner. Mom brought out the spaghetti (my favorite), and the four of us gathered around the antique claw footed dining table that had been a wedding present from my mother's parents. I sat near the old working rotary phone attached to the wall, the kind with the two bells on top and the cup-like earpiece that hung by a black wire down on the side. It resembled a face to me. Dad called me from work once pretending to be the Tooth Fairy on that phone, and I was mesmerized equally by the phone face and the realization that the Tooth Fairy had the voice of a man.

At dinner, my parents announced that we were heading to Georgia to see our grandparents, aunts, uncles, and cousins the next day. A cloud of excitement enveloped the room, since Travis and I were still at the age when going to see your grandparents was cool and when another state felt like a wild adventure. Heading back to Georgia was homecoming for my parents, and their excitement and anticipation were contagious.

No salt, no waves, no sand. Just red Georgia clay and muddy fishing holes. On the drive up from Orlando, I watched the rows and rows of shriveled up orange trees from where the freeze came through a few years before. I wondered if the citrus groves would ever recover and how they got those trees to grow in such perfectly straight lines in the first place.

Mom and I sang "Up on the Roof" in harmony, and my brother Travis cried and said that we were making him feel sick. Then I cried because, heaven forbid, he was looking out my window. Dad told us we both better be quiet or he was really going to give us something to cry about. So, we opted to play the Alphabet game on billboard signs, and neither one of us ever got past "X."

Then we counted cows, Travis against me. I was winning for a while until we passed a cemetery on my side of the road, which, according to the rules of car cow counting, wipes your score back to zero. We argued over cows so much that Dad pulled into the next cemetery and the graves on either side wiped both of our scores out. With the competition over, we eventually drifted off to sleep to the hum of the Oldsmobile diesel engine and the promise that we would get a quarter if we would go to sleep. We nodded off with the distant hope that we wouldn't wake up until we finally got there.

On the drive through Georgia, we passed many places speckled with Southern history and character, right down to their names. Some can be found on formal maps; others are known only in the folklore and language of their people. Too Nigh, Yahoo, Buttermilk Bottom, Roosterville, Wayback, Lick Log, Social Circle, Tell, and Snap Finger each have their own story. One area in north Georgia is known as Plum Nelly because it's "plum outta Tennessee and nelly outta Georgia." Places like Bloody Bucket, Ty Ty, Lick Skillet, and Booger Hollow cover the state. It makes you wonder if a regular sounding place like our destination, Hamilton, Georgia, could possibly have a story worth telling.

As the neighboring city of Columbus rapidly grew and expanded, it reached further and further north toward Hamilton (a small town in Harris County). Columbus is locked in on the south side by the army base formerly named Fort Benning. On the west side rolls the muddy Chattahoochee River and beyond that, Alabama. The great city balances like a shaken Coke can, spewing out its population and progress north. Traveling from Columbus toward Hamilton along Highway 27, the dense pine branches waved a spindly welcome for miles. It seemed there were more pecan trees than people. I loved watching rows of them speed by my window.

Now concrete developments pepper both sides of the road like shotgun spray as Columbus' growth invades the southernmost sections of Harris County. Developers clear cut century old forests. They paved over wild foliage and suffocated it under parking lots and custom landscaping. The subdivisions and office parks are upscale and tastefully done, but the new structures can't rival the former majesty of creation in its purest form. To me, fast food and box stores are no match for red bud, wild dogwood, and 100-foot Longleaf Pines.

About twenty miles into the drive from Columbus to Hamilton, our chain link property line comes into view from the two-lane highway. My grandfather erected the barrier years ago to keep trespassers out, but he simultaneously preserved an oasis inside the rusty barbed wire gate. When we reached the "Welcome to Harris County" sign, we knew we were almost there.

Back in the 80s, the Spectrum gas station was the most exciting store to visit in Hamilton. Situated a block away from my grandparents' house, it was our first stop when we unfolded ourselves out of Daddy's blue Oldsmobile sedan upon arrival in Hamilton. We sipped Icees and stocked up on Runts and Sugar Babies to last us the duration of our stay. That afternoon, we picked the figs the birds missed and took a walk around the town square, acquiescing to those sweet vacation days when your sibling is your only (and best) friend. Trips to Hamilton were some of the few times my brother and I got along because we were forced to play together.

The city of Hamilton had about 300 people then and not too many more now. You could walk from my grandparents' to the bank or the post office or the Spectrum in about three minutes, and those were evidently the only places anybody in Hamilton needed to go. There were no stop lights.

"Fate denied them victory but crowned them with glorious immortality" were the words etched in stone at the town's core. The ghostly Confederate statue faced ever north, clinging to his musket, still warding off the War of Northern Aggression. As I peered up at his eyes of stone, I wondered what all he had witnessed in his stationary existence and if he stood there as a lasting remembrance or a vengeful warning. He was the center of activity, the speechless, nameless guest at every town square gathering and every late-night lovers' stroll.

He loomed high on a pedestal, revered and guarded by a wrought iron fence, representing what may have been brave and stubborn about our Southern heritage. The likeness of a thousand men, he had marched three hundred miles, shot bullets of melted down church bells, and never returned to his sweetheart back home. He was a Southern icon, a man who may have gambled or sipped moonshine, may have even owned a slave or two. Despite his shortcomings, he was tough as nails and loved his family and his seceded country.

On Confederate Memorial Day, he was draped in the stars and bars of the South. At the Fourth of July parade, he witnessed the high school marching band and the mule-riding Bobby Haralson. Of course, no small-town parade was complete without the local Avon lady spraying perfume on the spectators as she passed. We got to see the entire thing from my grandparents' porch, three times in fact, as they made their laps around town. The children scrambled for candy tossed from the vehicles into the crowd. My grandfather even got out his bugle from his Eagle Scout days and played "Reveille" with surprising gusto as the parade passed by.

Growing up in Florida, we were somewhat removed from the deep Southern tradition boasted in this little town and in the seven generations of Georgians up our family tree. I always pictured it as a magnificent pecan tree, like the ones in my grandfather's yard, littering the grass with nuts. I was deeply curious about my Southern roots and heritage, and the Civil War statue seemed to always coax my eyes upward. There was nothing like this in Orlando.

His stature appropriately represented the history of the South. Everything about this small Georgia town felt strange and intriguing compared to our life growing up in preppy and sophisticated Winter Park, Florida. We had Park Avenue laden with fountains and brick streets; they had a town square with the Video and Tan. We had Ann Taylor and Barnie's Coffee; they had the Five and Dime and the Green Onion Café. We had Lake Eola with swan shaped paddle boats and Spanish Moss; they had muddy fishing ponds with bass boats and canoes. We had intimidating stone cathedrals, and they had trailer churches with signs reading warnings like "There's no bass fishing in the lake of fire."

Florida had lizards and roaches, and the people of Hamilton had plenty of huge black grasshoppers alighting bushes, sidewalks and blades of grass that summer. It looked like one of those plagues you learn about in Sunday school, and I imagined the gigantic insects could eat up every leaf of vegetation in the whole state of Georgia. It's too bad they didn't prefer eating kudzu.

Every step on the cracked sidewalks brought new adventures and awakened childish curiosities. Daffodils surrounded the foundations of old homes and ancient camellias burst forth in lacy bright pinks and cream. When the fireflies came out, we grabbed glass jars and poked holes in the top to house our captured loot.

As a child, I viewed my grandparents' stark white antebellum house with the same awe as if Atlantis rose from the depths and planted itself smack on Hill Street in their small town. Its style is "Greek Orthodox," but I'm nearly sure the slaves who built it in 1845 would not have cared. The original house had no kitchen or indoor plumbing, and the outhouse and smokehouse were originally around back. The couple who restored and renovated the house in the sixties added modern amenities like running water and electricity.

The front yard is mostly flat and the lot slopes toward the street where 40-foot magnolias shield the house from view. Four columns line the porch, and a small Romeo and Juliet balcony protrudes from an upstairs door right in the center of the second level. Heavy black wrought iron doors and large green ferns adorn the front porch. The house has black shutters and now dons white aluminum siding. A traveling salesman sold the siding to nearly every house on the street years ago, metal armor shielding the past against a changing modern world.

In two rooms, the pine floor slopes in such a way that you wonder how the house has survived 150 years of storms and settling. A steel beam through the middle of the living room supports half of the upstairs. If you are over 5'8," which I am, you have to duck when you come down the wooden staircase because the ceiling comes so low in one spot. One Christmas morning as a teenager, I traipsed down the stairs, and in my tired stupor I forgot to duck. I found myself laid out on my back and sliding down the bumpy stairs while I groaned in pain at the knots on my forehead and backside.

The grand old house, named the Mobley House, brims with unique character and charm. The fireplace surround in the living room is made from mosaic tiles by artist Henry Mercer. The tiles form a series of pictures, telling the story of the discovery of the New World. Only two pieces of this artist's work remain, this fireplace and another which tells the story of the Bible through tiles. Though the house is magnificent, my grandparents really bought this place because of the land behind it. Rolling hills, lush pastureland, towering oaks, and fishing lakes create the perfect backdrop for a family homestead.

When we were children, the years seemed to pass quickly between visits to Hamilton, and though we changed, the house never did. My grandmother kept everything just the same. The kitchen transports you back to the 1960's with brown speckled Formica countertops and yellow and brown linoleum floors. The purple shag carpet in the office and the baby pink tiled bathroom recall a foregone era. The home tours like a montage to the last hundred years of American style, and the rooms give you a feel for the eclectic mix of decades filling it.

The room where my brother and I stayed upstairs was outfitted with an old wooden bedroom suit including two single beds. Its ivory finish antiqued with age made it look like it could have been carved from genuine elephant tusks. The mattresses were at least as old as the beds themselves, and it was much like sleeping on a canoe. You had to master sleeping right in the middle or the whole thing would shift to one side, and you would roll right off. I awoke one morning on the floor to find I had a black eye, no doubt rendered from the side table after a sleepy change of position.

Out of our bedroom windows fronting the house, you could see the four white stately columns, and beyond them across the street a single-story white home with a rambling wrap-around porch. I remember the first time I walked there with my parents. We climbed up the back steps (because that is just the friendly nature of this small town) and knocked on the glass storm door.

It was the first time of many I would go to visit the Fort sisters in the years to come. They were living history of all that made up Hamilton and small-town Georgia. I was always surprised to see them answer the door so swiftly, even into their nineties. They welcomed us inside, always offered us a cold glass of Coca-Cola and a trip back in time on their antique rockers.

The Sisters embodied everything that made up the little town of Hamilton. Mary, the younger, had been a history teacher and to meet her was like talking to a real-life Aunt Bea. If she didn't know the answers to our questions, she certainly never let on. The elder sister, Edna, taught second grade for the majority of her life, and she wisely subscribed to the "younger shall serve the older" way of living. She survived happily on her sister's cooking, driving, and bill paying.

Our knock on their back porch door inevitably interrupted a very competitive game of Scrabble with one another. The game board and its letters were quickly cast aside in true Southern fashion to welcome their unexpected company. They lived in the house where they were raised, the house built by their father's hands and the garden tended by their mother when they were children. They remembered with a grin the first airplanes and the man who would come around every night and light the streetlamps. They rode horse and buggy to the tiny Methodist Church and took the train to and from the neighboring town, Chipley (now called Pine Mountain), for school every day during the week. Because neither of them ever married, it seemed natural for them to retire to the town of their birth and home of their youth.

I found myself wanting to explore their vast backyard and their house full of ancient treasures. Their house was more like a museum than a residence. Faded faces in black and white peered over the tops of dressers and shelves. The outside well they had drawn from as children was filled with cement years ago, and the water and electricity now flowed from pipes and wires inside the house. I am not convinced that the television in the living room actually worked. I don't know if anyone has ever seen it turned on.

The Fort sisters probably preferred their life the way it had always been, without the intrusions of world news or the sitcoms of the 1980's. They could do without their well-meaning relatives' attempts to modernize them with stereos and TV sets. Their records and newspapers would do just fine. They were happy clams growing a potted garden of African violets in the windowsill, cuddling up with the latest Reader's Digest, content to be alive.

The Fort Sisters were masterful artisans with words, and as surely as honey dripped from their lips, the earth's salt oozed from their souls. Though mild-mannered and soft-spoken, they would tell stories that captivated our attention as children. It seemed they knew more yet revealed less than anyone else in town, so when they allowed us rare glimpses of the past, we sat still and listened. Forty-five minutes later, we left the sisters smiling with the roses we clipped and brought over from the garden. Without fail, one of the sisters would say to the other, "I believe those are the prettiest roses I have ever seen."

These two ladies made me fall in love with Hamilton at a young age. When they passed away many years ago, I felt a personal loss, but the town really lost dear souls who embodied the spirit of the tiny town. The Fort sisters were the truest form of Southern ladies I ever knew. They had every bit of Scarlet's curtain-wearing strength for survival and all of Melanie's lovely warmth. As we descended their back stairs, Miss Edna would usually remark how the summer was "going by on wings." And it always did.

As an adult, I have learned of the many fascinating people who live in Hamilton and what a treasure trove of people have resided there. Within a half mile of my grandparents' home lived the retired sheriff, Sam Jones. He was the sheriff when my Uncle Boots tried to outrun the police as a sixteen-year-old.

Prior to that episode, Sheriff Jones had many adventures. "Mr. Sam" jumped out of a helicopter and stormed the beach at Normandy and avoided drowning only by shedding all of his gear in the water. Mr. Sam also was Sheriff at the time of an infamous murder in the neighboring Coweta County. A book was written about the complicated circumstances, and a later movie was made starring Johnny Cash and Andy Griffith ("Murder in Coweta County"). The story was about race and corruption and how they affected a southern small town murder case. Mr. Sam always sipped his coffee at the local cafe with his back to the wall, just in case the many vengeful ghosts from his past were lurking.

My dad used to love to tell a story on Mr. Sam. Many years ago, when Sam was the sheriff, he pulled someone over for speeding. Sam approached the vehicle and dutifully asked for the license and registration from the driver. He studied the license and then looked back at the man behind the wheel. "It says here you wear glasses," said Mr. Sam. "I have contacts," answered the man. "Well, I don't care who you know," said Sam, "if you are speeding in Harris County, you're gonna get a ticket!"

A quarter mile away lived George W. Garrett in another white antebellum home. Mr. Garrett was stationed at Pearl Harbor the day the Japanese bombers swooped in and slaughtered American naval forces. In the few times I was ever around him, I never heard him speak of that day or his experiences in the war.

There is also a successful lawyer turned singer, songwriter, judge and author, our dear friend Allen Levi, who tends the family property and his vegetable garden. Allen writes wonderful songs, some even about the interesting people in this town. Allen's brother Gary was a world traveled missionary and another dear friend. He lived in different corners of the world telling the Good News of the Gospel. Allen is now an acclaimed author who has written a memoir about his brother's life and another popular novel.

Sheriff Mike Jolley and his wife Cindy became dear and longtime friends of our family. Cindy is a retired Synovus executive and recipient of the Blanchard Award. Mike rides through every contiguous U.S. state nearly every year with a group of motorcyclists called the Miracle Riders. They have raised over a million dollars for The Children's Miracle Network. Sheriff took me to the state penitentiary on my 21st birthday and had me sit in the electric chair, an experience I will never forget for many reasons! Sheriff Jolley is one of the bravest and absolutely funniest people I have ever known. He has made FOX News several times, recently for the signs he erected in Harris County that read "Welcome to Harris County, Georgia. Our citizens have concealed weapons. If you kill someone, we might kill you back. We have ONE jail and 356 cemeteries. Enjoy your stay! - Sheriff Mike Jolley"

Hamilton, in the heart of beautiful Harris County, Georgia, didn't even have a stoplight until the late nineties. While it was the County Seat with a beautiful courthouse, it was a dot on a map to most people or a place they might drive through on the way to somewhere else. They could never imagine the extraordinary people who live in this town. They are the kind of people who build a wheelchair ramp for a home when a neighbor they have never met has a debilitating brain tumor. This is the kind of place where the postal workers pool their money together and bring you a sandwich tray when your dad dies unexpectedly.

This is the town where my grandparents chose to retire, where they would live out their golden years, and the place they would plant deep in the soul of our family. My granddad quietly joined the ranks of the hidden heroes in this speck of a town in the Georgia foothills of the Appalachian Trail. Andy and Grace Roddenbery became Hamiltonians. They are forever woven into the storied history of this place. And so, we, as their grandchildren, were grafted into the Hamilton family as well. That is just how it is in small southern towns. Your family becomes everyone's family.

Caretaker

His smooth fingers were wrapped around a small object when his hand emerged from his pocket. It was brown and shiny and somewhat round. My eight-year-old eyes had not seen anything quite like it, and he chuckled as he made me guess what I thought it was. "It's a buckeye," he finally said. My paternal grandfather, Otis Bryce Alston, or "Pop," used to carry it around in his pocket. I never knew exactly why he had it or where he got it, except that it was a good luck charm of sorts. I'll go out on a limb and say that a large portion of America had not heard of a buckeye before Ohio State won the national football championship in 2002.

As a young man, my Pop's pockets were filled with other things, like white lint from sweeping the floors of the Bibb cotton mill in Columbus, Georgia. Then the lint was replaced with a shiny brass key that rode deep down in his pocket, a key to an office he earned with sweat and smarts to become the Vice President at Swift Spinning Mills. Pop carried around spare change even when it wasn't spare, and he snuck it into our small hands to buy gum balls at the store. He certainly always kept a pocketknife (as did my father) every day I can remember as a child.

I believe you can tell a lot about people by what they carry in their pockets. I find my own pockets filled with hair ties, fruit snacks, and hand sanitizer. If I emptied my pockets, you would learn a lot about my daily life taking care of three daughters. I carry those things out of necessity, but they also, in a strange way, reflect what is important to me. For the same reason, people carry pictures of their family, an old pocket watch, or an iPhone, any sort of thing small enough to fit.

I know a man who carries a wad of Franklins rolled up thick like toilet paper in his pocket. He pulls them out and undoes the leather money clip holding them together anytime he can find a reason, then he peels them back one at a time like a monkey preparing his banana snack. His pockets hold the key to his brand-new sports car on a sterling monogrammed keychain and a few golf tees left over from his morning outing on the links. He is the kind of man whose family money bloats his bank account, and I'm not quite sure he has ever had a J-O-B.

Another man I know, John Riley, carries an acorn in his pocket. I heard him tell a group of people about it one time. An acorn is a curious thing to carry around. It serves no real purpose, is not particularly rare or valuable or interesting to look at. It is just litter from an oak tree, about one centimeter by one centimeter, with a single seed inside. John carried it daily as a reminder to live his life with purpose.

Where I grew up, acorns crowded sidewalks and yards, tore up your lawn mower blades, and knocked you off your roller skates. In Winter Park, Florida amidst acres of orange groves, Southern live oak trees drop acorns everywhere. The grand trees are symbols of the South's grandeur, surviving decades of storms, rope swings, and tree houses.

A Southern oak can grow to be 50 feet tall and span about 160 feet wide. After walking beneath and climbing on the branches of these old trees for most of my life, I have an appreciation for a tiny acorn. Now when I hold an acorn between my thumb and first finger, I realize I am holding the entire potential of an enormous tree. It is the seed from which every branch and leaf could grow. An acorn, separated from its source of life, is the hope that something grand and wonderful can grow from something dying, worthless, and small.

Most people believe some seeds are just plain bad and will never flourish. I guess in a way, we all have the potential to be a "bad seed," but our circumstances in life and the choices we make will dictate how we will live. For most trees to grow, the conditions need to be favorable: the soil fertile, the water and sunshine plentiful, and the climate just right. Even so, there are those rare seeds, which despite circumstances, hostile conditions, or a poor climate, still thrive. My grandfather was this kind of seed.

Had Andy emptied his pockets as a young man, there would not have been much to show except maybe a small arrowhead or a lucky penny. When he started his football and academic career at the University of Georgia in 1934, he showed up on those steps of Joe Brown dormitory in Athens with little more than a change of clothes and a small pocket size New Testament given to him at graduation. From there he would fill his life's suitcase with all kinds of treasures, but not necessarily the most desirable ones from a worldly standpoint.

Seventy years after starting college, my grandfather's pockets could hold a lot of valuable things. Instead, the elderly surgeon's pockets hold sentimental treasures. He keeps a cracked brown leather change purse that he has had for most of his life. The pennies and dimes he stuffs inside mean little more to him than the 1992 white Oldsmobile parked outside. He also keeps an oval metal medallion with a Methodist cross in his pocket. He found it years ago and has made it a personal keepsake. He does not have rolls of money or expensive car keys in his pockets. He does not even own a cell phone. He loves the right things.

I graduated from Winter Park High School in May of 1996, and we packed up and moved to Georgia a month later. My brother was a scholarship pitcher for the baseball team at Samford University in Birmingham. All four of my grandparents were still living but aging rapidly and requiring more care. My mom and dad wanted to be closer to help, and closer to us.

We drove away from the only place I had ever lived, past palmettos and orange groves up the eight-hour stretch of highway to Hamilton, Georgia. Once we started seeing rolling hills and front porches and pecan trees, I knew we were getting close. Even though I was raised in Florida, I was a Bulldog through and through, made more painful by

Steve Spurrier's reign of football domination at Florida for my entire childhood. Our move to my family's home state was as welcome as an outhouse breeze.

I come from seven generations of native Georgians, but since I grew up in Florida, I have the unique perspective of seeing southern culture as both an insider and an outsider. I was raised with southern ideals. I was never allowed to call boys on the phone, and I couldn't date anyone unless they opened the door for me. These rules along with my above average height drastically shrunk the dating pool of eligible Florida boys.

My friends used to come over to my house simply to taste the sweet tea that overflowed from a glass gallon jar in our refrigerator. My dad would sit and pop beans while he watched Georgia football on Saturdays. My mom would simmer them on the stove with ham hock and chicken stock, until they tasted less like vegetables and more like salty poetry.

I was bound for the University of Georgia that fall and could hardly wait to attend the same university my great-grandfather, grandfather and parents did. I had the grades and qualifications to go to a more prestigious school, and many of my friends did not understand my choice of a state school. Those friends never donned the red and black or walked the bridge over Sanford Stadium amidst the yell of a hundred thousand fans. They had never tailgated at "The Tree" with Larry the Legend and Sue Gaither. Those well-meaning friends had never sung "Glory, Glory" along with the Redcoat marching band or tip-toed around the Arch.

My high school record and achievements earned me a full academic scholarship from the University's Foundation Fellows program, and it seemed like I was on the cusp of all my dreams coming true. It's funny how life works sometimes. The most valuable thing is the one you look past to get to the next one. Like when you skip a rock across the water, you only really care about how many times it lands and how far it goes, but you forget about all that time floating through the air, the in between time when it soars. Those few months before I headed to Athens proved to be some of the most valuable of my life. It was the first whole summer I spent with my grandfather.

We bought the white antebellum house from my grandparents on Hill Street, and they moved next door to the house referred to as "the cottage" which they bought several years before for my great grandmother. They added a nice master bedroom and bathroom, a laundry room, and a ramped entrance, and finally got rid of the 1950's waiting room chairs in the front room. It was a perfect arrangement for all of us. I took long walks with my mom and dad in the mornings, our feet touching nearly every sidewalk in town. And we watched the sun set every evening over the old red barn and expansive pasture from our den with my grandfather, "Papa".

We saw the hardwood shadows stretch longer across the hills, crisscrossing with each rise and fall in the ground like a chess board. The Black Angus cows ate their way across green waves until they were safe near the barn, and we watched the smoking clouds catch fire under a smoldering red sun. Thick, humid air settled on Papa's ponds like a fuzzy afghan where gnats hovered and hummed, and dragonflies floated lazily. The hot summer Georgia air can feel stifling to an outsider, but I breathed it in deeply, pleased for it to reside heavy in my lungs like a blanket weighting my newly anchored soul.

We fished and gardened and rode around on the 400-acre tract of our family land in the rusty red Ford truck. We ran the dogs and walked the creek bed. We saw deer and turkey and slapped ticks off our ankles. We fed the catfish with brown pellets tossed out in a fan from a plastic cup. We ate sweet berries right off the vine. Our lives were about as country as cornbread.

My grandmother Grace, or "Mimi" as we called her, was suffering from ovarian cancer. She walked around with a terry cloth turban on her increasingly bald head from her treatments. She had them in three colors and wore them on rotation- baby blue, light pink, and mint green. My grandfather served her and did anything he could to make her more comfortable, including giving her necessary pain medicines and a lot of love.

Papa walked over to our house in the afternoons and spent time talking with me and telling me most of the stories written in this book over and over again. Then he would go next door and return minutes later, steadying his bride as they walked arm in arm across the driveway. They usually joined us for dinner, and we sat in the grand dining room under the sparkling crystal chandelier from Austria. We all listened to him recount his life over mom's cooking.

His eyes shined as he remembered. He smiled to himself for a moment with quiet excitement, like a skinny tick on a fat dog. And then he paused. He offered a moment of silence for a bygone era and all the charm and characters that went with it. His face illuminated with recognition and remembrance like it so rarely did in his last years.

Then spontaneously, the stories seeped out, one after the other, drop by drop, until his mind was satisfied and his heart was full, and all present were swimming (and occasionally drowning) in his lake of glad memories. Don't be deceived into thinking that they were all glad, his memories. But the ones that came the quickest and the easiest were the joyous ones. He rarely ever spoke of anything bad.

His captive after-supper audience was with him, running the jingle-wing at the Polo grounds clad in red and black. He took all along on his Boy Scout expeditions and to the top of the Coca-Cola building to meet with his powerful and generous benefactors. He reeled his audience into his canoe in the Canadian wilderness dragging in a 32-pound Muskie out of Manitou Lake in July 1935. He talked of lifelong friends, childhood heroes, and love at first sight.

Growing up without much can haunt you in several different ways. It can make you so starved for the stuff of life that you become obsessed with gaining it all, it can make you bitter and jealous; or it can make you generous and compassionate if you ever get a bunch of stuff of your own. Some who obtain the stature and success of a surgeon surround themselves with gadgets and trophies. Many buy sports cars and beach houses and some even trade in their wives for younger ones. My grandfather was never interested in that.

Living his dream at last in this thick Georgia woodland, Papa created a haven for us. The home he longed for but never had as a child is now being enjoyed by his great-great grandchildren. It is a place to bait fish and to pick muscadines, a place where we all want to come home. It's the perfect backdrop to shoot your first gun, catch crawfish in the creek, ride your pillowcase down the stairs of the antebellum home, and fight rainbow trout jumping and spinning at the end of your line in the stocked lake. It is paradise.

Many times, I have driven this land with my grandfather behind the wheel, his words flowing like wine in an Italian countryside, recounting story upon story. The cousins piled in the truck bed with loose tools rolling around and stacks of hay to sit on. We bounced around on the dirt roads, our untethered bodies catching air as stray branches slapped us in the face. In the words of my cousin Paige, "He didn't baby us. We had to figure it out."

Nearly 30 years since my parents moved there, I still feel like a young girl at the threshold of his Narnia. Captive in the pickup truck, I expect a startled deer to stand upright and speak. I assume the bass in the small, muddy brown pond will jump out to greet us. It is the childlike way he approached his domain that makes me think that all of it is possible. It is a place of near magic, where in fact dreams have come to life and a family has been healed. He always considered himself a caretaker of this land, not the owner of it. It's a different kind of care than he was used to giving- not in binding up fleshy wounds but in wrestling tangled vines and chopping up downed trees. He is the keeper of the red clay kingdom.

Husband.

When August rolled around, I prepared to go to college, and UGA proved to be everything I didn't even know to dream about. I was having the time of my life, but I was still pleased when my parents and grandparents made the trip to Athens for every home game. They would roll into town on a Friday, make a stop at The Varsity for a chili dog, fries, and an orange freeze. Then off they would go on a ride down Milledge Avenue and head to their rooms at the Georgia Center, just down the hall from where UGA, Georgia's famed bulldog mascot also stayed.

I rarely went to football games with a date like my friends since I preferred to make my way to our family seats during the game. We were spoiled there with an air-conditioned room and complimentary snacks. On the club level I would find my parents, grandparents, aunts, uncles, and cousins watching the game together with many other former UGA lettermen and their families.

When I was a student, my grandfather received the Bill Hartman Award, given to former UGA lettermen who have made remarkable achievements in both profession and work in their field and community. It was a special weekend for our family and honor for my grandfather as he played on the same backfield as Hartman. The pre-party was at Vince Dooley's house and my entire extended family was there. Later at the game, I sat in the stands with my cousin Paige, and we watched Papa on the Jumbotron at midfield accepting his award. He stood waving to the crowd with his same gracious smile, his white hair with the wind in it, and a look of pure joy. Perhaps he even recalled a time when the stadium was just a field with bleachers.

I remember the day my grandmother died. It was April 7, 1998. She had been suffering from cancer for several years and this visit to the hospital in Columbus would be her last. We were told the end was near, and my grandfather agreed they had done everything they could do for her. I rushed from Athens where I was in my second year of college.

She had lost her hair, her will, and ultimately her life to the cruel disease. Moments before the end, she called out a muffled, "Andy!" from her almost comatose state. My grandfather made his way over to her bedside. He bent down to kiss her, and for the first time in St. Francis Hospital, he was not the attending physician, he was not her faithful caretaker, he was a tearful spouse.

"Grace," he started. "I want you to know you have been a good wife and I love you very much. I also want you to know it is okay for you to go on now." And then he paused, "You are really going to like it in heaven. There is no dust there...the only dust you will see there is gold dust." He choked up for a moment then softly said, "So you go on now, it's okay. And I won't be far behind."

She died in a quiet room with her family close by. I arrived just minutes after she passed away, and the mood was still somber and quiet. Uncle Ed and Aunt Becky were there to tell us she had departed. Standing on the cold floor in St. Francis Hospital, I kissed her hand. It seemed like she aged a century in the months since I had seen her. Her pale body, bald from the months of chemotherapy, was lifeless, and painless... at last.

The always-doctor, my grandfather called my mom over to the hospital bed to my grandmother's body just minutes after her death. When Grace was alive, she would never let my grandfather feel her abdomen where the cancerous tumors grew rampantly. He finally had the chance to push down on her hard, knotted stomach and made my mom feel it, too, much to her dismay. His medical mind took over and he was teaching my mom about cancer at the deathbed of his wife.

The service was in the small Methodist Church in Hamilton. Someone sang "Amazing Grace." A few kind words were said, and many people came to pay their respects. I saw family I had not seen in years. I remember my mom's friend Ruth Chapman drove up from Florida to help take care of things around the house. That kind of love is not easily forgotten.

As a young child, I could not understand how Papa came to marry my grandmother, Grace. I finally reasoned that he has always held tightly to his great faith in the potential of the human spirit. I used to be convinced she somehow tricked him into believing she was someone else during the short months of their courtship. I am ashamed to say now, I secretly disliked her for casting some Yankee spell on him and robbing him of a marriage to a warm and loving Southern woman.

She really did not like children because they made her nervous. When I was a child, I saw her as somewhat of a tyrant. She would make breakfast for the whole family and then monitor how much everyone could eat. We famously called it the "one, one, and one," courtesy of my dad and Uncle Ed. One piece of toast, one egg, and one slice of bacon, served with a one swallow sized glass of orange juice. My Uncle Boots told me when he graduated high school, he was 5'9" and weighed 125 pounds because of the meager portions she rationed out in his youth. This was a trait birthed during the Depression era she was raised in.

She was thrifty in the New England sort of way. In a Southern family of make it from scratch cooks, she was a can opener. My dad recounts his first time to dinner at the Roddenbery house with humor. He was used to several meats, fresh veggies, and homemade desserts to choose from, with plenty left over. There he sat at the dinner table with a family of six plus himself with bowls full of one can of this and one can of that. He kept waiting for more food to come out, but it never did. If you took one look at my family, you would know that we had to sneak out later to eat again after almost every meal served under her care.

She counted the silverware after every meal and did not welcome help in the kitchen since the dishwasher had to be organized just so. I will never forget the day she took one look at my eight-year-old 1980's perm and called it "kinky nigger hair." If something came to her mind, she said it, even if it hurt someone else. When we packed up to go fishing at the lake, she rarely came, and if she did, she brought cards to play instead.

My cousin Laura reminded me how she used to always try to quit smoking while we were there. I guess her habit made her feel guilty with kids around the house, so she would stop smoking for a few days which only intensified her grouchiness. She would inevitably go back to smoking sometime after we left and then start the pattern over again on our next visit.

She also counted pecans and put them in Ziploc bags in the freezer with the tallied number emblazoned in permanent black ink on the outside. After suspecting a nighttime snacker, she recounted the pecans and announced that someone had been eating pecans out of the freezer. I am certain it was my dad, though none of us spoke up or said a word.

I am sure she felt like an outsider of sorts in her own family because she was the only one who would read the "Yankee" magazine she received regularly. We used to quietly make fun of her for it. I once heard a joke that Yankees were like hemorrhoids: a pain in the butt when they come south and a relief when they go back up north.

Where was the grace, I could not help but wonder? My dad hand carved for her a wooden plaque as a kind gesture during a period when my grandfather was getting a lot of awards and attention. It read, "If there ain't no grace in

Grace's house, then it ain't Grace's house you're in. 'Cause if
Grace is home then it's grace you'll find .... when Grace's is
where you've been." She loved it- and my dad- so much that
she hung it on the wall in her kitchen. All her children will tell
you she was a good mother and very dedicated and devoted to
her family.

It is only now I can see how much he loved her, with the
kind of love that doesn't go away. Not with circumstance, not
with time, not with the sting of death's separation. He missed
the way she scolded him for popping a fresh trash bag too
loudly when putting a new one in the can. "Dammit Andy!
You're gonna make a hole in it!" she would shout. He would
sometimes pop them behind a mischievous smile, just to see
her react. He would sing "Amazing Grace" and whisper that
Grace would have liked that. His hand boasted his antique
gold wedding band, a family heirloom, and he wore it fondly
a decade after Grace's death. It is engraved on the inside
with the Latin words "VIRTUS JUNXIT. MORS NON
SEPARABIT." This means "Virtue joins. Death does not
separate." And it didn't.

It was only after her death that I grew to appreciate the
woman she was, and I came to understand that such a difficult-
to-love woman in my eyes was deeply, if not passionately
loved, by my grandfather. Their love at first sight all those

years ago did not falter or fade after decades of life together. That initially superficial love grew into a deep and abiding one. They were deeply committed to one another and as I saw my grandfather's pain in the months and weeks after her death, I realized how wrong I had been. Even in her cancer-ridden state, she was never outwardly mean or cruel, but sweet and peaceful. I began to miss her, too, and see her for all her strengths rather than her weaknesses.

I miss the woman I didn't get to know in my own adult life, and the wife and mother I never truly saw for who she was. I regret the way I viewed her. I thought she seemed unfeeling and unkind, but she really cared very deeply. She sometimes lacked the proper way to communicate or show her affection, but she worried and meddled out of a magnitude of love for us. While I thought she was cheap and tyrannical, she was really very wise and frugal. I later learned it was her thrifty lifestyle that enabled my grandparents to give large amounts of their money away for the good of others. My grandfather established a memorial scholarship fund in my grandmother's name after her death which funded others to pursue their dreams of higher education.

As an adult, I remember her differently. I miss the ease of knowing dinner would be warm on the table at 6:00 p.m. sharp or that her Christmas card would include a check for $20 or so. I miss the fierce love that put "Dear Abby" clippings on my bed because she was too old-fashioned to talk about the things she thought I needed to know. I miss my Mimi who put plastic solo cups and scraps of tin foil in the dishwasher. I realized she really was grace, just as my dad had wisely written so many years ago. That plaque now proudly hangs on my wall.

Only two months after my grandmother passed away, I was studying for finals in my sorority house bedroom when I received a phone call telling me that my first cousin Tate (my mother's sister Ann's son) had been in a motorcycle accident. Tate and his brother Tripp were older than me, but because they both were from Athens, we got to see each other more often at sporting events and family get-togethers.

Tate had been thinking of buying a motorcycle from a friend and he took it out on a test ride. He was unfamiliar with the roads and quickly came to an intersection with speed too fast to stop. The bike lurched out into the oncoming traffic, and he was hit by the car head on. My dear roommate Catherine drove me to the hospital in Athens. My dad and grandfather were already driving the two and a half hours from Hamilton.

I will never forget seeing Tate in the hospital room, unrecognizable with tubes everywhere. My dad and grandfather arrived in time to meet with the doctors and with Ann and Frank. I look back now at the chaos of that evening, and I don't know how I was in the room with my aunt and uncle when they were receiving Tate's terrible prognosis. I watched Papa's dismal nods of understanding as the doctors spoke in their confusing medical jargon. Having lost his wife two months before, he knew before the rest of us that he would be losing a grandson as well.

Tate was a bright light in our family. He was an organ donor, so others are alive today because of his giving spirit. We all miss his playful, fun-loving presence. He was a great soccer player, ran track in high school, and earned a scholarship for technical support for the football program at UGA. He is honored with a Memorial scholarship in his name to the University of Georgia for students in Agricultural and Applied Economics. His death affected our family profoundly. My brother and sister-in-law Melanie named their oldest son Tate Anderson after him. Tripp, Tate's older brother, also named his little boy Tate.

Papa.

Grace and Andy had eight grandchildren, fanned out in four pairs across Georgia and Florida during our growing up years, and spread out in age over a decade and half from 1967-1982. Each of us remembers similar characteristics but different stories from our individual lives with our grandfather whom we called "Papa" (except Laura and Paige who called him "Granddaddy"). We are now spread out from Arizona to North Carolina, so we don't get to see one another often, and we all stay busy raising children of our own.

My cousin Laura, who is ten years my senior, got a very bad case of food poisoning as a child in Columbus when they were visiting our grandparents. Papa treated her with a suppository, and Laura was horrified he didn't wear any gloves! He could easily shift from being a grandfather to being a medical practitioner. When it came to sickness, even of a loved one, it was sometimes a matter of science and treating an ailment for Papa.

Laura reminded me of the same short but effective prayer he said before every family meal. "Lord make us thankful for these and all our many blessings. We ask in Christ's name, Amen." He loved to sing and hum old show tunes and hymns, especially in his later years. He had a habit of softly rubbing his hands together while he was talking to us. Laura remembers him saying he was going to have a "night cap" before bed, even though she didn't know what that meant until years later.

Calcification in his neck from football tackles prevented him from turning his head very far to the left and right, so he had to turn his torso to look at you while driving his car. It was terrifying to ride with him. Not only did he often speed down familiar country roads and highways, but he would also tilt his whole body to tell you a story which meant he was not looking ahead!

Laura married her high school sweetheart, Jay Bell, who was drafted after high school to play Major League Baseball. He had a long career playing for the Indians, Pirates, Royals, Diamondbacks, and Mets, and as a result, he traveled frequently. Jay and Laura had been apart for months since he was on the road, and she had to be on bedrest for pregnancy. They had only seen each other one day in a two-month period, when Jay flew home for their child's birth.

Several weeks after the birth, Laura flew to Arizona from Florida with her newborn Brock, three-year-old Brantley, and six-year-old Brianna to spend time with Jay. Our grandmother passed away shortly after Laura arrived in Arizona. Papa called to reassure Laura that she needed to stay with her husband instead of coming to Georgia for Mimi's funeral. He said Mimi wasn't here on earth to know the difference, and they needed to spend time with Jay. He put others' needs before his own.

Papa loved Jay as his own grandson. When Jay was playing in Atlanta against the Braves, Papa and Mimi made the short trip to Atlanta to watch him play. He told everyone Jay was his grandson and he got a lot of special perks, including up front VIP parking at the game. He welcomed all our spouses lovingly into the family and treated all our children (his great grandchildren) with the same unconditional love he gave each of us.

Many more of our family members have enjoyed athletic success at the collegiate level and beyond. My uncle Ed played golf at Georgia. My brother Travis earned a baseball scholarship at Samford University and then played in the minor leagues with the Philadelphia Phillies. Travis pitched for

Samford in Athens against UGA when I was a student there. His son Miller is attending Wofford College on a baseball scholarship, and Paige's son Brent is playing basketball at Barton University. My cousin Laura's two sons Brantley and Brock are both playing professional baseball. Athletics have been a large part of our extended family and a great legacy of my grandfather.

All the grandchildren share similar memories of his storytelling, the way he often told us, "I'm so very proud of you," and going to Georgia football games with him, of course! He even sent a pilot friend down to Pensacola in a small plane to pick up Boots and family and bring them to and from the Georgia football games. We all remember going to Vince Dooley's home in Athens the weekend Papa received the Bill Hartman Award.

We recall how quickly he ate, and how fast he climbed the hills of Athens to get to his seat in the football stadium. He had a strict game day routine of eating at the Georgia Center hotel, parking in a special spot, and getting to his seat in the club level before the game started. He was equally in a hurry to beat the traffic after the game.

Paige remembers wanting to get her ears pierced when she was a young girl, but she was scared to death. Her dad Boots talked her into having Papa pierce her ears when they drove up to Hamilton. She said Papa was very patient with her and numbed her ears before he pierced them. I also remember him cutting a wart off my foot one time. He performed these small procedures for most of us grandkids at one time or another.

Papa used to sit at a small antique desk at the top of the stairs or at the big roll-top desk in his home office and write letters to people. My brother Travis reminded me how Papa penned hundreds of letters of encouragement to family members and friends. He wrote to Travis telling him how proud he was when he signed a contract to play in the Minor Leagues and when he graduated from college. He wrote to me upon my acceptance to UGA, when I was inducted into the Arch Society as a UGA student ambassador, and other times while I was in college.

We can remember him lining us up for family pictures. He loved taking photographs, and he was meticulous about how he wanted everyone to stand. He did not tolerate us screwing around and cutting up when he was trying to take our picture. It was brutal for a young child, although he did have a knack for taking good pictures! He kept incredible records, almost always writing the names, date, and location on the back of each photo. This has helped us immensely as the years have passed to remember the names of distant family members and the dates pictures were taken.

When Uncle Boots and Donna would drive for a visit to Hamilton in the wee hours of the night with Laura and Paige, Papa always waited up for them to arrive safely. He would stand and greet them on the back porch when they arrived. He had gas pumps installed at the back of his driveway in the 1970's, and we all remember how he often filled up our gas tanks before we drove back home.

I was a young girl when Mimi and Papa got a hummingbird feeder and hung it just outside the big picture window of the den. I had never seen anything like the tiny buzzing birds. At times there were seven or eight of them hovering, chasing one another, and vying for a sip of sugar sauce. I used to lie down on the floor and inch my way up to the window to get as close to them as possible. When the ants also found the sweet spot and marched up and down the feeder, Papa fastened a sponge soaked in ant killer around the hanging wire. He was resourceful and a good problem solver.

As a child, I rode the tractor around the pasture from the safety of his lap, and no matter how old I got or how convincingly I asked, he never saw fit for me to cast my own fishing rod. It was partly his overwhelming feeling of paternal protection and partly his code for being always a gentleman. Later in life as an old widower, he walked his daily helpers

Lillie and Sherry to the door in the evening when it was time for them to go home.

I never saw my grandfather without him telling me he loved me and that he was proud of me. His warm smile has always been a natural part of his greeting to everyone he meets. He related to all types of people with a clasp of the hand, pat on the arm, or touch on the shoulder.

I grew up hearing my grandfather's stories and assuming he was special simply because he was special to me. As an adult, I now understand that he is an utterly amazing man, in fact one of the most remarkable men I have ever known. It was a rare occasion to go anywhere with him without one of his former patients expressing appreciation and love for him. I have witnessed firsthand his unassuming greatness.

The most common sentiment among us is how he treated all people the same. It didn't matter to Papa how rich, poor, black, or white someone was, he valued and treated each person with the same dignity and respect. He was equally at ease talking to a Nobel Laureate as he was an uneducated laborer. Many times, people from the community would knock on his back door in need of help or medical advice. He always made time to listen and offer his services or his wisdom. He could connect deeply with virtually everyone.

My cousin, S.A. Roddenbery V ("Little Andy," or

"Andy V") may have spent the most time with Mimi and Papa growing up. He lived in Columbus only about twenty miles from their farm in Hamilton, and he enjoyed hunting and fishing with his dad Ed. They spent a good many days out on the land with Papa. During his time in Hamilton, Little Andy got to know Eugene, a man who helped Papa on the farm doing odds and ends. Andy V told me the following story about Eugene:

When Papa got on in years, he needed a little help around the farm. He loved making gradual improvements to the land, and sometimes there was debris or fallen trees to clean up, especially after a storm. Sleepy had aged right along with him, and Sleepy moved to Grantville to be near his sister when he could no longer live alone.

Papa found a local man named Eugene to work alongside him as needed in Sleepy's stead. Eugene was a pulpwood man by profession, and he had his own truck for hauling debris. Though he was only about 140 pounds, he was strong as an ox. Each taut muscle of his bare abdomen protruded when he lifted heavy objects. Andy V said he was chiseled from stone, and that Eugene was the darkest man he had ever seen.

Papa loved being out on the land with Eugene. He was surprised by what Eugene could do, and he regularly boasted about his superhuman abilities and incredible physical strength to other people. Not only was Eugene hardworking and strong, he was dependable and trustworthy, and he earned the deep respect and admiration of Papa. They grew a friendship out under the brutal summer sun, cutting up and hauling trees and branches, mending fences, and toting hay.

Andy V found some first and second grade level reading textbooks at Papa's house lying around when he was about ten years old. He questioned Mimi and Papa about why they had these books and what they were using them for, but they redirected the conversation to other topics. Andy V could not get past the strangeness of the books in the house and continued to press. They finally told him Papa was using those books to teach his friend Eugene how to read.

In disbelief, Andy V asked Papa how he knew Eugene could not read. Papa explained how he had seen Eugene mark his name with an "X" at the bank because he was unable to write his name. It never occurred to Andy V that there were grown people who could not write or read just down the road from him in Georgia, or especially someone he knew personally. For as much as Eugene could do physically, he had not been given the opportunity to improve his mind through a good education.

Papa was determined to help Eugene learn to read. Education was such an important part of his life, and he wanted every willing and able person to have the basic foundations of learning that he was given. He noticed once he started doing the lessons with Eugene, his friend stopped coming around as often. Papa was frustrated as he feared Eugene was intentionally staying away to avoid the reading lessons. After a few months, Papa had a conversation with Eugene and found that his suspicions were correct.

He made a deal with Eugene that they would cease all studies if he would come back and work with him on the farm just as before. That is exactly what they did for many years. They toiled, sweated, and laughed until they both were unable to do the difficult manual labor the land required. Their friendship transcending race, education, age, and ability was forged over many years together.

When Eugene died, there was no money for a headstone, so Papa took it upon himself to have one created. He found a large rock from the creek, the same waters they used to drive through side by side in the red pickup truck. Papa had a plaque engraved and mounted on the stone. Engraved on the headstone was each letter of the name of his good friend. It read, "Eugene."

Nonagenarian

There is something old in my spirit. I prefer a bath to a shower, a good book to a movie, a walk to a drive, hot tea to coffee, a manual can opener to an electric one. I enjoy a slower pace of life, which I am rarely afforded with three children. I appreciate things from past generations like antiques, old books, and family heirlooms.

For this reason, I love the homes of the elderly. They are marked by efficiency, character, and the past. There are no decorator's paint palettes, designer pillows and drapes, or other vanities. Simply and frugally, their homes depict a life scarred by the hunger and fear of a Depression and more horrific wars than any other American generation has yet seen. Their treasures are pictures, and stories, and people.

In 2006, my husband Marcus and I had our first daughter Neely. We had two more daughters, Sadie and Maggie. As anyone who has ever had children will tell you, there is truly nothing so fulfilling and so remarkable in life. I wonder what kinds of trophies and honors they might earn. What things will they value enough to keep or display? What will their homes someday say about their lives and the way they lived?

If you had knocked on my grandfather's door before his memory began to fail him, he would no doubt have invited you inside with a gracious Southern smile and even offered you a cold Coke. He might have taken you into his office to show his life collections, achievements, and memories on display. Later in life, some pictures were added and even scotch-taped to the walls. In a rhythmic dance of sorts, he would walk the perimeter of the room, stopping to collect his thoughts at each memento, sharing with a smile his stories and recollections of an era I can only wonder about.

In his front hallway sat the Harvard chair, as we fondly referred to it. It was an antique chair with "VERITAS" engraved on the front. Along the walls were various antiques, as old or older than my grandfather himself. On a dusty shelf leaned his tattered Harvard Medical School yearbook from 1941 with a date of death written next to the faces of his deceased classmates. He was one of the last still living. There was a picture of Knute Rockne and Papa's life-long friend, Ted Twomey who was an All-American football player under Rockne at Notre Dame.

High above the pictures of his friends and family beamed his UGA football team, lined up single file across the field where Sanford Stadium now stands, before it was much of a stadium at all. As a young man with a number "17" emblazoned on his chest, he posed with a leather helmet and a pigskin ball. He became the oldest living football letterman from his beloved university.

He would also have shown you proudly his picture with Gene Roddenberry, the creator of Star Trek, his distant cousin, though he usually didn't mention the "distant" part. He would point you to a picture of himself in front of a Stearman 2-passenger, open cockpit biplane from World War II he trained in along with a framed explanation he asked his wife Grace to type many years ago. It tells how President George H. Bush flew in the same kind of plane as a Naval pilot that my grandfather flew in as a flight surgeon. He was a patriot.

There was an original painting given to him by Lamar Dodd, his long-time friend for whom the University of Georgia

Art School is named. It was once appraised for $30,000. Spilling into the dining room, his trophies occupy shelves and tables, among them the Georgia Medical Association's Lifetime Achievement Award for Muscogee County.

He was President of the Georgia Surgical Society, and he had a gavel to show for it. He was awarded the National Football Foundation and Hall of Fame Distinguished American Award. The University of Georgia's Bill Hartman Award also hung on the wall, named for my grandfather's college teammate and given to former lettermen who have distinguished themselves in their chosen field while also contributing much to their communities.

One fellow Hartman Award winner, Dr. Tommy Lawhorne, a surgeon in Columbus and UGA football letterman was mentored by my grandfather. Lawhorne wrote a poem to my grandfather that he had framed, a portion of it read, "I'm so fortunate our paths did cross, He called me a peer, but to me, he is the Top Dawg, the Boss!" Another dear friend, Bobby Joe Baxley, also wrote him a poem that he had framed.

On the walls were pictures of his grandchildren, great-grandchildren, and his ancestors: his great-grandfather, Seaborn Anderson Roddenbery, the country doctor and founder of the Roddenbery Pickle Company; his grandfather, Seaborn Anderson Roddenbery II, the Georgia U.S. Congressman; and his father, John Roddenbery, in a naval uniform as a lieutenant commander. It is one of only a few pictures of his father I have ever seen.

He had a shadow box with his Phi Beta Kappa pin, Phi Kappa Phi pin, Sphinx Award, and pocket watch for "Best All-Around" student a Lanier High School in Macon, one of his prized possessions. His Boy Scout awards hung on the wall, including every badge he could earn, giving him the title of Eagle Scout. He was a Trustee of the University of Georgia Foundation beginning in 1957, earning emeritus status in 1970. In 1980 he was elected to membership in the Gridiron Secret Society. He directed the Muscogee County Chapter of the Red Cross and was President of the local UGA Alumni Society. All these awards peeked out behind dusty glass.

Lindbergh flashed a faded smile down from the wall. My grandfather paused silently at this picture with a boyish grin. I could tell he was lost in his memory of meeting the larger-than-life man as a child. Peering down from the wood paneled wall was the same smile he flashed my grandfather that fateful day in Atlanta, the day when young Anderson grabbed Lindy's coattails and followed him toward greatness.

Of the times he walked me through his halls of memories, I have never heard an ounce of arrogance in his voice, only the truth of a lifetime's experiences in a matter-of-fact tone, as if he were describing a simple medical procedure or a life as ordinary as yours or mine. He was recounting these memories less for his own benefit and more to inspire us to greatness. A quick tour of his keepsakes would tell you that his life has been nothing short of extraordinary. For a man with so many heroes strung up on his walls, he unknowingly became one for many. At five foot eleven, he was a giant among men.

Even for all his trophies and beautiful furniture, he knew all too well that someday his old records might be taken to the Salvation Army along with his dusty sofa and his dated suits. He was fully aware that his heirs would not treasure his Reader's Digest condensed books the way he did and that some lucky garage saler could soon eat off his china. He made it clear his treasures were not on earth.

In the month of his ninety-second birthday, my grandfather asks me, "What year is it?" When I tell him it's 2008, I can see him figuring up his age in his head, recalling the year of his birth. The optimist hesitates, then chuckles and says, "Eight more years 'til I'm a hundred."

I reach over and grab his hand, realizing all the great things his hands have done. The gracious surgeon's hands skillfully executed thousands of procedures, took out the weekly garbage for a needy neighbor, and tossed a pigskin in Sanford

Stadium at the University of Georgia. His steady hand penned the life and legacy of Dr. Delmar Edwards. And his hands will still open wide to greet you on the square of Hamilton or in the Steak-n-Shake in Columbus. If you catch him there, you can hear him slurping down a chocolate milkshake, seemingly without taking a breath.

His faded brown eyes are compassionate and strong, and his soul looks out through them steadily and filled with hope. He is slightly taller than average, of average build, with hands smaller than his frame would predict. He fidgets with them while he sits, but his movements are always careful and precise, the calculated maneuvers of a surgeon at rest. His nails are clean and well-manicured, his hands soft and wrinkled with age.

He always gives a firm shake, and when he looks you in the eye, his smile is eager and, in some way, boyish. The deeply carved lines surrounding his mouth boast of found happiness. His hair as a young man was dark chestnut brown and then turned fully white at the early age of thirty-five, a trait I unwillingly inherited. In his older age, his fluffy hair gives away his adventurous spirit, looking like he has been out riding with the windows down, hair feathered back and refusing to lie down properly.

He appreciates the simple things in life, finding certain

pleasure in bending down to pick up a dirty penny off the street. In fact, I've never seen him walk past one. He hardly missed an evening in his retired years of watching his herd of Black Angus approaching the barn, the setting sun illuminating their outlines on the horizon. He walks steadily, slowly up to the herd, whispering calm words of friendship and handing out a peace offering of hay. He finds joy in being among them and watching them come into the pasture and the safety of the barn in the late afternoons.

My grandfather is a surgeon through and through. Even in his old age, he cannot recall the President's name, but he will diagnose skin cancer on your nose. He doesn't always remember the names of his grandchildren or his great grandchildren, but he always smiles and laughs and treats them with kindness and love. Long after retirement, he eats at a doctor's pace as if still anticipating an emergency call, and never stops chewing and swallowing long enough to breathe without wheezing and jaw popping.

He has a keen understanding of the things that matter most in life, long after a shiny car rusts and new clothes fade. He does not value too highly the things in his life, but rather the people in his very large circle and ultimately his God. My grandfather is as dependable as a big pitcher of sweet tea in my mother's fridge. He is a member of the greatest generation, those who signed up to bleed for justice across a broad sea, and many of whom had a heap of injustices to overcome.

He believes the best about people, which has made him both wise and occasionally gullible in his lifetime. I think he believes that people would rise to his high expectation of what they could become. This is why he writes letters to his wife's nephew in prison. He invites him to come live with him to help him get his life together when he gets out. He means it, too. His word is as strong as goat's breath.

He is Georgia born and Georgia bred, and when he dies, he'll be "Bulldog dead," or so it reads on a plaque on his wall. If ever anyone loved the University of Georgia, my grandfather does with his whole heart. It served him well and then he served it right back for many years.

"I have a clear conscience. I hold no grudges," he will say, matter of factly. "I count my blessings every day, and I have so much to be thankful for." Though his hearing fails him, and he walks on a slant until he really gets going, he only looks for the good in life. I have never heard him utter a single complaint. Ever. He has grown old without contempt.

He is one of those men who was born with all the level-headedness and maturity of an adult. His own mother adored him, and I think admired him in a way that surprised even her. The grandeur she and his father chased during their lives eluded them, and their son possessed it almost effortlessly.

One afternoon my mom was driving Papa into Columbus to run some errands, and they saw a homeless man on the side of the road walking in the same direction. Mom spent a fair amount of time trying to help the homeless in Orlando when we were growing up, and her heart of compassion would not let her keep driving past this man on that day. She explained to her dad what she wanted to do, and they circled the car back to talk to the man.

The vagrant was on his way to Columbus to hopefully find some place to spend the night, so they agreed to give him a ride. I don't think my grandfather had ever experienced being around someone as destitute, smelly, and needy as this man, and his heart was broken for him. They drove to several shelters that turned him away, and Papa was indignant that no one was willing to help. His sense of justice and love for his fellow man took over and he firmly insisted that one place take him in. They succeeded in their quest to find him help on Second Avenue at Valley Rescue.

After my grandmother died, Papa wanted to take all his children on a tour of Boston to show them where he met Grace and several other sites of importance. All four children and their spouses packed up and flew to Boston. Papa was an extremely organized trip planner. He had an itinerary for each day and was enthusiastic about the planned activities.

Papa was sharing a room with my parents on the trip. After a long day of traveling, they all melted into their beds and planned on getting some solid shut eye before the next day's activities. My parents were awakened by Papa standing at the foot of their bed at 5:00 a.m. sharp singing "Oh what a beautiful morning, oh what a beautiful day!" with gusto!

He was fully dressed in his windbreaker, hat, and his precious camera hanging from a strap around his neck. He was ready to get the day started, but Mom and Dad encouraged him to go downstairs, read the paper, and eat breakfast. The trip created some lasting memories as they all got to tour Harvard, the Brigham hospital where he worked and met my grandmother, and other sites of importance.

Many local widows started showing up regularly with meals for my grandfather. They were vying for his attention, since he was probably the most eligible eighty-three-year-old around. He quickly latched onto a widow named Hazel Lewis because he wasn't used to all the attention from women. She had been a well-respected retired schoolteacher in Columbus, and her deceased husband had been his patient for years.

Hazel's husband was one of only two patients who died under Andy's care surrounding surgery. Her husband was having some kind of routine surgery like a gall bladder removal, and when he was put under with anesthesia, he died on the table before surgery was to begin. Andy always felt badly about that because it was a routine procedure, not considered high risk or dangerous. Andy and Hazel turned out to be good companions for one another for several years during the time my grandfather's memory began to fail him and dementia was setting in.

She came to Athens for football games from time to time. My parents would drive them up on Friday and take them home on Sunday. My mom had to stay with Hazel in a room at the Georgia Center and my dad stayed with Papa. On one game weekend, my grandfather was down in the lobby early with two of his children and their spouses. When he saw Hazel get off the elevator and she approached them, he stood up and said, "Hazel, it's so good to see you! What are you doing here?" Dementia got him in a heap of trouble that day!

One time my parents took him to his wife's grave on their anniversary. He picked out some flowers to place at the spot marked "Grace George Roddenbery." The three of them stood there in silence among the rows and rows of artificial flowers. Papa turned to my parents after a few minutes and said, "I don't remember what we are doing here." Mom and Dad reminded him that it was his anniversary, and they were putting flowers on his wife, Grace's, grave. Taken aback, he said in disbelief, "I had a wife????" Mom assured him that he did have a loving wife and a very long marriage. He paused for a moment and then said, "She was a good ole girl."

Similarly, one evening my parents and Papa were sitting in the den watching the cows come in. Papa looked at my dad, his son-in-law, and asked, "Robert, are you my only child? Or do I have other children?" My mom could not believe what he had just asked, and she started to giggle. My dad, always joking around, assured Papa that he was in fact his favorite child while proudly smiling at my mom across the room and laughing quietly.

As a family, we had to laugh about the dementia so we could survive. Otherwise, it was just too painful. There were other times when he couldn't remember things, but he was gracious and kind even when he wasn't sure what was going on. He was still brilliant in many ways even when he couldn't remember basic facts.

On one trip to Athens for a football game, my dad was

driving. Papa was in the passenger's seat, and my mom was sitting in the middle in the back. During that time in 1998, a sex scandal involving then President Bill Clinton and a White House intern Monica Lewinsky was all over the news. Because of the nature of the story, all journalistic modesty went out the window. Sexual content of all sorts was being talked about on prime time television.

During the two- and half-hour car ride while listening to crude radio news chatter, Papa leaned in and said, "Robert and Berta, I've been meaning to ask you something."

"Sure Doc!" said Dad.

"Well, what is the meaning of 'oral sex' anyway?" he asked.

My dad caught my mom's eye in the rear-view mirror. In her embarrassment and horror, she pointed at my dad to let him know he was definitely gonna answer this one! She laid down in the backseat, wishing to hide from the whole situation. Papa continued, "Because if it's just kissing, I don't see what all the fuss is about."

My Dad could always diffuse a tense situation with humor. "Well, Doc," started Dad, "It's not just the kissing that's the problem...," he paused, choosing his next words wisely for maximum understanding and minimal embarrassment. "it's

WHERE the kissing is taking place." Papa sat there for a long, uncomfortable moment and then started to chuckle until his shoulders shook with laughter.

Suddenly Papa said, "Well in that case, I don't think he should still be our President."

The rare occasion he was obstinate or resistant was when his four children decided it was time to take his car keys away. He had been in a fender bender recently, and they were concerned about safety as well as his fading memory. He became angry and asked, "On whose authority are you taking my keys away?" My mom Berta explained that he had been to see his friend Dr. Ben Pike. After the doctor's examination and upon his recommendation, they all agreed it was in his best interest to stop driving. Feeling cornered by his children and his friend, Papa said indignantly, "Well, he has never ridden with me! I have just lost all respect for Doctor Ben Pike!" Reluctantly, he handed over the keys.

My uncle Ed found a little black cat one time when he was hunting, and he brought it to my grandfather to have as a companion. Papa named the cat Amos, so that together they were "Amos 'n' Andy," like the famed radio and television show. The cat brought a lot of joy to Papa. They took the cat to the vet for a checkup, and Papa told the doctor he had some questions about Amos. There were all these ticks on Amos' belly and though he kept pulling and pulling, he could not get them off. The vet flipped the cat over to look at him, and with a big grin he reported to Dr. Roddenbery that "those aren't ticks. And this cat is not a boy. Those ticks are Amos' nipples!" Everyone had a great chuckle, and Amos finally got relief! I called her "Amy" after that.

In his last months, dementia clouds his mind, and the stories and people and pictures are melted together in a maze of memories. The disease shreds his thoughts and his days, and sometimes the sunshine and strength that were once in his face seem ages past. On bad days, a weak, empty space now occupies the windows to his soul, and his silver hair often looks wiry and disheveled. On good days, he is mostly present but seems distracted by something that seems to shine beyond the veil.

The curious thing about memory disorders is the afflicted's desire to cling to the past for lack of knowledge about the present. In the end of his life, there is little sense of home, diminished value in the trophies he has long since forgotten. There are only the Hamilton woods, his photographs, and the six summers in the lake country of Canada hidden in the deep recesses of his mind.

Canada is part of him. In his college summers, the lakes of Ontario permeated his being so that seventy years later, it is the place my grandfather dreams about. A thousand miles north in the Canadian wild, the grand and magnificent maze of lakes and streams flood his mind, and water meanders through them the way blood does the old man's veins. My grandfather remembers Canada and the many summers as a camp fishing guide, and his love for the wilderness that distracted him from the wounds of his imposing father.

It was there in a cabin on a jagged lake in the north country where he performed his first impromptu surgery as a college student, and in the moments that followed, the trajectory of his life changed forever. He believes he is there after looking through his old camp pictures and recounting the lore of his youth. Now in his nineties, he will sit on his living room chair in Hamilton, Georgia and call my mom next door. "Berta," he says, "I am up in Canada at Camp Twomey, and someone needs to come pick me up right away."

In his old age, his very being is still somehow entangled with his memories of Canada, and his tract of land in Georgia pays homage to the camp he loved. Eventually Canada is the place he longs for in his elderly, bewildered state. In fact, he feels a certain connection with a pair of Canada Geese who have made their home near his, and he joyfully watches them bask in the beauty and security of his land. Here, the water rolls, the soil yields, the sun warms, and winter welcomes.

My grandfather is fascinated with these birds and somehow identifies with their journey. At first glance, they seem too elegant to me to be confined to such an ordinary place. But in the gentle rolling hills of Hamilton, Georgia, just south of a little ridge called Pine Mountain (the first in the Appalachian chain), they saw a place worth making a home. Of all the locations in the entire South, out of every lake and hillside, they chose this one. They still come back year after year, drawn to his haven.

The geese are made for the wilds of Canada, meant for adventure on a bigger scale than here. That is where they come alive. Yet they feel equally at home in the two-acre manmade fishing pond bobbing up and down to cricket sonnets. They can be spotted swimming alongside their trio of golden fuzz goslings, basking in the cool water amid budding spring oaks.

The backdrop of simplicity doesn't diminish their grandeur. The modest country setting somehow accentuates it. They are not alone in their quest to assimilate to small town Georgia and ease into a quiet life. They may be the smartest birds in the bunch since they discovered an idyllic home place hundreds of miles from Canada. After all, they have the same inclinations as a Harvard-educated surgeon. They chose the same Eden.

We find the humor in all of it, because we must, but the pain is ever present. In the silence of the night when the police knock on my parents' door with my grandfather, disoriented and sweaty from a brief time of wandering outside, there is also sadness and uncertainty about the future. My parents live with the constant responsibility of his care and well-being, and they wonder how long he will be able to stay at home and if it is the safest place for him.

How do we live with the pain of losing someone who is not really gone? He exists: eating, breathing, sleeping, talking, and of course always singing. But the boyish spark that ignited in his eyes when he used to tell one of his stories has long since faded and drifted into blank stares. Now those eyes are more distant and less vibrant. Even when you are with him, he feels far away at times. The clear tone in his tenor voice is more garbled, and the once politically correct lyrics to "Suwannee River" change from "Oh Lordy" back to "Oh, darkies...how my heart grows weary" from the original version.

There are, however, constants in his life. He is very gracious, often talking about how blessed he is and how he has lived a charmed life. His words reflect optimism about life, telling my mother they have a "bright future." In his last years, there is a seamless attitude of thankfulness, while at the same time he longs for the next life his faith assures him will someday come.

While he has lost much, he still retains his fabulous vocabulary, his gentlemanly traits and impeccable manners, walking any guest to the door to say goodbye. My mom set up a monitor in his room so she can listen out for him during the wee hours. It warms her heart to hear him read his tattered Bible aloud at night and pray.

Though he doesn't remember much, he is preparing to leave this place, sometimes with a small suitcase packed and ready to go. He will stuff a few clothes in the same leather bag he took to Joe Brown Hall his freshman year at Georgia, and he will fasten his belt around his favorite stack of books like he did in elementary school. Occasionally he will hear a school bus in the morning and fear he will be late for school. He is relieved to be reminded he has already graduated.

Every so often he looks at me with a fearful vacancy, unsure of where home is even now. On a good day, he remembers Grace is gone and that he lives next door to my parents in Hamilton, Georgia. More common lately are the bad ones, the days when he longs for home from his living room couch and when he asks for his mother. Surrounded with his treasures collected over almost a century of living, he seems unsettled, homesick. He wants something else, needs something from the thick, red dirt and the trickling creek that four walls and a roof cannot offer him.

I marvel how the minds of the elderly in some ways return to childhood. My babies loved to be outside. They would sit contently for hours gazing at the clouds and trees, feeling the breeze on their faces. I loved to watch their amazement at the sights and sounds of nature. In many ways, my grandfather returns to those simple pleasures at the end of his life as my daughters were in their beginnings. Under a roof, he grows restless and confused, but outside he is at perfect peace.

When I think about it, it makes sense to love and long for the outdoors. It is what God made in its unspoiled form for us to enjoy. Nature is what Eden was filled with, and it was paradise indeed. Much of the most beautiful art and the most inspiring writings are imitations or interpretations of the divine around us. Everything else is manmade, twisting the good and natural elements to make something more comfortable and convenient, and in many instances, less inspiring.

A few years ago, when my parents were out of town, my grandfather's daytime helper called to say he was missing. Without hesitation, we knew where to look. Even though it had been several years since he stopped driving, the old red

Chevy pickup truck, the one we only used to drive out on the land, was missing. Uncle Ed would come to the rescue, but he was also traveling. My grandfather's longtime friends, Bobby Joe and Pat Baxley went looking for him. Bobby Joe knew the land well and was eager to help.

As darkness was setting in and they were about to quit searching for lack of daylight, they noticed in the distance a man's profile slowly walking across the pasture toward the house. They quickly drove toward him, and the old Eagle Scout waved, brandishing the walking stick he had fashioned from a fallen branch. There he stood in his red University of Georgia windbreaker, confused at what they were doing there but glad to see them, nonetheless. "Hi Bobby Joe," the doctor greeted them. "Hello, Doc! Could we give you a ride home?"

He had gotten the truck stuck crossing the wide part of the creek and was soaking wet, walking unsteadily toward the house. We were all very concerned, but he was not lost or afraid. He was more at home in his kingdom than in his white three-bedroom house, content in the wild majesty of this land that the good doctor calls his own. After a hot shower and a snack, he was ready for bed and walked his guests to the door. He never remembered the incident. That was the last time my parents left the keys in the truck.

The large oak tree out in front of my parents' home got struck by lightning a few years back, proof that even the most beautiful and most firmly rooted can't outlast death. Even nature is fallen. As the men in the bucket truck came and carved each branch away, I grinned, reminded of the many rose bushes I clipped for my dad one summer. There might as well have been a thousand of them. I remembered how I would pile the leaves and stems up in five-gallon buckets and dump them in the backyard compost pile. When I finally got to come inside, my hands were blistered and cut from the thorns, my nose burned from the summer sun. I hated the work of caring for them, but their undeniable beauty somehow made it all worth it.

I now know when Dad asked me to pick off the black spotted leaves from those rose bushes it was less for the roses and more for me. The same way I clipped those thorny branches, Dad knew in the years after my loved ones were gone, including his unexpected death a decade ago, life would prune me, too. He knew I needed tough hands for washing dishes and the heavy load of parenting and eventually burying the ones I love. He knew that a little dirt under fingernails never hurt anyone.

In much the same way, my grandfather knew it was the hard stuff in his life, the trials, that made the joys of life so sweet. Papa knew he was a soul that had a body, not just a body that contained a soul. And he knew that a soul doesn't become beautiful by coasting through life comfortably and without suffering. I was told once, "If you want to make your child's life really hard, then make it really easy!"

Papa says he was born under a shining star, and I don't doubt this is so. But deep in his past, buried so far back even he rarely speaks of it, there is sorrow. Some memories are so dark and painful that they erase the deep laugh lines from his face, and his quick leaking words slow into a painful dripping quiet.

Certainly, in his lifetime, he has known loss. Even so, he has taken the hard times with the good. His character was founded and built upon with great perseverance through trials. There was the untimely death of his sister, Mary, and the death of a firstborn son who arrived too soon in an era unequipped to help. He has trembled with the pain of losing his spouse. Only a few friends his age are still living, and he has stood over most of their graves as they were lowered into the earth. His last living sibling, Martha, passed away in her sleep at age 92. He lives with the childhood memories of an abusive father who abandoned him.

My grandfather told me a story, only once that I recall, that pricked my heart in such a way that I have never forgotten it. It is about a man who was hero to none, who made more mistakes and caused more hurts than anyone else in my grandfather's life. You could say he caused the bleeding. Papa told me the story of going to visit his father John when he was on his deathbed. It must have been his father's words that pierced him over the years. "I have lived a wasted life," his father said, looking him straight in the eye with a tone of great regret and repentance.

The unrealized dreams he chased after in his life left his father empty handed on the last day. The things he thought mattered all those years in fact amounted to nothing, and the faces of the people whose lives he had shattered haunted him as he stared bleakly into eternity. For years, the last words of Papa's father John ate away at him. Like ocean waves eroding the delicate walls of a sandcastle bit by bit, his father's nagging regrets finally broke down the castle walls, and once the sand settled, clarity stared up at my grandfather from the shallow pool. My grandfather purposed not to waste his life.

To be sure, we have all pondered it, the meaning of life. To live it well costs us everything and yet our life is all we really possess, if it is ever ours to begin with. What is the meaning of it all?

One evening Mom was sitting with Papa on a good day in his final year. He looked at her like a young boy and asked, "Berta, what do you think is the purpose of life?" Wanting to keep it simple, she said, "Well Dad, I think our aim is to please God and glorify Him- and I believe you have done that." Satisfied with the brief and profound answer, they sat there together for a while, quietly and peacefully watching the sun sink behind the trees and into the earth through the great picture windows of the den.

Immortal .

April 4, 2010, was Resurrection Sunday. In the wee hours of the morning when little churches all around the valley were preparing to celebrate life, an ambulance blazed down Georgia Highway 27, escorting my grandfather from his beloved home in Hamilton to the hospital in Columbus. The beds of his fingernails turned blue and at one point his face did, and he was unable to get up and walk.

My mother was in Huntsville helping my brother and sister-in-law Melanie with their newborn identical twin girls when she received the call from my dad. After an emotional morning, my mom felt an urge to come home to help take care of her dad. So, she left the sweet high of being with her two newest grandchildren and began an ominous four-hour drive that would lead her on the uncertain path to an end, and all of us to a new beginning.

Mom called me Easter morning and told me what happened and that she was driving home. At the time, my grandfather was being examined for a possible heart attack or small stroke. His unusually low blood pressure (his normal blood pressure was that of a teenager) and vital signs caused some concern. Marcus and I were in Destin with my in-laws for spring vacation. I broke down and cried on the way to church when I told my husband Marcus, but I continued to the rest of the activities for the day.

Later at the beach with my two girls, the thick, powder white sand felt heavy around my feet and the endless water that looked so beautiful and clear just the day before now rolled with sorrow. I picked up a handful of sand and sifted it through my fingers like an hourglass, letting it fall and float off in the breeze. There was nothing to do but wait.

Mom and Ed stayed with him through the night, but my grandfather never slept. The Broadway music and old hymns that played in his father John's mind years ago and haunted him in the end was the same music my grandfather joyfully heard in his mind constantly on repeat. Papa just hummed and sang along in the dark hospital room with my mom or her brother Ed by his side. Mom could not fall asleep because of the chance he might fall trying to get out of bed or pull his IV out. If she tried to turn on a light or the television, he would call out uncharacteristically, "Turn that off! I can't sleep with that on!" Of course, he was not sleeping anyway, but my mom sat patiently in the dark alone with her thoughts and praying through the night.

By mid-week, it became increasingly clear that at almost 95 years old, my grandfather would not recover. The doctors would "let nature take its course," and my grandfather left the hospital where his name was engraved on the wall as an honored surgeon to return to his bedroom at home. Hospice care arrived with a brand-new hospital bed, oxygen, and full-time care. His regular caregivers would also take turns sitting with him and helping. When the nurses attempted to put a catheter in, he began bleeding profusely, so they made the decision to take him to Columbus Hospice where he could get the best possible care.

When I first heard "hospice," I felt sad but tried to convince myself not to be. How many people live nearly 95 years? He lived an amazing life, worth writing about, and his quality of life had been diminishing. In my mind I knew it was probably time for him to go. His condition was declining rapidly, and he was no longer opening his eyes or speaking. My mom said it was like he was in a deep sleep.

I initially decided I would just wait for the funeral to go to Hamilton. I had a three-year-old and a one-year-old at home and the thought of taking a trip after just getting back from the beach felt like too much to pull off. I tried to convince myself he wouldn't even know I was there if I went, and he has not known who I am for a long time now. What difference did it make?

Mom called me on Friday night and told me that his kidneys were shutting down and he would probably have a week or so left to live. I wept. When I woke up on Saturday, I knew I needed to drive to Columbus. My husband Marcus encouraged me to go, and he graciously offered to watch our girls on the weekend of the Masters, a rare weekend when he usually relaxes and glues himself to the TV.

I cried a lot on the three-hour drive from Tuscaloosa to Hamilton. I have heard that grief comes in waves, and I believe that is true. I went from having a happy memory and almost laughing to tears flooding my eyes and dripping from my hot face down onto my shirt. I got to Hamilton about 2 p.m., and after a quick late lunch my mom drove me to Columbus Hospice to see Papa.

She wanted to warn me before I saw him that he would look different, like he was dying. I didn't care, I just wanted to be in his presence. We walked into the beautiful facility where people enter alive and only the empty shells of their bodies leave. It was a strange feeling to pass room after room of the dying, walking the hallways where souls leave their bodies and go to their final resting places. It felt holy.

We arrived at room 6 and walked in the open door. My grandfather was lying in his hospital bed, his caregiver, Lilly, was in the corner in a chair, and my Aunt Donna and Uncle Boots were seated on the couch. It was midday, but it was dark in the room, with the only light peeping in through the cracks in the plantation shutters. The yellow rays hit the wall and slid down the floor in perfectly angled lines, the only thing that made sense to me in that whole room.

I said hello to everyone and then went over to my grandfather. He was lying with his head propped up on a pillow with words that read "A Bulldog Sleeps Here." His mouth was open and there was a low gurgling sound in his throat when he took a breath, one of the stages of death, I have learned. His eyes were closed. He looked small and weak lying in that bed. It was hard to imagine how such a giant of a person was confined to such a withering body. I pulled up a chair next to him and grabbed his hand. It was smooth except for the raised veins that looked like a purple chicken's foot spreading out across his hand. Brown age spots peppered his hand and forearm. His skin felt soft and warm. His nails were perfectly manicured.

I leaned over to talk to him close in his ear. "Papa, it's your granddaughter Mary Grace. I wanted to see you and tell you how very much I love you. My whole life, every time I have seen you, you have always told me how proud you are of me. I always thought it was really the other way around. We are the ones who are proud of you and proud to be a part of your family." I had never told him of my plans to write about his life, and I knew I would regret not telling him. I forced out the words through sobs, "I am going to do my best to write a book about your life so everyone can know what an amazing life you have had. I love you and I will see you again."

He moved his mouth a little bit like he might be trying to say something or acknowledging that he heard me. Then I just sat for a long time and held his hand. It was an honor to sit with him on the narrow precipice between time and eternity, to kiss his head, just to be close. Those were sacred, holy moments with a precious and rare soul. I will never forget that opportunity to tell him goodbye.

We made a circle around him and held hands: Boots, Donna, mom, Lilly, and me. Boots leaned over close to his ear and said, "Dad, I just want you to know it's okay to go on now and be with Jesus. All your children, me, Ann, Ed, and Berta have all been here and we are all doing fine and taken care of. We are all well and so are your grandchildren. You don't have anything to worry about. It's okay. Mom is waiting in heaven for you and so is your mother, Mary Carle. We love you and we will see you there someday."

After Boots kissed him on the head, he turned to leave. He stopped at the door. "Of all of the children, I am the most blessed," he said as he wiped his tear-strewn face, "because I got to be with him the longest." In fact, we were all blessed to know him, to have just sat in his presence a while, to have felt his genuine kindness, to have basked in the warmth of his boyish laughter and to have listened to his larger-than-life stories. We had been the objects of his unrestrained pride and love.

I noticed as I was leaving the room his white hair, no longer fluffy and feathered, was finally lying down properly. The wind finally abandoned his white locks, a sign that his adventures here would be nearly over. In fact, his best one was about to begin. I knew in my heart it would be the last time I would ever see him.

I went home on Sunday, and Monday lingered on with no change in his condition. Tuesday morning, I received a message from my dad that Papa had gone on to be with the Lord at 1:30

a.m. that morning with Uncle Ed by his side. I immediately called my parents even though I was not at home. My mom answered the phone, and I wept on the other end with heaving shoulders in the corner of a public restroom.

I thought about Papa and how he viewed death. When most folks see a long black hearse coast by, tightness fills their stomachs. They must face up to the fact that their mortality is just as real as the one riding coach. Not my grandfather. He gazed respectfully but with anticipation and deep knowledge of a bright future, as if he had the secret recipe for Coca-Cola written on a napkin in his pocket. He did not shrink from death or cling so tightly to his own life that he did not willingly give it away when his Master called.

Even knowing this, I was surprised by the depth of my sorrow, that I could be so sad over the death of a 94-year-old man who lived a life most only dream about. It was evidence that we were never created to experience death and pain and sadness. We were made for Eden. And the land he cared for and left us would be the closest reflection of that paradise here on earth for the remainder of the time we have left.

St. Paul Methodist Church was filled with respect-payers at Saturday's funeral. There were no ornate decorations, only a brass easel displaying a portrait of my grandfather, gray-haired, with glasses, in a powder blue suit. I think it was just the way he would have wanted it. And truly, you don't need anything much to honor a life that so clearly speaks for itself.

At the funeral, Uncle Boots gave a breathtaking tribute to the man my grandfather was behind closed doors. "I rarely heard him raise his voice in anger. I never heard him say anything bad about anyone." He talked about his father's competitive nature and how as a young boy at 11, he challenged his father to a race down the beach while on vacation. His dad graciously accepted this challenge, and he beat his young son by about 3 or 4 strides. Sensing Boots' disappointment at losing to his forty-year-old father, my grandfather said, "Son, you are faster than I am. I just got a quicker start." Boots said he wanted to challenge him to another race, but in looking at his dad, he could tell he gave it all he had the first time around.

Through the years, my grandfather had become a role model for many other Bulldog football players who turned doctors, among them: George Skipworth, Clyde Harrison, Hurley Jones, Happy Dicks, Rosie Gilliam, Chuck Heard, Scott Rissmiller, John Lee, Bill Simpson, and Tommy Lawhorne. Andy mentored Lawhorne and guided him into a career as a physician in Columbus, Georgia.

Dr. Tommy Lawhorne, linebacker under Vince Dooley and valedictorian of his 1968 class, spoke these words at the funeral, "Dr. Roddenbery in many ways influenced my life more than my own father." Lawhorne said, "I have never met another human being with his courage, his sensitivity and his determination. His vast knowledge, innate understanding of people and gentleness of manner endeared him to patients and friends alike. All those who know him have been blessed."

We all sang "In the Garden" at the close of the service. It reminded me of a joke my dad told years ago about how God's nickname must be "Andy," since the chorus of that old hymn says, "And he walks with me, and he talks with me, and he tells me I am His own." If you sing it just right, it does sound like "Andy walks with me...Andy talks with me..." I could clearly recall my grandfather's unbridled laughter when my dad told him that joke and sang it to him years ago. And I thought how Papa would have liked that. His wife Grace used to say with a smile it was her favorite hymn.

A reporter, Loran Smith wrote of the service, "the atmosphere of the church dripped with respect for the fisherman-turned-doctor, an endearing story that is a reminder that football, even today with its skewed attitude toward money, can often become a conduit to usher a boy from a modest upbringing into professional achievement."[8]

After the funeral, we had a reception at the church that my Aunt Becky organized. Sally White, a former UGA cheerleader and friend of my grandfather called it "the last great tailgate for Dr. Roddenbery." We reminisced about my hero over pimento cheese sandwiches, chocolate chip cookies, and punch. "Your grandfather caught hell for what he did," said John Spencer, talking about Papa taking on a black surgical partner. "But your grandfather was a hell of a man."

It was at this reception that I heard a story about my grandmother that may never have been told before. John Spencer was the son of Addie, the Roddenbery family maid who helped raise my mother and her siblings. John said that he was the first black student at Columbus College (now Columbus State University). After he was admitted, he got a call from my grandmother. "John, I want you to meet me at Columbus College this afternoon." So, he got ready and met her up at the college. He then told me that she got out her wallet and paid for his tuition and books. She did this every semester until he graduated. John is now in charge of a program at a local institution to keep kids in school.

John also told me how he split his head open as a young man and he went to see my grandfather. After Papa sewed him up, John said, "How much do I owe you, Dr. Roddenbery?"

"Aw, get outta here," Papa said with a smile. He never would let him pay for any medical care, and he did this for many in Columbus who could not afford good care.

"Your grandparents took care of me and my family, and even my wife and all her family," he told me. My grandfather made good on his promise to his benefactors who funded his education. He paid back every penny to those who would let him, he paid it forward for any who refused his offer. He and my grandmother did this in secret, escaping the knowledge of even their own children. This is how they wanted it.

Many articles were written about my grandfather after his death, rows of black and white letters trying desperately to capture the man he was and the stories he lived. There was a lot to put on paper about his legacy, his awards, his accomplishments. Famed UGA tennis coach and friend of my grandfather, Dan Magill, wrote a beautiful memoir in the Athens paper. But perhaps my favorite was a simple letter to the editor in the Columbus paper written by a former nurse, S. Rogers. She spoke less of achievements and more about the way he treated people, the way he did what was right.

She said that he, along with Dr. Delmar Edwards and Dr. C.D. Johnson (who both passed away within seven months of Papa), were "the gold standard for patient care and compassion. They never saw people for the wealth they did or did not have. They never treated people differently because of their religious beliefs, nor did they differ in their treatment of one race over another. They treated every patient with the same concern and genuine empathy. They also were known for their deep respect for nurses."

I would gladly take that epitaph over a whole room full of awards.

Epilogue

After my grandfather's death, the land ownership continued in a trust for his children to caretake. I once heard someone say, "There's nothing sacred about that land," as if to imply that it is no different than any other land, its sentimental worth declining with every dollar increase in value. Everything can be for sale, for the right price, and his dream has seen its day.

I disagree. In fact, there is something sacred here. If you are quiet, you can hear the hardwoods beckon you inside. Bending pines make up its rooftop and layers of decomposing leaves create its floor. No walls can keep the sunshine out. In a day when black asphalt entombs budding azaleas and rows of painted lines on cement replace those of cotton, this piece of ground is truly hallowed.

For thousands of years this land has existed, and in these woods is written the story of countless joys and sorrows. The rolling pastureland provided healing in the old county hospital once located up on the hill. The last rope in Harris County unjustly tightened around an unfortunate black neck in one of these tall oak branches. And under the mangled thicket of wild azaleas, the bones of Creek Indians groan beneath piles of stones.

Among the ghosts of the dead and history's shame spawns a wellspring of life. This wild land is a resting place for the living, a sanctuary of rebirth. Chunks of earth, wood and water have healed my family wounds and may somehow still heal today. The land provides a place for our clan to come home. It is a place for the family to hunt, fish, build a cabin, or gather to enjoy. We are heirs in the same commonwealth, not made by hands, but cultivated for decades with my grandfather's constant loving care.

We are not a perfect family. We hurt each other, argue over selfish wants, and hold grudges. But eventually, if we follow Papa's example, we will forgive. Even his estranged father John walked these paths as an old man and made amends in the bracken. Every year a new crop of acorns falls to the ground, each year a fresh possibility for a new tree to sprout and grow.

The last time I walked through Papa's house soon after his death, I listened to the orange linoleum kitchen floor creak beneath my feet. On the counter sat boxes of Honey Buns, packets of popcorn, and dishes drying on a rack by the sink. It felt as if he had just been there and was out for the afternoon. I gazed out the window expecting him to come zigzagging up the walk.

I meandered through his whole house room by room, stopping at each picture, walking through his self-proclaimed "charmed life," displayed in images and letters from those he loved hanging in frames and scotch-taped on the walls. I wanted to remember the feel of his shag carpet under my feet and the way his closet smelled faintly of moth balls and dusty suits. I needed a permanent picture in my mind of his home before his things were divided and scattered among the family. I cherish those minutes I spent paying a quiet homage to his life well lived.

I don't know why I tried to talk myself out of the pain in the weeks surrounding his death. I guess I just felt guilty knowing that there are so many other people in the world with more lingering problems than mine. Just weeks before, my friend Cabell lost her incredible husband Mike at age 35 to a violent battle with cancer. My tears felt more justified then. Why should I mourn the death of one who lived a long, full life?

But pain is pain, and the thing with pain is you can't control it. I came to realize the deepest pain for me is not being able to call, write, or stop by and see him. The pure, cutting pain of not being able to reach over and hold his hand. Presence is a gift we take so for granted in this digital age.

I know in my head that things must constantly change, and people will pass in and out of our lives. I resolved to count my blessings the way my grandfather did instead of peeking in at the hurt that had not yet eased with time. It just didn't seem right that he should still feel so present when I thought of him and yet he was physically absent. Or maybe that was the biggest blessing of all, the legacy of remembering him, of realizing the parts of him still living in my family, in me, and in my children.

After the weekend of the funeral, I went back to Tuscaloosa and out for a long drive with my daughters. As I thought about the many memories I have with Papa, the earth started to feel emptier and more lackluster without his presence on it. Sadness eroded my demeanor, and I found myself more reserved and pensive. If somehow the measure of deep pain in loss equally reflects the heaps of love we shared, then I wanted to honor the love by feeling every ounce of the pain.

Eventually in the coming months, the sun started to feel warmer and brighter on my face than it had in a long time, and strangely more life-giving. Uncertainty lifted, like the dark smoke from a smoldering fire, and I could glimpse in the glowing embers the end to the story. I do not believe that time heals all wounds, but I do believe that God can.

As the seasons wore on, the piercing sorrow in losing him could not swallow up the joy of new life and the sweetness of spring. Eventually, the dogwoods burst forth in exuberant praise and the azaleas replied with pink exclamation. Wisteria hung from trees with delicate lavender petals cascading down a promise of hope. God smiled all around me, a reminder that life won't always feel broken and empty.

One night I remember walking outside in the quiet darkness to think and pray. Heat lightning exploded suddenly across the sky. Out of the pitch black appeared the most spectacular, pure light in a flash. It's as if nature itself was screaming that no matter how bleak life seems, there can come certain, unexpected joy. It looked obscure at first, even frightening to eyes dulled from seeing darkness. But after a while, the heat lightning was soothing, even beautiful, and I started to expect and look for the light in the void. This is what Papa taught me to do- to look for the good, to find the light, to hope. In recognizing the dignity of all people, in building bridges, and in pushing dirt and planting seeds, he was making space for life, and for his family, to bloom. He was driving back the darkness.

Maybe being the first to fly over the Atlantic in an airplane makes you a hero to a whole lot of people, certainly to a twelve-year-old boy. But that same little boy grew up and left a legacy of love and care that makes him a hero, too, if only to some. Who can say one feat isn't just as remarkable as the other? To live a quiet life, to do the right thing over and over again when no one may be looking, to fill the hurt in other people's hearts, these are not small tasks. The legacy of his love overflows from us. His legacy is still one of healing.

A few months went by, and my cousin, Seaborn Anderson "Andy" Roddenbery V opened his surgical practice in Columbus, Georgia. He now has a son, Seaborn Anderson Roddenbery VI, so my grandfather's name lives on in his great-grandson. The same week Papa died, he became a great-grandfather two more times when my brother Travis and his wife Melanie had identical twin girls, Anne Marie and Alexis. Mom says death and new life always seem to go hand in hand.

Most of Papa's ashes were buried in Park Hill cemetery on the plot with my grandmother, but my uncle wanted to spread some of his ashes over the land. We all agreed this was extremely appropriate, since spellbinding creation was the place my grandfather longed for at the end of his life. Papa never really considered this place any sort of permanent home, but the earth is what God looked at and called "good." His land is not worldly and materialistic, not altered to be more comfortable and more useful. It is pure and raw, and innocently gratifying.

I have never asked my uncle where exactly he laid some of his ashes to rest. If it had been up to me, I know right where I would have taken them. There is a spot deep in the woods, a holler where the creek makes a sharp turn to the south and sunlight peeks in with long, sweeping beams. It is over the hill from the pond my grandfather built, where we used to catch catfish and pick wild blackberries. There are beautiful smooth rocks in the shimmering creek bed, towering oaks overhead, and scattered prunifolia azaleas alongside the water. They are giant and magnificent.

Thirty years ago, Papa planted these azaleas that his friends Cason and Virginia Callaway (who founded Callaway Gardens just to the north) gave him. This rare breed of azalea grows only in a small area in southwest Georgia and blooms in August, the month of my grandfather's birth. As high as 15 feet tall, some tower above the vegetation, and their vibrant red flowers showcase the old Bulldog's favorite color. In full bloom, they look like firecrackers against the shadows of a towering forest. They brighten the darkness.

I have been shattered many ways in the last decade plus since Papa passed into eternity. My dad died unexpectedly only three years after my grandfather, and it still takes my breath away each time I think about my life without both patriarchs in it. But who's to say when God picks up the shattered pieces of our lives and puts them back together that it can't be just as beautiful, or dare I say even more beautiful, than it was before?

He created all the beauty in this world, and all we can hope for is to find it and pay homage to it in a way that whispers some small echo of His glory. My new world has more depth, more color, more compassion, more empathy, more love. My pain doesn't seem to get a lot smaller very quickly, but I have found God can and does get bigger around it if we let Him.

I know that when I experience the things Papa loved- whether it is drinking a cold Coke or watching the Georgia Bulldogs play football- I will pause in reverence. Gosh how he and my dad would love those back-to-back National Championships for Georgia football in recent years! I think about them up there with Larry Munson and Vince Dooley celebrating, although I am not sure they know or would care much about college football compared to the magnificence they are experiencing.

I still smile when I bait my own fishing hook or when I see a fresh halved cantaloupe just waiting to receive a sweet scoop of vanilla bean ice cream (one of his favorite summer snacks). And I may always tear up when I hear an old Broadway tune like "Some Enchanted Evening" or "If I Loved You," recalling the sweet sound of Papa's tenor voice making wonderful music in the hallways of his home. And the land, oh how I love to walk the land. I feel more at peace there than any place on earth.

When I was a young girl walking in the woods with my dad, if we ever ventured off the worn path, he would tell me to walk behind him for my safety. "Step where I step, Gracie," he would say. I strained and stretched my strides to his giant ones and tried to put my shoe exactly where he had walked. I made tiny footprints inside of his big ones. Papa's life and legacy, and my dad's, essentially says to us, "step where I step." Follow the paths they blazed for us.

I don't think I will ever be able to walk these trails without feeling both of their presence. When Marcus and I bring our three daughters Neely, Sadie, and Maggie here, I hear the hum of his rusted red truck and feel the smooth vinyl seats against my sticky back. I can almost make out Papa's immortal, soft whisper telling me the story of how he came to purchase paradise piece by piece fifty years ago. I see dark shadows resembling his herd of Black Angus meandering through the tall grass, and I hear ripples in the lake from a pair of Canada geese just taking flight.

Though the leaves annually dry up and fall to the ground and the creek sometimes slows to a trickle, the love still echoes loudly in each jubilant sunflower bloom and every squish of red clay. To know that this place he cultivated was here long before us and these trees will wearily hunch over this ground long after we are gone is a comforting thought.

It's these woods and something deep within them that called my grandfather, softly and steadily, to venture inside and come home. Each time he saw the land, he marveled at its beauty. When he spoke about it, he had the look of summiting a great mountain, as if this exact location was the pinnacle of creation itself, and everything else waned in comparison. In truth, his land never belonged to him as much as he belonged to it, and both of them to God.

My grandfather considered himself one stone piled on a monument to something much greater than himself. Each new stone balances on the strength of the ones beneath it and girds itself for the task of lifting the next ones. His offspring are the next pebbles in the stack of stones, in his Ebeneezer. We are marking our past and pointing upward in a hopeful Hallelujah, giving glory to the Creator of it all.

When I stand on the spring soil and look out over the

rolling pasture, I think about my grandfather's ashes mixed with the dust of his beloved ground. I search for aged footprints barely visible in the dirt to guide my shoes while I walk. These woods, of all places on earth, are where he has always been at peace and now where his bones will rest until the last day. It is in this hilly land in middle Georgia where he mastered the art of living and of dying.

His faith is sight. The healer healed. The keeper kept.

He is finally and forever Home.

Afterword: Family History.

I always thought "Seaborn" was a curious sort of name. I imagine its origins were of an ancestral babe born in an American-bound boat bobbing about in the middle of the Atlantic Ocean, bow pointed toward freedom. I think about some poor woman, torso tight with expectancy, tossed about by the whims of an unforgiving sea, water breaking, pains mounting, and finally the relief of a newborn's cry. Seaborn.

Seems like no matter how far inland a seaborn man gets, his bones should long for the roll of white caps, enticed by the sea and drawn into the churning mystery of heavy heaves sliced beneath the ship's bow. His soul should yearn for tight lines and salty skin and lungs thick with enchanting ocean air. The elusive indigo horizon should pull him like a magnet, frenzied wind and soaked skin a restorative tonic for his sea thirsty soul.

As a native Floridian, I have seen many men drawn to the water. They are like wild pelicans riding unpredictable waves: tugged by gravity one moment, mounted to the sky the next, and then diving beak first into the vast unknown, only to emerge with dinner in their grasp. Most other kinds of men tolerate only a toe-dipped sort of ocean. They find contentment and safety in a view, a beachy scent, vastness of sand, a broad rim hat, shell collecting, and tame, predictable tides. These men enjoy watching waves break on the shore from their beach chairs. They see a dolphin playing in the surf and gleefully explode out of the water, but they do not wish to be one.

If this were poetry, the heart of a man named Seaborn would be most alive untethered, gliding anchor up across unruly waters. But my grandfather Seaborn Anderson was born in South Georgia, far from the coastline, with only a trace of the sea in him. "Anderson" enjoyed the ocean as one enjoys a good book. He appreciated and marveled at it, but he never yearned to be one with it. By the time the Seaborn line stretched into his veins from his rambling father John, it was taut and tired from anchorless adventures. The salt in his bloodline diluted so much that he wanted to run aground those unpredictable family sea legs and walk solidly.

Anderson grew up needing a rooted sort of adventure. For my grandfather, the red clay of his home state planted him. He instead craved a sea of muddy earth and a fishing pond, blackberry bushes, high corn, and a rolling skyline of reaching forests. Unlike the sailor who thrives unanchored, my grandfather needed his roots to grow down deep into the carefully tilled Georgia soil of his ancestors to feel truly alive.

With the heritage of hard work and the success of his predecessors, my grandfather Seaborn "Anderson" Roddenbery III could have been born into an easy life, eating from a silver spoon, and handed a college education. Instead, largely because of his father's absence, he struggled, gritted his teeth, forgave, and rose above. It's hard to make sense of what happened before my birth, but piecing together my grandfather's history is a good place to start.

There is little, if any, anecdotal rhetoric to draw from, but the lives of five generations of Georgian Roddenberys most certainly have their place in this book and in the molding of my grandfather. History gives a straightforward, factual account of my predecessors, the pickle people who dug their roots down deep into Georgia dirt and built themselves from that fertile ground up. The Roddenbery family used the land near Cairo to amass an estate and a fortune in the family business of selling crops. The ground in southern Georgia gave much of what it had to the Roddenbery family and even claimed at least one life in the process.

About two hundred years ago, Robert Roddenbery, Anderson's great great-grandfather, the first Georgian in our family, was born in South Carolina. He moved to Georgia as a young man. After Andrew Jackson and his army defeated the Creeks and forced the treaty of Fort Jackson in 1827, the wild country in Georgia previously occupied by Native Americans became available for white settlement. Robert was a wage earner, saving large amounts of what he made and gradually accumulating land, buying it at times for as little as a dollar an acre. Over time he pieced together a large estate. The lion's share of his land was in southern Thomas County, Georgia.

He married Levicey "Vicey" Anderson who was born in that area, and they had seven children: Louisa, Mary Ann, Seaborn Anderson, John, Nancy, Margaret, and Georgia. Robert built a log house on his land and later cleared much of it himself. At the time of the Civil War, Robert owned many slaves who worked several hundred acres of his land. He freed nearly one hundred of those slaves at the end of the war, willingly or not. In his later years, he moved to Thomasville. The ground that helped make Robert claimed him when he was thrown from a carriage and fatally injured after he landed hard on the dirt.

Robert's eldest son, Seaborn Anderson Roddenbery (Anderson's great-grandfather and his original namesake) left the safety net of his father's plantation to pursue a career in medicine. Seaborn was born February 18, 1836, on the family Thomas County farm, in deep rural Georgia, not by the sea at all. He was the third of seven children. From the hall in my grandfather's home, I have often seen Seaborn staring down at me with dark eyes that seem sunken into his face. His expression is very solemn, characteristic of the times when no one smiled in pictures, or possibly an indication of a serious personality. He had a long, sharp nose like a possum, and a lengthy black and grey, wiry beard. He stood at average height and was of average build, thin even.

Seaborn studied as a young boy in the rural schools of Thomas County, and though he grew up on a farm, he had always wanted to be a doctor. His father wanted him to study the classical school of homeopathy and would have paid for his education if he studied this branch of medicine. However, Seaborn wanted to study allopathy, a method which became the forerunner of modern medicine, and so chose to become independent financially of his wealthy father.

He became a clerk in a store in Thomasville while attending Thomasville public school and studied under Dr. Robert Bruce in town. He saved enough to eventually pay his way through medical school at Oglethorpe Medical College in Savannah. He earned his M.D. in 1858 and moved to Decatur County (now Grady), Georgia to start his medical practice.

In the early 1800's, this area in Georgia was brimming with Seminole Creek Native Americans. At this time, the fear of attack from "Indians" was so great that all men aged sixteen to sixty were required to serve in the local militia. The first white settler there was William Hawthorne, a Baptist preacher who cut roads through the thick Georgia wilderness stretching about 40 miles. He built a home for his family at Tired Creek, about four miles from the city of Cairo. After arriving from North Carolina, William wrote to friends expressing a desire to start a settlement there, calling it Miller's Station. He must have been a man of persuasive words because many friends followed him and moved their families south.

When Seaborn first arrived around 1860, he boarded with a farmer there named Samuel Braswell, one of the early settlers who came from North Carolina. Seaborn began practicing medicine and rode horseback or traveled by horse and buggy to visit his patients. A year after arriving in Decatur County, Seaborn married Samuel's daughter, Martha America Braswell, born in 1837 in Thomas County. My grandfather's sister, Martha, was later named for her.

Seaborn and Martha had five sons and two daughters: Walter Blair, Bertha, Robert S., Seaborn Anderson, Jr., John William, Charles D., and Kate. Walter Blair was born in 1862, named for his father's favorite professor at Oglethorpe, Dr. Hugh A. Blair. That same year, Henry Miller, one of the original settlers of the area sold some of his land to Seaborn, and he built a two-room log cabin for his family on this land two miles from Cairo on the Thomasville-Bainbridge Stage Coach Road. The town of Cairo was formed four years later.

Seaborn had two professions: country doctor helping the sick and manager of a general store, which prepared him to go into business for himself. He needed both sources of income to support his growing family. Many of the country folks could not afford to pay for his medical services and did not pay cash. They offered chickens, eggs, or corn in exchange for suppressing a cough or bandaging up a wound.

Seaborn had an entrepreneurial spirit, and he decided to buy a mule and a cane grinder and began grinding juice from sweet sugar cane. He poured the juice from the sugarcane into a large black pot where he boiled the juice until it became thick and sweet. He began collecting any size jars and cans he could find, and after scalding them, he filled them with "Roddenbery Pure Cane Syrup."

His recipe became known as Georgia's first pure cane syrup, and he started storing it in cypress barrels in his general store around 1890. Customers would bring their own containers to fill with his syrup. His cane syrup business prospered so much that ten years later, he acquired a 10,000-acre sugarcane farm and closed his medical practice.

The business produced about 120 barrels of cane syrup a day, and sold many kinds of syrup, including maple and corn. In 1904, Seaborn traveled to the World's Fair in St. Louis, Missouri.[9] There, he served pancakes topped with his Roddenbery cane syrup. The Roddenbery Company became a local landmark, so much so that the high school in Cairo's mascots are named the Syrupmakers or Syrupmaids (and still are to this day). This was the beginning of what would become a multi-million-dollar company and the largest employer in Cairo, Georgia.

In 1920, son Walter Blair began running the company after Seaborn's health began to fail, and the company became known as the W.B. Roddenbery Company. Walter Blair was studying at the University of Virginia in his second year intending to study law when the poor health of his father required him to come home and run the business. He also took care of the family homeplace where he lived his entire life. Walter Blair married Maude Bostwick in 1887. She was from Louisiana, the granddaughter of Jimison Scaife, a pioneer of Methodism in Georgia. While Walter joined the Baptist church, Maude never relinquished her membership in the Methodist church. True to Southern form, the Baptists and the Methodists did not mix their religion, even with marriage.

By all accounts, Walter Blair Roddenbery was a man of great influence and affluence. A third generation Georgian, he used his position to help form Grady County out of then Decatur and Thomas counties in 1906. After Grady County formed, he became the chairman of the Board of County Commissioners. During his reign as chairman, the Grady County courthouse was built, and he remained as chairman until the project was completely paid for. My grandfather told me there was no more magnificent courthouse in the entire state of Georgia than the one in Grady County. The original one was unfortunately destroyed by fire in 1980.

By the 1930's, the Roddenbery Company grew watermelons and made cigars. While Walter was running the W.B. Roddenbery Company, he was also president of the

Roddenbery Hardware Company and of the Cairo Guano Company. He marketed the cane syrup under the brand "Nigger in de Cane Patch." Interestingly he was also chairman of deacons in the Baptist church and superintendent of the Sunday school during this time.

The empire also had a thriving hardware business. The company added pickles in 1936, peanut butter in 1937, and by 1960 canned boiled peanuts were being produced in mass. For many decades, the company was owned and operated by three generations of Roddenberys in Cairo, Georgia. The family members were also philanthropists, and they donated the funds to build a new public library in Cairo in 1964 among other projects. By 1986, they were making 45 kinds of pickles, 12 kinds of syrups, and boiling millions of peanuts.[9]

Toward the end of the Roddenbery family's ownership of the company in 1986, they had a large family reunion in celebration of 100 years of the Roddenbery Pickle Company. My family drove up from Orlando to join the droves of family members who gathered for the celebration. It was a fair of sorts, on the grounds of the company in Cairo, surrounded by huge cypress barrels of pickles. The barrels looked like the tallest above ground swimming pools you have ever seen, but instead of water, they had pickles stored inside of them, and instead of plastic exterior, they were made of aged cypress wood planks.

There were hundreds of Roddenbery family members in attendance. I remember dill pickle stands serving huge pickles free of charge, which seemed a bit like heaven to a twelve-year-old girl. We also took a special tour of the plant with my grandfather. I vividly remember seeing Walter Blair's tall, imposing wooden desk and cabinet. We got several token gifts to take home. One was a centennial Roddenbery Pickles card deck, and I'm fairly sure my mom still has it with all 52 cards plus jokers intact. That evening there was a large family dinner followed by the famed Ray Charles singing "Georgia on My Mind" and playing the piano. Gene Roddenberry, creator and producer of Star Trek also made the trip from California.

I remember the Roddenbery Pickles commercials from my childhood in Florida. There was an old man's voice saying "pickles are for smiles" at the end of the commercial along with a smiley face drawn in the shape of a green pickle. In 1993 when the Roddenberys sold to Texas based Dean Foods, the largest private pickle supplier in the country at that time, the Roddenbery Pickle Company was doing about $57 million in annual sales.[10] For some time, Dean Foods continued to market products under the Roddenbery label but closed the Cairo plant in 2002.

Seaborn Anderson, Jr. was the younger brother to Walter Blair and the fifth child born to Seaborn and Martha (Decatur County in 1870). He was the grandfather of Anderson (my grandfather). My great aunt Martha described him as "strong and robust but small of stature." He grew up devoted to outdoor life, camping, hunting, and fishing. He went to Cairo public schools and then graduated from Mercer University in Macon. In his junior year of college, he began teaching at the Singletary School in Ochlocknee, Georgia.

He married Johnnie Butler, and they had 6 children: my grandfather's father John William (born October 1, 1892), Louette, Grace, Mary, Ruth, and William. Grace died as an infant. In 1881, Seaborn built a ten room, two story house to accommodate his large family. The house burned to the ground the night they moved in. In the wake of the smoke and ashes of his hard work, he decided to build an exact duplication on the same sight, moving there again from his farm several years later.

He believed very strongly in the importance of good education and was hard on his children regarding their academics. For three years in 1886-1889, he moved his family to a rental house in Macon near Mercer University and Wesleyan College to further the education of his three youngest children. This paid off as all of his children, who grew up during Reconstruction years, attended colleges in Virginia, Tennessee, Kentucky, and Georgia.

Seaborn Jr. was elected to the Georgia state legislature in 1892 at the age of 21. After two terms, he became a professor of Language and Mathematics at Southern Georgia College in McRae. In his spare time, he read law books, and he was admitted to the Georgia Bar in October 1894 because of his rigorous study. Soon thereafter, he was appointed United States Commissioner until 1896.

He served for three terms as a Democrat Representative for his district. He was president of the Board of Education of Thomas County (1895-1898), appointed judge of the County Court for four years (1897-1901) and was the third mayor of Thomasville (1903-1904). President U.S. Grant appointed him Postmaster of the new Cairo post office. He achieved great success and popularity in his public and private life.

He was elected to the United States Congress as the representative from the second district of Georgia to fill the unexpired term of James Griggs after his death. He returned to the 62nd and 63rd Congress without opposition. He was known as a persuasive and powerful orator and one of the top three parliamentarians in the U.S. House of Representatives.

Congressman Roddenbery was known to filibuster when he opposed legislation. He was vehemently opposed to increasing the pensions of Civil War Union veterans because thousands of Confederate veterans were ineligible to receive federal pensions under the 14th Amendment. The south's economy was hit hardest after the war, and Georgians were opposed to having their tax dollars used only to support former Union soldiers. Seaborn also strongly supported prohibition.

Even with his love of family and his fellow man, he was a product of the times in rural Georgia. He did not believe black and white people were on equal footing, and he definitely did not believe they should intermarry. This issue was brought to the forefront of political discussion when John Arthur "Jack" Johnson, a black heavyweight boxer, married his second wife Lucille Cameron, who was white, in December of 1912.

Later that year, Roddenbery urged the adoption of an amendment to the U.S. Constitution that would outlaw interracial marriage, also known as anti-miscegenation laws across the country. He introduced H.J. Res 368 in January 1913. Similar laws making interracial marriage a felony were enacted in most southern states as well as many states in the west and the Great Plains. In one speech, he said, "Intermarriage between whites and blacks is repulsive and averse to every sentiment of pure American spirit."

Despite his efforts, a nationwide law was never enacted, and H.J. Res 368 failed a few weeks before he retired from active participation in Congress. He was a heavy cigar smoker and decided to take a short rest at home in Georgia before a planned return to Washington. He died a few days later from throat cancer at the young age of 43 while serving his second term in the U.S. Congress.[11]

When we talk about family history, we usually refer to him as "the Congressman" because there are so many "Andersons" and "Andys." On his deathbed, he said, "I have lived my convictions." I have a hundred-page hardback book containing the Memorial Addresses delivered in the House of Representatives and the Senate of the United States in his honor. Page after page of speeches describe him in similar words to Mr. Frank Park's of Georgia, as "earnest, tireless, forceful, now enshrined a martyr in the hearts of the people... As a judge he tempered justice with mercy, and all the ends he aimed at were his country's, God's, and truth's. He devoted his life to service, and be it said to his honor, he labored to uplift humanity." The Senate passed a bill to name the post office site in Thomasville "Roddenbery Park." After his death, his widow Johnnie received a federal appointment as the Postmistress of Thomasville and stayed in that post for many years. She held three successive four-year appointments under Presidents Wilson, Harding, and Coolidge.

The Congressman's first-born son, John William, Anderson's father, was attending law school at the time of his father's untimely death. John had a meager desire to pursue law school except for his father's insistence. John happily dropped out to help take care of his family when his father died. As it turns out, being a caretaker was not one of his strongest attributes.

My grandfather Anderson used to visit his grandmother as a child and read many of the mementos about his own grandfather, the Congressman's, life. He would sit in her attic pouring over the records and articles about his grandfather. His grandmother gave him any of them he wanted, and he kept each as a prized possession. His grandfather's success was always a source of pride and inspiration for Anderson.

Acknowledgements

Faith often comes before seeing. I guess that's why I wrote the acknowledgements before I finished the book. Life took me on some unexpected journeys, and it has taken me much, much longer than I expected, but races are for finishing no matter how long the course. And I fully intend to finish empty.

As I have pondered the life and legacy of my grandfather these many years, I have been thinking a lot about the American myth of the self-made man, about how others are always involved in the making, whether they get the credit or not. This book is my attempt to burn an incense of gratitude to the many people who invested in my grandfather's life; and ultimately to thank Papa and the others who have poured themselves into me.

I am profoundly moved by the reality we aren't meant to go through life alone. When it comes to finishing a large project, most of us cannot do it completely by ourselves. I know I am extremely dependent on help from others to accomplish most anything, especially finishing this book. It has been over two decades in the making and so many have contributed.

I've been pondering the idea of legacy too, and how in our extremely digitized world, most people project some utopian ideal of themselves to the masses. Their perfectly curated image may be electronically engraved for all of time, but how much of their story is true? And how much of the self-invented story is for someone else's glory and not solely for their own? What percentage of our lives are lived for the legacy we may never see? Are we willing to sacrifice ourselves for that kind of investment in others- a mentorship that may glean no instant gratification and results that will likely outlive us?

The very first spring I lived in my home, I was delighted to see vibrant daffodils randomly push through the hard winter soil in my backyard. Several patches of yellow blooms fought back winter and ushered in spring. I often think about the mystery person who planted those bulbs, and how his or her legacy may be in a row of daffodils that makes a stranger smile every year. A legacy can be children. Or poems. Or sacrificially giving of yourself or your fortune.

No one may appreciate the ways you give your life away. Or many may appreciate them. But here's the thing- we can't let the desire for our offerings to mean something to the masses eclipse our desire for them to mean something to a few. I have an audience of one. My deepest desire is to please God and to give Him glory in all things.

My only regret in writing this book is that I didn't finish it sooner. My Dad, even from the other side of the veil, has been the main encouraging voice in my head and heart. He knew I would be a writer long before I ever imagined it. He told me I could do this, persistently, in a thousand little (and sometimes big) ways. He taught me to find joy and pursue love in everything. He did not give up on me, and even though his physical presence is sorely missed, he is more alive now than ever. Dad, you have always been my biggest fan. This book is for you.

Thank you, Mom, for your love of our family, your constant, compassionate care for your father, and your help with every need and question I have ever had. Without you having the foresight to collect written and taped versions of our family history and being the keeper of all the family pictures, this would never have been possible. You also painstakingly read each chapter, edited, and fact checked me, more than once. You gave me no excuse. This book is for you, too.

Thank you, Papa for living your life well, one that history books and granddaughters should tell about. My meager words can never do justice to your legacy. You truly lived this short life's adventure well and are now living the next one. I hope you have a rusty red truck in heaven and a Georgia cap. I hope to ride with you again, with windows down on streets of gold. You will forever be my hero.

Thank you to Marcus whose own sacrifices helped make writing this book possible. And to our three girls, Neely, Sadie, and Maggie, who gave me space to be slumped over my computer when they probably needed more from me- and who believe in me more than I believe in myself at times- I love each one of you. Dreams are for reaching.

Thanks, Travis, for giving me stamina and fight and for your contributions and memories of Papa. You have always made me want to be better.

Thank you to my aunts and uncles: Andy "Boots" and Donna Roddenbery, Ed and Becky Roddenbery, and Ann and Frank Brookins for their contributions, and for helping me to see my grandfather through different lenses. Thanks to my cousins: Tripp Brookins, Tate Brookins, Laura Roddenbery Bell, Paige Roddenbery Eilertson, Dr. S.A. "Andy" Roddenbery V, and

Ruth Roddenbery Mathews for sharing in these stories and many of my memories growing up. My goodness, how very blessed we are!

And Alexis Bolz, thank you for knowing the song in my heart and singing it back to me when I have forgotten the words. No one on earth has ever had a truer friend!! Thank you for nudging me along and celebrating each little victory.

Thanks also to my Uncle Leighton Alston for his recollections, my Aunt Jane Youmans for influencing my life, and to my other Uncle Bryce whom I promised to mention! Thanks to Bonnie McCroskey, and John and Nealie Roddenbery, half siblings of my grandfather who helped me gain perspective on their father John.

Wow, Rick Bragg, I cannot believe you didn't run from my fish sandwich tears. You helped me find my voice and gave me the gift of your coveted friendship and advice. I feel honored to know you.

Special thanks to my Great Aunt Martha, truly a Sister of Mercy, who gave me the invaluable gift of her childhood memories.

Thanks to my teachers Sally Berg, Rosalie Gwinn, Renee Bell, and Patty Schoene for teaching me how to slide words together like pearls on a string. You taught me to see the valuable stories and my own worth in telling them.

To our dear family friends Coach Charles Friedley, Mike and Cindy Jolley, Sue and Larry the Legend Gaither, and Allen Levi, thank you for taking up Dad's torch and nudging me to pick up the pen. And thanks to Aron Ritchie for her invaluable advice.

And to my faithful friends Kerry Boulware, Anita Kay Head, Catherine Sanders, Emily Howell, Kristen Reynolds, Brooke Castino, Sarah Cohen, Kristen King, Susie Lovekamp, Melanie Martin, Chrystal Senter, Julie Letourneau, Rachel Norris, and Mary Beth Minnis, you all know what you mean to me. I am who I am in part because of each one of you.

And finally, thanks to you, reader, for pausing in a fast-paced world and finding this humble morsel worthy of your time and attention. I pray you go away glad to have spent a few hours with my family and inspired to love and live like my grandfather. I hope you plant a lot of daffodils.

And if I had a thousand tongues, each would thank the Author of all things. Thank you for scripting out this story, and all others, for Your glory. There is only one plan, Yours. It has been painful and difficult beyond my meager comprehension at times, but You are always with me, Emmanuel... Your presence brings unsurpassed peace and joy.

And finally, to the growing descendants of Andy and Grace Roddenbery, keep looking for the footprints and try to step where they walked.

Papa with me before a
home UGA football game
in Athens, GA, fall 1999

S.A. RODDENBERY, M.D.
341 HILL STREET, P.O. BOX 246
HAMILTON, GEORGIA 31811
706-628-5208

June 6, 1998

Dearest Mary Grace,

Your beautiful letter brought me great joy. As I read it, tears of happiness streamed down both cheeks. It has been a great privilege for me to see you grow and mature from infancy to become the beautiful talented person that you are today. You inherited good genes from your parents and they provided an environment which with their guidance and your ambition and motivation you have become my "Miss Georgia" and my "Miss America". You are the finest and best and are taking full advantage of the opportunities with which you have been blessed. You deserve and have earned the right to the best things in life. I am so very proud of you and I love you always,

Sincerely,
Papa

The Roddenberys

The Roddenberys: mother Johnnie, John (Andy's father), sister Louette, and father S.A. Roddenbery II (U.S. Congressman, Andy's grandfather)

Mary Carle Hurst (Andy's
mother), Atlanta, Georgia

John Roddenbery, my
great-grandfather, Andy's father,
in his U.S. Navy uniform

Mary Carle Roddenbery with
Baby Anderson March 5, 1916,
The Atlanta Constitution   — newspapers.Atlanta Constitution (1868 - 1929)

Pretty Mother and Child

MRS. JOHN RODDENBERY,
Thomasville, and little son, Seaborne Anderson Roddenbery. Mrs. R
denbery was Miss Mary Carl Hurst, of Atlanta.

Anderson Roddenbery
as a young boy

Martha, Anderson, and Mary Roddenbery

My grandfather Anderson with family:
Anderson Roddenbery, Rosalind Hurst,
Jewel Hurst, Mary Carle Roddenbery,
Mary Roddenbery, "Martha
Roddenbery, unknown, and Jack Hurst

Anderson "Andy," the Eagle
Scout bugler at Camp Benjamin
Hawkins Boy Scout Camp
Byron, GA, Summers 1925-1929

Andy Roddenbery, Malcomb Pfunder,
Bill Candler, Asa W. Candler, Emile
Pepin, Bill Barnes, and John McPherson,
Camp Twomey in Ontario, Canada,
Summer 1936

Andy Roddenbery, Rhodes
Scholar Nominee, University of
Georgia, 1936

Ted Twomey, Grace Roddenbery,
Andy Roddenbery, Drew Field, 1944

Andy and Grace
Roddenbery, 1944

Andy Roddenbery, Randolph Field, Texas, November 29, 1945

Mary Carle Roddenbery Hofer, her
daughter Martha Roddenbery (Sister
Madeline, Andy's sister), Jewel Hurst
(sister of Mary Carle) in the 1950s.

Andy, Ann, Grace, Berta,
and Andy, Jr. (or "Boots")
Roddenbery, 1949

Ann, Ed, Andy, Berta, and Boots
Roddenbery, Stark Ave., Columbus,
Georgia, March 1955

Grace and Andy Roddenbery,
Southern Surgical meeting,
Boca Raton, Florida, 1960

S.A. "Andy" Roddenbery III, M.D.

Back row: Andy and Grace, Front
Row: Ann, Ed, Boots, and Berta
Columbus, Georgia, 1964

Dr. Andy Roddenbery, Dr. Delmar
Edwards, and Dr. Abe Conger,
Medical Center, Columbus, GA

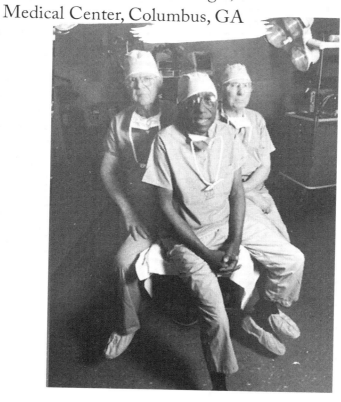

Me with Nip and Tuck, my
grandfather's dogs, Hamilton,
GA, 1983

Travis and Papa on the tractor
on the Land, Hamilton,
GA, 1983

Travis, my mom Berta, me, Grace (Mimi), and Andy (Papa), the Land, 1985

Cousins: Tate, Me,
Little Andy V, Travis
Truck ride with Papa, the
Land, Hamilton,
GA, 1987

Me and Dad, Fishing at the
pond, the Land, Hamilton,
GA, 1988

Three generations of Andys:
Seaborn Anderson Roddenbery,
Jr. ("Boots"), Seaborn Anderson
Roddenbery V ("Little Andy,'"
or "Andy V," now an M.D.), and
Seaborn Anderson Roddenbery,
III, M.D. ("Andy" or "Papa"), at
Papa's retirement party, 1986

Papa, Tate Brookins, Me, Travis
Alston, Andy Roddenbery V,
Robert Alston, Ed Roddenbery
Hamilton, GA, 1987

Roddenbery Family: Boots, Berta,
Grace, Andy, Ann, and
Ed Roddenbery

Me, Travis, and Papa with a
catfish I caught in our lake,
Hamilton, GA, 1991

Boots, Ed, Judge Aaron Cohn,
Grace, Andy, Berta, and Ann

Robert, Ed, and Andy
Trip to Camp Twomey (now
Northern Lite Camps),
Canada, 1990s

Andy and Grace Roddenbery
at their home in Hamilton,
Georgia, 1992

Papa's half siblings Bonnie and
John Roddenbery, John's wife
Nealie, Grace and Andy, 1994

Andy and his daughter
(my mom) Berta

Andy Roddenbery, Coach Vince
Dooley, Bill Hartman
Bill Hartman Award presentation,
University of Georgia Sanford
Stadium, 1998

Me and Papa, Athens,
GA, 1998

Andy V, Ed, Andy, Boots (The
Roddenbery men)
Lifetime Achievement Award,
Muscogee County Medical Society

Me with my hero, University
of Georgia, Sanford Stadium,
Athens, Georgia, 2001

Back row: Boots, Ann, Berta,
and Ed, Front row: Andy

Back Row: Ed, Andy V, Ann,
Donna, Boots, Travis
Front Row: Becky, Ruth, Papa, Me,
Marcus, Berta, Robert, and Melanie
St. Luke Methodist Church,
Columbus, GA, May 2003

My daughter Neely with her great grandfather Andy Roddenbery, Hamilton, GA, 2008

Roddenbery cousins in birth
order: Tripp Brookins, Laura
Bell, Paige Eilertson, Travis
Alston, Andy Roddenbery, Me,
Ruth Mathews
Papa's funeral, 2010

Jay Bell, Laura Bell, Me, Maggie
Lyon, Sadie Lyon, Marcus Lyon,
Neely Lyon, Berta Alston, Paige
Eilertson, Philip Eilertson,
Hamilton , GA , 2022

References .

1. "Lindy Decorated by U.D.C., Pays Tribute to War Heroes." *The Atlanta Constitution*, 12 Oct. 1927, p. 4.

2. Britannica, The Editors of Encyclopedia. "Adelina Patti". *Encyclopedia Britannica*, 15 Feb. 2023, https://www.britannica.com/biography/Adelina-Patti. Accessed 1 August 2023.

3. Camp, Edwin. "Old Timers Column." *The Atlanta Constitution*, 1934.

4. "The Legacy of Horace King." *Reflections: Georgia African American Historic Preservation Network*. Volume III No. 2, March 2003.

5. Lupold, John. "Columbus." *New Georgia Encyclopedia*, last modified Jun 21, 2022.
https://www.georgiaencyclopedia.org/articles/counties-cities-neighborhoods/Columbus/

6. Lloyd, C. (2007). Thomas Brewer. In New Georgia Encyclopedia. Retrieved Aug 25, 2020, from https://www.georgiaencyclopedia.org/articles/history-archaeology/. thomas-brewer-1894-1956/

7. Roddenbery, S. A. *I Swear by Apollo*. Grandy Press, Inc., 1994.

8. Smith, Loran. "Roddenbery's Influence Continues On." *Albany Herald*, 26 April 2010.

9. Bowers, Paige. "W. B. Roddenbery Company." New Georgia Encyclopedia, last modified Oct 4, 2018.https://www.georgiaencyclopedia.org/articles/business-economy/w-b-roddenbery-company/

10. "Dean Foods Company History." International Directory of Company Histories, Vol. 21. St. James Press, 1998. http://www.fundinguniverse.com/company-histories/dean-foods-company-history/

11. "S.A. Roddenbery Dead. Georgian Who Served in Three Congresses Dies at Home." *The New York Times*, Sept. 26, 1913.

About the Author.

Mary Grace Lyon grew up in Winter Park, Florida with seven generations of Georgia in her blood. She developed her passion for writing at an early age by listening to the master storytellers in her extended family. Her favorite time of year is college football season.

She holds a degree in journalism from the University of Georgia and a master's in education. She lives with her family in Tuscaloosa, Alabama. This is her first book.

Follow Mary Grace at marygracelyon.com